SAINTS AND FEASTS
OF THE LITURGICAL YEAR

SAINTS

and

FEASTS

of the Liturgical Year

Joseph N. Tylenda, S.J.

GEORGETOWN UNIVERSITY PRESS
WASHINGTON, D.C.

Georgetown University Press
© 2003 by Georgetown University Press.
All rights reserved.
Printed in the United States of America.
10 9 8 7 6 5 4 3 2 1   2003

This book is printed on acid-free recycled paper meeting
the requirements of the American National Standard for
Permanence in Paper for Printed Library Materials.

Designed and composed by Melissa Ehn at
Wilsted & Taylor Publishing Services.
Cover design by DesignPoint, Inc.

LIBRARY OF CONGRESS CATALOGING-IN-PUBLICATION DATA

Tylenda, Joseph N.
    Saints and feasts of the liturgical year / Joseph N.
Tylenda.
        p.   cm.
Rev. ed. of: Saints of the liturgical year. c1989.
Includes index.
    ISBN 0-87840-399-X (pbk. : alk. paper)
    1. Christian saints—Biography. 2. Church year—Prayer-
books and devotions—English. 3. Catholic Church—
Prayer-books and devotions—English. 4. Christian saints—
Prayer-books and devotions—English. I. Tylenda, Joseph N.
Saints of the liturgical year. II. Title.
BX4655.3.T95 2003
263'.9—dc21   2003004677

Contents

Introduction

AFTER A LONG SLUMP of interest from the late 1960s through the 1970s and into the 1980s, the saints have begun to recapture the minds and hearts of Roman Catholics as sources of inspiration and encouragement. Collections of biographical essays, like *Saints for All Seasons*, and full-length biographies of popular saints—such as Francis of Assisi, Thérèse of Lisieux, Ignatius of Loyola, and more contemporary figures like Padre Pio and Mother Teresa—have also been published to critical and popular acclaim. This revival of interest, however, runs parallel to a large amount of ignorance about the lives of the saints, especially among Catholics who grew up during the period of their virtual eclipse in catechetical and liturgical instruction.

This convenient volume is intended to help remedy that situation, at least insofar as the saints of the Liturgical Calendar are concerned. The book—which is organized according to the memorials and feast days of the liturgical year—provides a brief biography of each of the saints commemorated in the Mass. It gives the kind of information that would be of great use to celebrants who wish to say a few words about the saint of the day at the beginning of Mass, or who might want to point out in their homilies how the life of the saint is reflected in the special prayers and readings chosen for the day's Mass formulary. The aim is to be succinct and informative about the events of the saint's life, leaving the celebrant or homilist free to develop whatever themes seem more appropriate.

Certainly, teachers in Catholic schools or in Confraternity of Christian Doctrine programs will find the same information helpful for introducing students to the history of the Church as it has been exemplified by her heroes and heroines. The mystery of the Church is most fully alive and most approachable through these remarkable individuals, and connecting their stories with the central story of Christ's Paschal Mystery will enliven and deepen catechetical instruction.

Finally, many Catholics who attend Mass regularly during the week find that the brief sketches of the life of the saint of the day, which appear in the daily missals, are much too brief. The sketches given in this volume are considerably more detailed and informative, but they are still brief enough to be looked at five or ten minutes before leaving for Mass. The book is designed to fit handily on the shelf alongside the Bible and the Sunday Missal.

❧

This *Saints and Feasts of the Liturgical Year* is based upon the *General Roman Calendar*, as found in the *Missale Romanum, editio typica tertia* (Vatican City, 2002) and presently in use in the Roman Catholic Church, together with the *Proper Calendar for the Dioceses of the United States of America* as decreed by the Bishops' Committee on the

Liturgy of the National Conference of Catholic Bishops. Also included are the feasts, saints, and blessed from the *General Liturgical Calendar of the Society of Jesus* as promulgated within the Society of Jesus.

✒

There are three grades of liturgical celebrations. First, a *memorial* is the rank given to the Mass commemorating a particular saint, and the day of the celebration is usually the day of the saint's death, or birthday into Heaven. If the particular saint has universal significance, the Mass is to be observed by the universal Church (e.g., St. Augustine and St. Teresa of Jesus), and such a *memorial* is said to be *obligatory*. The commemorations of the other saints in the calendar are listed as *optional* (e.g., St. Norbert and St. Rita of Cascia); these saints are usually only venerated by particular churches, religious communities, or countries. Second, a *feast* is of higher rank, and it commemorates mysteries in our Lord's life (e.g., Transfiguration, Presentation in the Temple), events in the life of the Blessed Virgin (Nativity, Visitation), as well as certain more important saints, such as the Apostles and Evangelists. On *feasts*, the Gloria is added to the Mass. Third, the highest rank is that of a *solemnity*; these Masses commemorate the chief mysteries of the faith and of our redemption (e.g., Christmas, Easter, Holy Trinity), the more important celebrations in honor of Mary (Assumption, Immaculate Conception), and the principal celebrations honoring SS. Joseph, John the Baptist, Peter, and Paul. On *solemnities*, the Gloria and the Creed are added to the Mass.

In this book, the grade (*memorial, feast,* or *solemnity*) of the celebration is given together with the name of the day's feast or saint. When no grade is given for the celebration, it ranks as an *optional memorial.* An asterisk (*) precedes those memorials and feasts that have been taken from the *General Liturgical Calendar of the Society of Jesus,* and that are not already included in the *General Roman Calendar* and the *Proper Calendar for the Dioceses of the United States of America.*

This book is a revised and expanded edition (with thirty-four new entries) of the volume that appeared in 1989 titled *Saints of the Liturgical Year: Brief Biographies,* which also was published by Georgetown University Press.

Liturgical Calendar

*as generally observed
in the United States of America
including that of the Society of Jesus*

JANUARY

1	Blessed Virgin Mary, Mother of God . .	*Solemnity*
2	Basil the Great and Gregory Nazianzen, bishops and doctors of the Church . . .	*Memorial*
—	Epiphany of the Lord	*Solemnity*
3	Most Holy Name of Jesus	
—	Baptism of the Lord	*Feast*
4	Elizabeth Ann Seton, religious	*Memorial*
5	John Neumann, bishop	*Memorial*
6	André Bessette, religious	
7	Raymond of Peñafort, priest	
13	Hilary, bishop and doctor of the Church	
17	Anthony, abbot	*Memorial*
19	*European Martyrs of the Society of Jesus	
20	Fabian, pope and martyr	
	Sebastian, martyr	
21	Agnes, virgin and martyr	*Memorial*
22	Vincent, deacon and martyr	
24	Francis de Sales, bishop and doctor of the Church	*Memorial*

25	Conversion of St. Paul, apostle	. . . . .	*Feast*
26	Timothy and Titus, bishops	. . . .	*Memorial*
27	Angela Merici, virgin		
28	Thomas Aquinas, priest and doctor of the Church	. . . . . .	*Memorial*
31	John Bosco, priest	. . . . .	*Memorial*

FEBRUARY

2	Presentation of the Lord	. . . .	*Feast*
3	Blaise, bishop and martyr		
	Ansgar, bishop		
4	*Jesuit Martyrs of the Missions	. . . .	*Memorial*
5	Agatha, virgin and martyr	. . . .	*Memorial*
6	Paul Miki, religious and martyr, and companions, martyrs	. . . . .	*Memorial*
8	Jerome Emiliani, priest		
	Josephine Bakhita, virgin		
10	Scholastica, virgin	. . . .	*Memorial*
11	Our Lady of Lourdes		
14	Cyril and Methodius, bishops	. . . .	*Memorial*
15	*Claude La Colombière, priest	. . . .	*Memorial*
17	Seven Founders of the Order of Servites, religious		
21	Peter Damian, bishop and doctor of the Church		
22	Chair of St. Peter, apostle	. . . .	*Feast*
23	Polycarp, bishop and martyr	. . . .	*Memorial*

MARCH

| 3 | Katharine Drexel, virgin | | |
| 4 | Casimir | | |

7	Perpetua and Felicity, martyrs	*Memorial*
8	John of God, religious	
9	Frances of Rome, religious	
17	Patrick, bishop	
18	Cyril of Jerusalem, bishop and doctor of the Church	
19	Joseph, husband of the Blessed Virgin Mary	*Solemnity*
23	Toribio de Mogrovejo, bishop	
25	Annunciation of the Lord	*Solemnity*
—	Resurrection of the Lord	*Solemnity*

APRIL

2	Francis of Paola, hermit	
4	Isidore, bishop and doctor of the Church	
5	Vincent Ferrer, priest	
7	John Baptist de la Salle, priest	*Memorial*
11	Stanislaus, bishop and martyr	*Memorial*
13	Martin I, pope and martyr	
21	Anselm, bishop and doctor of the Church	
22	*Blessed Virgin Mary, Mother of the Society of Jesus	*Feast*
23	George, martyr	
	Adalbert, bishop and martyr	
24	Fidelis of Sigmaringen, priest and martyr	
25	Mark, evangelist	*Feast*
27	*Peter Canisius, priest and doctor of the Church	*Memorial*

28   Peter Chanel, priest and martyr

Louis Mary de Montfort, priest

29   Catherine of Siena, virgin and doctor
of the Church . . . . *Memorial*

30   Pius V, pope and religious

MAY

1   Joseph the Worker

2   Athanasius, bishop and doctor
of the Church . . . . *Memorial*

3   Philip and James, apostles . . . . *Feast*

4   *Joseph Mary Rubio, priest

10   Damien Joseph de Veuster of Moloka'i,
priest

12   Nereus and Achilleus, martyrs

Pancras, martyr

13   Our Lady of Fatima

14   Matthias, apostle . . . . *Feast*

15   Isidore

16   *Andrew Bobola, priest and martyr . . . *Memorial*

18   John I, pope, martyr

20   Bernardine of Siena, priest

21   Christopher Magallanes, priest and
martyr, and companions, martyrs

22   Rita of Cascia, religious

24   *Our Lady of the Way

25   Bede the Venerable, priest and doctor
of the Church

Gregory VII, pope, religious

Mary Magdalene de' Pazzi, virgin

26	Philip Neri, priest	*Memorial*
27	Augustine of Canterbury, bishop	
31	Visitation of the Blessed Virgin Mary	*Feast*
—	Ascension of the Lord	*Solemnity*
—	Pentecost Sunday	*Solemnity*

JUNE

1	Justin, martyr	*Memorial*
2	Marcellinus and Peter, martyrs	
3	Charles Lwanga and companions, martyrs	*Memorial*
5	Boniface, bishop and martyr	*Memorial*
6	Norbert, bishop	
9	Ephrem, deacon and doctor of the Church	
	*Joseph de Anchieta, priest	
11	Barnabas, apostle	*Memorial*
13	Anthony of Padua, priest and doctor of the Church	*Memorial*
19	Romuald, abbot	
21	Aloysius Gonzaga, religious	*Memorial*
22	Paulinus of Nola, bishop	
	John Fisher, bishop and martyr, and Thomas More, martyr	
24	Nativity of St. John the Baptist	*Solemnity*
27	Cyril of Alexandria, bishop and doctor of the Church	
28	Irenaeus, bishop and martyr	*Memorial*
29	Peter and Paul, apostles	*Solemnity*

30	First Holy Martyrs of the Holy Roman Church	
—	Most Holy Trinity	Solemnity
—	Most Holy Body and Blood of Christ	Solemnity
—	Most Sacred Heart of Jesus	Solemnity
—	Immaculate Heart of the Blessed Virgin Mary	Memorial

JULY

1	Junípero Serra, priest	
2	*John Francis Regis, Bernardine Realino, Francis Jerome, Julian Maunoir, and Anthony Baldinucci, priests	Memorial
3	Thomas, apostle	Feast
4	Elizabeth of Portugal	
5	Anthony Mary Zaccaria, priest	
6	Maria Goretti, virgin and martyr	
9	Augustine Zhao Rong, priest and martyr, and companions, martyrs	
11	Benedict, abbot	Memorial
13	Henry	
14	Kateri Tekakwitha, virgin	Memorial
15	Bonaventure, bishop and doctor of the Church	Memorial
16	Our Lady of Mount Carmel	
18	Camillus de Lellis, priest	
20	Apollinaris, bishop and martyr	
21	Lawrence of Brindisi, priest and doctor of the Church	
22	Mary Magdalene	Memorial

23 Bridget of Sweden, religious

24 Sharbel Makhluf, priest

25 James, apostle . . . . *Feast*

26 Joachim and Anne, parents of the
Blessed Virgin Mary . . . . *Memorial*

29 Martha . . . . *Memorial*

30 Peter Chrysologus, bishop and doctor of
the Church

31 Ignatius of Loyola, priest and founder of
the Society of Jesus . . . . *Solemnity*

AUGUST

1 Alphonsus Liguori, bishop and doctor
of the Church . . . . *Memorial*

2 Eusebius of Vercelli, bishop

Peter Julian Eymard, priest

*Peter Faber, priest

4 John Mary Vianney, priest . . . . . *Memorial*

5 Dedication of the Basilica of
St. Mary Major in Rome

6 Transfiguration of the Lord . . . . . *Feast*

7 Sixtus II, pope and martyr,
and companions, martyrs

Cajetan, priest

8 Dominic, priest . . . . *Memorial*

9 Teresa Benedicta of the Cross, virgin
and martyr

10 Lawrence, deacon and martyr . . . . . *Feast*

11 Clare, virgin . . . . *Memorial*

13 Pontian, pope and martyr, and
   Hippolytus, priest and martyr

14 Maximilian Mary Kolbe, priest
   and martyr . . . . *Memorial*

15 Assumption of the Blessed
   Virgin Mary . . . . *Solemnity*

16 Stephen of Hungary

18 Jane Frances de Chantal, religious
   *Albert Hurtado Cruchaga, priest

19 John Eudes, priest

20 Bernard, abbot and doctor
   of the Church . . . . *Memorial*

21 Pius X, pope . . . . *Memorial*

22 Queenship of the Blessed Virgin Mary . *Memorial*

23 Rose of Lima, virgin

24 Bartholomew, apostle . . . . *Feast*

25 Louis of France
   Joseph Calasanz, priest

27 Monica . . . . *Memorial*

28 Augustine, bishop and doctor
   of the Church . . . . *Memorial*

29 Martyrdom of John the Baptist . . . . *Memorial*

SEPTEMBER

3 Gregory the Great, pope and doctor
  of the Church . . . . *Memorial*

7 *Stephen Pongrácz, Melchior Grodziecki,
  and Mark Križevčanin, priests
  and martyrs . . . . *Memorial*

8 Nativity of the Blessed Virgin Mary . . . . *Feast*

9 Peter Claver, priest and religious . . . . *Memorial*

10 *Francis Gárate, religious

12 Most Holy Name of Mary

13 John Chrysostom, bishop and doctor
of the Church . . . . *Memorial*

14 Exaltation of the Holy Cross . . . . . . *Feast*

15 Our Lady of Sorrows . . . . *Memorial*

16 Cornelius, pope and martyr, and
Cyprian, bishop and martyr . . . . . *Memorial*

17 Robert Bellarmine, bishop and doctor
of the Church . . . . *Memorial*

19 Januarius, bishop and martyr

20 Andrew Kim Taegon, Paul Chong
Hasang, and companions, martyrs . . . *Memorial*

21 Matthew, apostle and evangelist . . . . . *Feast*

23 Pio of Pietrelcina, priest . . . . . *Memorial*

26 Cosmas and Damian, martyrs

27 Vincent de Paul, priest . . . . . *Memorial*

28 Lawrence Ruiz, martyr, and companions,
martyrs

Wenceslaus, martyr

29 Michael, Gabriel, and Raphael,
archangels . . . . *Feast*

30 Jerome, priest and doctor
of the Church . . . . *Memorial*

OCTOBER

1 Thérèse of the Child Jesus, virgin and
doctor of the Church . . . . . . *Memorial*

2 Guardian Angels . . . . *Memorial*

3 *Francis Borgia, priest . . . . *Memorial*

4 Francis of Assisi, religious . . . . . . *Memorial*

6 Bruno, priest

Marie-Rose Durocher, virgin

*Diego Aloysius de San Vitores, priest and martyr

7 Our Lady of the Rosary . . . . *Memorial*

9 Denis, bishop and martyr,
and companions, martyrs

John Leonardi, priest

14 Callistus I, pope and martyr

*John Ogilvie, priest and martyr . . . . *Memorial*

15 Teresa of Jesus, virgin and doctor
of the Church . . . . *Memorial*

16 Hedwig, religious

Margaret Mary Alacoque, virgin

17 Ignatius of Antioch, bishop
and martyr . . . . *Memorial*

18 Luke, evangelist . . . . *Feast*

19 Isaac Jogues and John de Brébeuf,
priests and martyrs,
and companions, martyrs . . . . . . *Memorial*

20 Paul of the Cross, priest

23 John of Capistrano, priest

24 Anthony Mary Claret, bishop

28 Simon and Jude, apostles . . . . *Feast*

30 *Dominic Collins, religious and martyr

31 *Alphonsus Rodríguez, religious . . . . *Memorial*

NOVEMBER

1   All Saints . . . . *Solemnity*

2   Commemoration of all the Faithful
    Departed (All Souls) . . . . *Solemnity*

3   Martin de Porres, religious

    *Rupert Mayer, priest

4   Charles Borromeo, bishop . . . . . . *Memorial*

5   *All Saints and Blessed of the
    Society of Jesus . . . . *Feast*

9   Dedication of the Lateran Basilica
    in Rome . . . . *Feast*

10   Leo the Great, pope and doctor
    of the Church . . . . *Memorial*

11   Martin of Tours, bishop . . . . . . *Memorial*

12   Josaphat, bishop and martyr . . . . *Memorial*

13   Frances Xavier Cabrini, virgin . . . . *Memorial*

    *Stanislaus Kostka, religious . . . . . *Memorial*

14   *Joseph Pignatelli, priest . . . . . . *Memorial*

15   Albert the Great, bishop and doctor
    of the Church

16   Margaret of Scotland

    Gertrude, virgin

    *Roch González, John del Castillo,
    and Alphonsus Rodríguez, priests
    and martyrs . . . . *Memorial*

17   Elizabeth of Hungary, religious . . . . *Memorial*

18   Dedication of the Basilicas of SS. Peter
    and Paul, apostles

    Rose Philippine Duchesne, virgin

21	Presentation of the Blessed Virgin Mary	Memorial
22	Cecilia, virgin and martyr	Memorial
23	Clement I, pope and martyr	
	Columban, abbot	
	Michael Augustine Pro, priest and martyr	
24	Andrew Dung-Lac, priest and martyr, and companions, martyrs	
25	Catherine of Alexandria, virgin and martyr	
26	*John Berchmans, religious	Memorial
30	Andrew, apostle	Feast
—	Our Lord Jesus Christ the King	Solemnity

DECEMBER

1	*Edmund Campion, Robert Southwell, priests and martyrs, and companions, martyrs	Memorial
3	Francis Xavier, priest	*Feast
4	John of Damascus, priest and doctor of the Church	
6	Nicholas, bishop	
7	Ambrose, bishop and doctor of the Church	Memorial
8	Immaculate Conception of the Blessed Virgin Mary	Solemnity
9	Juan Diego, hermit	
11	Damasus I, pope	
12	Our Lady of Guadalupe	Feast
13	Lucy, virgin and martyr	Memorial

SAINTS AND FEASTS
OF THE LITURGICAL YEAR

JANUARY

✝ JANUARY 1   ✐   *Solemnity*
The Blessed Virgin Mary, Mother of God

Today is the octave of Christmas. On December 25, we commemorate our Lord's nativity according to the flesh, and today we remember his mother, and particularly under her ancient title of Mother of God (Theotokos), for it was she who bore the person of the Word in her womb and from whom he received his human body. As early as the fourth century, this Marian title (the most important of all her titles) was in common use; however, Nestorius (381–after 451), Patriarch of Constantinople (from 428), challenged it because of his erroneous understanding of the relationship between Christ's divine and human natures. He proposed that Mary should only be called Christotokos, because, as he held, she was not the Mother of God, that is, she did not bear the divine Word in her womb but merely his human nature. Inasmuch as this teaching was contrary to the faith handed down by the Church's First Ecumenical Council, that of Nicaea (325), the bishops of the East, and especially St. Cyril of Alexandria (see June 27), called Nestorius to task. In a desire to bring doctrinal harmony to the East, the Byzantine Emperor Theodosius II (reigned 408–50), convoked a council to meet at Ephesus (in modern Turkey). At this, the Church's Third Ecumenical Council (431), the faith of Nicaea was solemnly confirmed, namely, that because Christ, the God-Man, was one divine person, his mother could rightly be called the Mother of God, and that the holy Fathers of the Church have never hesitated to grant her this title. The same council condemned Nestorius as a heretic, then deposed him and sent him into exile. This octave day of Christmas likewise commemorates our Lord's circumcision, which took place on the eighth day after his birth, and it was on this occasion that he received the name Jesus (Matt. 1:21; Luke 1:31).

✝ JANUARY 2 ✿ *Memorial*
SS. Basil the Great and Gregory Nazianzen, Bishops and Doctors of the Church

SS. Basil and Gregory Nazianzen share a common feast, not only because they were contemporaries but also because they were fellow students and close friends. Basil, known as "the Great," was born in Pontus, Asia Minor (today's Turkey), in about 329. He studied rhetoric in Caesarea (now Kayseri, Turkey), Constantinople (modern Istanbul), and Athens. Basil and Gregory were baptized together in about 358, and Gregory subsequently joined Basil in living an ascetical life at Annesi in Pontus. Basil was ordained a priest about 365, and then in 370 he was chosen Bishop of Caesarea, the capital of Cappadocia (now central Turkey). As bishop, he championed the faith defined at the First Ecumenical Council of Nicaea (325) and opposed the heretical

Arian teaching that did away with the divinity of the Son and the Holy Spirit. Through Basil's preaching and writings, he prepared the way for the Arians to return to orthodoxy. Many of his homilies and treatises are still extant, and his *Asceticon*, in which he expresses his understanding of the cenobitical life, and which eventually became known as the Rule of St. Basil, is much observed in the Oriental Church today. Basil died in Caesarea on January 1, 379.

St. Gregory Nazianzen, known as "the Theologian," was born in Arianzus, near Nazianzus (modern Nemisi, Turkey), also in Cappadocia, in about 330. His father, also Gregory, was bishop of Nazianzus. Gregory, the son, first met Basil in Caesarea, and later joined him in Athens. Gregory was ordained a priest in 362, and in 372 he was consecrated Bishop of Sasima, but he remained in Nazianzus assisting his aged father. In 379, Gregory was called to Constantinople to encourage the Nicene Catholics in their battle against the Arians. He was elected Bishop of Constantinople in 381 and took part in the Council of Constantinople (381), the Church's Second Ecumenical Council. Controversy, however, arose within the council about Gregory's installation as Bishop of Constantinople. His installation was said to have been contrary to the fifteenth canon of Nicaea, which forbade the transfer of bishops from one see to another. Rather than press the legitimacy of his translation, Gregory resigned his see and returned to Nazianzus, where he spent his time writing in defense of the Church's teaching. After Basil's death, he became the spokesman for the Nicene Catholics. Forty-four of his orations are still extant—a small fragment of those he had actually delivered—as well as 241 letters and some poetry. Gregory is especially remembered for his clear and explicit teaching about the Trinity. He died at Arianzus on January 25, 389 or 390. Because of Basil's and Gregory's important writings, they are honored as doctors of the Church.

✝ SUNDAY BETWEEN
JANUARY 2 AND 8   * Solemnity*
Epiphany of the Lord

Today's feast derives its name from the Greek word *epiphaneia*, which means a manifestation or revealing, and though this feast continues the mystery of Christmas, it presents Christ, the God-Man, in a new light. In Bethlehem, Christ's first visitors were shepherds from the fields, but now he reveals or manifests himself to non-Jews or Gentiles, in the persons of the Magi, who had come from the East. Today's Gospel (Matt. 2:1–12) describes this event. Having seen and followed his star, the Magi arrive in Jerusalem and inquire: "Where is the newborn king of the Jews?" for they have come to do him homage. When told that the place would be Bethlehem, they continue on their way, following the star until it rests directly above where the child lays. On seeing him, they kneel and adore him, and offer him three gifts. By gold, the Magi acknowledge that the Christ Child is of royal heritage; the gift of frankincense is offered because they recognize him as God; and myrrh is given because they affirm his humanity. By commemorating Christ's manifestation of himself to the Gentile world, this feast, then, proclaims that his is a universal mission and that he is the Savior of all. The feast was first established in the East, but by the fourth century it was also commonly celebrated in the West. Although the prayers of today's Mass only speak of the Magi's visit, the Liturgy of the Hours (at Vespers) also refers to Christ's divinity being made manifest at his baptism in the Jordan and at Cana, when he changed water into wine, his first miracle.

✝ JANUARY 3
Most Holy Name of Jesus

Jesus was the name given to Mary's child; it was not of her choosing; rather, it was given him from on high. The Archangel Gabriel said to her: "You will conceive in your womb and bear a son, and you shall call his name Jesus" (Luke 1:31). The Hebrew form of the name is Y'šua', which means "Yahweh is salvation," and this corresponds with the angel's message to Joseph: "You shall call his name Jesus, for he will save his people from their sins" (Matt. 1:21). Thus, from the very beginning this name enshrined our Lord's identity—he was destined to be our Savior. The name is one of power for, referring to his disciples, our Lord said: "In my name they will cast out demons" (Mark 16:17), and it was in virtue of that name that Peter healed the lame man at the Beautiful Gate of the Temple, saying: "Silver and gold I have none, but what I have I give you; in the name of Jesus Christ of Nazareth, get up and walk" (Acts 3:6). It is a name of holiness, for Peter, shortly after Pentecost, in preaching to his fellow Israelites, proclaimed: "There is salvation in no one else, for there is no other name under heaven given among men by which we must be saved" (Acts 4:12). It is likewise a name of glory, for Paul writes: "God has highly exalted him and bestowed on him the name which is above every name, that at the name of Jesus every knee should bend, in heaven and on earth and under the earth, and every tongue confess that Jesus Christ is Lord, to the glory of God the Father" (Phil. 2:9–11).

During the Middle Ages, the most ardent promoter of devotion to the Holy Name was the Franciscan, St. Bernardine of Siena (see May 20). Using his gift for oratory, he strove to instill in the hearts of his hearers devotion to Jesus's name. At the end of his sermons, he often displayed a tablet bearing the trigram of the Savior's name (IHS) in letters of gold. The devotion was subsequently approved by Pope Martin V (1417–31) and became so popular in Italy that that sacred trigram was frequently inscribed over the doorways of houses. In 1530, Pope Clement VII granted the Franciscans permission to celebrate a feast in honor of the Holy Name, and in 1721, at the behest of the German Emperor Charles VI, Pope Innocent III extended the feast to the universal Church. Today, the feast is celebrated as near as possible to January 1, the day when the Church commemorates our Lord's circumcision, for it was on that occasion that he was given the name Jesus. Our present custom of bowing our heads at the Holy Name goes back to the twenty-fifth canon of the Second Council of Lyon (1274).

✝ *Baptism of the Lord*

With this feast of our Lord's baptism, the liturgical season of Epiphany comes to an end. Christ is once more revealed to others, but this time more publicly. John the Baptist has been preaching on the shores of the Jordan River, and the people who have come to listen to him are sufficiently moved by his words that they willingly submit to his baptism of repentance. These individuals have now chosen to follow a new way of life. As Christ's precursor, John was sent to prepare them for Christ's appearance. Then, one day, the Sinless One does appear on the shores of the Jordan and asks to be baptized. Inasmuch as he has come to redeem sinners, he chooses to stand among them—as one of them. As the water flows over him, the heavens open, a dove descends and rests on him, and a voice from Heaven is heard: "This is my beloved Son. My favor rests on him" (Matt. 4:17; Mark 1:11; Luke 3:22). The crowd on the shore witnesses the event, but did the bystanders actually comprehend what was then taking place? The Triune God is present—the Father, Christ the Son, and the Holy Spirit under the form of the dove. Because Christ is about to begin his public life, the Father here approves the Son's mission, and the Holy Spirit anoints him to go forth and preach the coming of God's Kingdom.

✝ **St. Elizabeth Ann Seton, Religious**

St. Elizabeth Ann Seton founded the American Sisters of Charity and was the first native-born American to be canonized a saint. She was born Elizabeth Ann Bayley on August 28, 1774, in New York City; both her parents were Episcopalians, and she was brought up in that faith. She married (January 25, 1794) William Magee Seton, a wealthy New York merchant, and the couple had five children. During a visit to Italy, Mr. Seton died (December 1803), and there Mrs. Seton, having become acquainted with the Filicchi family, accepted their hospitality while she and her children sojourned in Leghorn, Italy. It was from this Italian family that Mrs. Seton learned about the Catholic faith. She returned to New York and was received into the Church at St. Peter's on March 4, 1805. When her friends abandoned her because of her conversion, she accepted the invitation (August 1807) of Fr. William DuBourg, Sulpician superior in Baltimore, to open a school for girls near St. Mary's Seminary on Paca Street. The school opened in 1808. After several young ladies joined in her educational work, they agreed to form a sisterhood. In the following year (1809), Elizabeth Ann went to Emmitsburg, Maryland, where she founded her congregation. As the number of sisters grew, so did the number of their schools and orphanages. Mother Seton's schools were the first in what eventually grew into the American parochial school system. She died at Emmitsburg on January 4, 1821, and was canonized by Pope Paul VI in

1975. The opening prayer of today's Mass summarizes St. Elizabeth Ann's life when it refers to her as wife and mother, educator and founder.

✠ JANUARY 5   *Memorial*
St. John Neumann, Bishop

St. John Nepomucene Neumann is the first U.S. bishop to be canonized a saint. He was born on March 28, 1811, in Prachatitz, Bohemia (in today's Czech Republic), and while studying at the seminary in Prague, he decided to go to the United States as a missionary. He finished his studies in 1835, and shortly afterward, though not yet ordained, left his homeland. When he arrived (June 2, 1836) in New York City, he was wearing the only clothes he owned and in his pockets he had but one dollar. He was immediately accepted by Bishop John Dubois of New York and shortly afterward was ordained a priest on June 25, 1836. Fr. Neumann spent the next four years as a parish priest in Buffalo, working among German-speaking immigrants. He then entered (1840) the Congregation of the Most Holy Redeemer (Redemptorists), and when he took his religious vows on January 16, 1842, he was the first Redemptorist to be professed in the United States. Subsequent pastoral assignments took him to Pittsburgh and Baltimore, where he also ministered to German immigrants. Pope Pius IX appointed him fourth bishop of Philadelphia, and he was consecrated in Baltimore on March 28, 1852. During his eight years in Philadelphia, he built eighty churches and organized the diocese's school system. He introduced the Forty Hours Devotion into this country and began construction on that city's new cathedral, that of SS. Peter and Paul. At first, Bishop Neumann was not well received—he spoke with an accent and looked more like a laborer than a bishop—but in time the people came to realize that they had a saint in their midst. He died of a heart attack on January 5, 1860, while walking along a Philadelphia street. He was canonized by Pope Paul VI in 1977.

<h2>✝ JANUARY 6
Bl. André Bessette, Religious</h2>

The name of Bl. André is closely linked with that of St. Joseph. He was born Alfred Bessette on April 9, 1845, near the village of Saint-Grégoire d'Iberville, in the Diocese of Montreal. By the time he was twelve years of age, he had lost both parents, and because he had to go to work when still a young teenager, his formal education was necessarily limited. His jobs were varied, and there was a period when he worked (1863–67) in the United States, in several New England cities. On his return to Canada, he entered (November 1870) the Congregation of the Holy Cross as a brother, and it was then that he received the name André. For most of his years in religious life, he served as porter at the College of Notre Dame in Montreal. Br. André always had a great devotion to St. Joseph, and he helped construct the first chapel dedicated to St. Joseph on the side of Montreal's Mount Royal. The small chapel opened in 1904, and because he spent much of his time there, Br. André was made its custodian. The chapel soon became a place of pilgrimage; the number of pilgrims increased and so did the miracles, all attributed to the prayers of the humble and holy Br. André. He cared for the shrine until his death on January 6, 1937. He was beatified by Pope John Paul II in 1982. What was once a small simple chapel to St. Joseph is now the magnificent Oratory of St. Joseph, where pilgrims from all parts of Canada and the United States gather to honor both St. Joseph and the humble and devoted Br. André.

✠ JANUARY 7
St. Raymond of Peñafort, Priest

St. Raymond was born at his family's Peñafort Castle in Villafranca de Penades, near Barcelona, between about 1175 and 1180. After completing his studies in Barcelona, he taught for a while, but then went to Bologna to study canon law. He received his law degree in 1218, and then returned to Barcelona, where he became a canon at the cathedral. When he was in his forties, he entered (1221) the Order of Preachers (Dominicans), and inasmuch as he was a renowned canonist, Pope Gregory IX called (1230) him to Rome to be his confessor and to gather his many decrees into a single volume. This he accomplished, and the work, known as the *Decretals of Gregory IX*, was promulgated in 1234. This collection eventually became the foundation for the Church's Canon Law. Raymond returned (1236) to Barcelona and was elected (May 22, 1238) third master general of the Dominicans. After giving the Dominican Constitutions its final juridical form, he resigned his office (June 2, 1240) and spent the remaining thirty-five years of his life working among the Moors and Jews of Spain. With a view to converting the Moors, he established (1245) a school of Arabic studies in Spain and asked St. Thomas Aquinas (see January 28) to write a text (*Summa contra Gentiles*) to be used in their conversion. He died in Barcelona on January 6, 1275, and was canonized by Pope Clement VIII in 1601. Because St. Raymond had written a very famous book to help confessors, the prayer of today's Mass mentions his ministry to sinners.

✠ JANUARY 13
St. Hilary, Bishop and Doctor of the Church

St. Hilary was born in Poitiers, France, about 315, and setting aside his Neo-Platonist ideas, he became a Christian after reading the Bible. He was chosen Bishop of Poitiers about 353, and his years as bishop were taken up in disputes with the Arians and in upholding the Church's teaching on Christ's divinity. While attending (356) a council of bishops at Béziers, in southern France, he refused to join the other bishops in condemning St. Athanasius (see May 2) with regard to the latter's orthodox stand against the Arians. As a result, Hilary was, by order of the Arian-leaning Emperor Constantius II (337–61), sent into exile to Phrygia in Asia Minor (now part of modern Turkey). During his four years (356–60) in exile, he became familiar with Greek theology and wrote two of his most important books. *On the Trinity* was directed against Arian teaching, and *On Synods*, which continued his combat against the Arian heresy, also included a history of the Eastern

Church up to his time. Hilary returned to his see in 361 and continued to undo the havoc caused by the Arians in Gaul and northern Italy. He died in Poitiers on January 13, 367. He was the leading Latin theologian of his age, and Pope Pius IX declared him a doctor of the Church in 1851. When the opening prayer in today's Mass says that St. Hilary defended the divinity of Christ, this is a reference to his writings and long struggle against the Arians.

✠ JANUARY 17 ✐ *Memorial*
St. Anthony, Abbot

St. Anthony was born in Comus, Upper Egypt, in about 250. As a young man, he was much given to prayer, and one day—hearing the Gospel passage, "If you seek perfection, go sell your possessions, and give to the poor. You will then have treasure in heaven" (Matt. 19:21) read in church—he immediately resolved to give away all that he had and to live as an ascetic. He found (269) a solitary place for himself near his village, and there spent his time in prayer, penance, and manual labor. About 285, he left for the Egyptian desert, where he lived as a hermit. In due time, stories began to spread about his holiness, his battles with the devil, and his miracles. The consequence was that other solitaries came to seek his advice, and eventually they built hermitages near his. Because Anthony now had disciples and became their spiritual guide, he formed (305) them into an organized group and led them along the way of perfection and holiness. But Anthony was made for the solitary life, and after about five years with his monks, he returned (310) to the Egyptian desert (between the Nile and the Red Sea), and there he received visitors and engaged in spiritual conversations. He is said to have twice visited Alexandria to preach against the Arians. He died at his desert hermitage in 356, at about the age of 105 years. In the year following his death, St. Athanasius (see May 2) wrote his biography, *Life of Anthony*, in which Anthony is portrayed as the ideal monk and the "father" of Christian monasticism. This book had immense influence in the early Christian world, and it has always been valued as a spiritual classic. Since the fifth century, St. Anthony's feast has been celebrated on January 17, as the date of his death. The opening prayer of today's Mass reminds us that Anthony renounced the world and sought solitude, and the prayer after Communion speaks of his conquering the powers of darkness.

✝ *JANUARY 19
European Martyrs of the Society of Jesus

Today, the Jesuit family commemorates the martyrdoms of seventy-eight of its brethren, all blessed, who died for the Catholic faith between 1570 and 1792.

Fr. James Salès (b. 1556) and Br. William Saultemouche (b. 1557) were martyred in Aubenas, France, on February 7, 1593, and were beatified by Pope Pius XI in 1926.

Fr. Ignatius de Azevedo (b. 1527) and thirty-nine fellow Jesuits were martyred (July 15 and 16, 1570) off the Canary Islands, while on their way to the mission in Brazil. They were beatified by Pope Pius IX in 1854.

Fr. James Bonnaud (b. 1740) and twenty-two French Jesuits were martyred (September 2–5, 1792) in France during the years of the French Revolution. They were beatified by Pope Pius XI in 1926.

Fr. Joseph Imbert (b. 1720) and Fr. John Nicholas Cordier (b. 1710) died in 1794 as a result of maltreatment received while detained on the Rochefort Prison Ships during the final months of the French Revolution. They were beatified by Pope John Paul II in 1995.

Fr. Thomas Sitjar Fortiá (b. 1866) and ten Jesuit companions died in 1936 during the Spanish Civil War. They were beatified by Pope John Paul II in 2001.

✝ JANUARY 20
St. Fabian, Pope and Martyr

St. Fabian was a Roman and was elected to the papacy on January 10, 236. Because he was a layman, he was not among the candidates under consideration to become pope. However, when everyone was gathered in the assembly hall and the election process was about to begin, a dove unexpectedly entered the hall and alighted on Fabian's head. The electors needed no other sign. A few things are actually known about Fabian. It was he who divided Rome into seven ecclesiastical districts, with a deacon in charge of each, and it was he who brought the bodies of the martyrs SS. Pontian and Hippolytus (see August 13) from Sardinia and gave them a fitting burial in Rome. When the persecution of Decius (emperor 249–51) broke out in 250, Pope Fabian was arrested and was among the first to die (January 20, 250), most probably while in prison and as a result of maltreatment. His body was placed in the papal crypt in the cemetery of Callistus and was later transferred to the Basilica of St. Sebastian, where it was discovered in 1915. St. Cyprian (see September 16) describes St. Fabian in this manner: "an incomparable man, the glory of whose death corresponded with the holiness of his life."

† JANUARY 20
St. Sebastian, Martyr

St. Sebastian may have been born in Milan. Not much is actually known of his life, but it is certain that he suffered martyrdom in Rome during the persecution of Diocletian (emperor 284–305), sometime between 297 and 305. The earliest account of Sebastian's martyrdom was written around 450, about 150 years after his death. According to this compilation, he was a Roman army officer, having entered the emperor's army about 283. When it was discovered that he was a Christian and that he had converted several of his fellow soldiers to Christianity, he was sentenced to die at the hands of the archers, his fellow soldiers. Through the generous ministrations of a widow named Irene, he recovered from his wounds and, rather than leaving Rome, he again presented himself before Diocletian, who then had him clubbed to death. Sebastian was buried in the catacombs on the Appian Way, where the Basilica of St. Sebastian now stands. Devotion to him spread very quickly among the Romans, and by 354 his feast was celebrated on January 20, the presumed date of his death.

✝ JANUARY 21 ✎ *Memorial*
St. Agnes, Virgin and Martyr

St. Agnes was, at one time, one of the more popular saints in the Church. Nevertheless, the only certain facts we have of her are that she was a Roman, and that she was martyred and was buried on the Via Nomentana sometime during the second half of the third or the beginning of the fourth century. A church was built (349) over her tomb by Costanza, Emperor Constantine's daughter, and as early as 354, her feast was celebrated there on January 21, the supposed date of her death. Tradition claims that when Agnes was about thirteen or fourteen years of age she was being pressed into marriage, but because she chose to remain a virgin consecrated to God, she declined the marriage offers and revealed that she was a Christian. When she subsequently refused to offer incense to idols, the Roman governor sought a variety of ways to break her will. He first placed her in a brothel, and when she was exposed before everyone's eyes, her hair miraculously grew to cloak her nakedness. When she was ordered to be burned alive, the winds carried the flames away from her and scorched the would-be executioners. Finally, she was beheaded. The year of her martyrdom is given as 304 or 305. The opening prayer of today's Mass tells us that God can transform what the world considers weakness into a strength that can put worldly power to shame, as Agnes's virginity withstood the threats of Rome's pagan governor.

JANUARY 22
St. Vincent, Deacon and Martyr

St. Vincent was born of a prominent family in Huesca, Spain, sometime in the second half of the third century. As a youth, he studied under Valerius, Bishop of Saragossa, who also ordained him a deacon and placed him in charge of distributing alms to the poor and of caring for widows and orphans. At the outbreak (304) of the persecution of Diocletian (emperor 284–305), Dacian, the governor of Valencia (Spain), initiated the persecution in his region by arresting Valerius and Vincent. Both bishop and deacon were bound in chains and taken to Valencia, where Dacian interrogated them. Unable to get either to renounce his Christian faith, Dacian then exiled Valerius and ordered Vincent to be tortured. Neither the rack, nor iron hooks, nor being roasted on a gridiron could persuade Vincent to deny his God, but they did allow him to pass from this earth to paradise (304). After Dacian had Vincent's body thrown into the sea, it was retrieved and appropriately buried. Of the many who suffered martyrdom in Spain during the Church's first centuries, St. Vincent the Deacon was one of the most popular. Devotion to him spread widely, and the Hieronymian Martyrology (about 450) records January 22 as the date of his death.

✝ JANUARY 24 ✐ *Memorial*
St. Francis de Sales, Bishop and Doctor of the Church

St. Francis de Sales was born on August 21, 1567, near Annecy, Savoy, France. Because his family was of the nobility, he was educated to be a gentleman. After early studies at Annecy, he went (1582) to Paris for his humanities, and then he went (1588) to the University of Padua to study law in preparation for a government position. He earned a law degree (1591), but a career in the world was not for him, and in December 1593 he was ordained to the priesthood. The following year, he went as a missionary to France's Chablais district, which had several years previously adopted Calvinism. There, he visited village after village trying to make converts. To help him in his task, he wrote and distributed leaflets explaining the Catholic faith; these were later collected and published as *Controversies*. After four years (1694–98), his missionary labors bore fruit for many of the inhabitants returned to the Catholic faith. On December 8, 1602, he was ordained bishop of Geneva. He was an ideal bishop. He brought his diocese into line with the reforms legislated by the Council of Trent, worked for the education of his clergy, and made regular visits to the parishes under his care. Though successful as a bishop, he is better known today for his writings. His sermons and conferences are numerous, and his most famous works are the *Introduction to a Devout Life* (1608) and the *Treatise on the Love of God* (1616). These books were popular when first written, and they are still appreciated and read today. In 1610, he helped St. Jane Frances de Chantal (see August 18) found the Visitation Order. He died in Lyon on December 28, 1622, and was buried at Annecy on the following January 24, the date when his memorial is liturgically celebrated. He was canonized by Pope Alexander VII in 1665, and Pope Pius IX declared him a doctor of the Church in 1877. Today's prayer speaks of St. Francis's compassion to befriend all people on the way to salvation; this was his motive in writing the two spiritual classics mentioned above.

JANUARY 25 ✦ *Feast*
Conversion of St. Paul, Apostle

Today we commemorate the day when our Lord, by the power of his grace, transformed a zealous persecutor into an impassioned apostle. Saul of Tarsus was brought up as a Pharisee and an enemy of Jesus Christ. After the death of St. Stephen (see December 26), at which Saul was present (Acts 7:58), he participated in a fierce persecution against the Christians. He "began to harass the Church. He entered house after house, dragged men and women out, and threw them into jail" (Acts 8:3). He was then empowered by the Jerusalem Council to go to Damascus to arrest and bring to Jerusalem anyone who lived according to the new way (Acts 9:2). As Saul approached Damascus, it was then that the Lord intervened. By means of a sudden flash of light, Saul was thrown to the ground, and at the same time he heard a voice saying: "Saul, Saul, why do you persecute me?" In response, he asked: "Who are you, Lord?" Then the voice identified itself: "I am Jesus whom you are persecuting" (Acts 9:3–6). This was the moment of his conversion, and he who was once a determined persecutor now became a vessel of election. Today's Mass offers a choice of first readings (Acts 22:3–16 or Acts 9:1–22); both narrate the events of Paul's conversion. This feast originated in Gaul in the sixth century and is celebrated on January 25, the presumed date of the transfer of the relics of St. Paul to the Constantinian basilica on the Ostian Way.

✠ JANUARY 26 ✒ *Memorial*
SS. Timothy and Titus, Bishops

SS. Timothy and Titus were two of St. Paul's faithful co-workers. Timothy was born in Lystra in Lycaonia (in modern Turkey), and when Paul visited that city (in about 50), Timothy, a recent convert, was so highly recommended that Paul took him with him on his second missionary journey (Acts 16:1–4). Timothy was Paul's constant companion and undertook special missions for him, for example, to the Thessalonians (1 Thess. 3:2) and to the Corinthians (1 Cor. 4:17). He was also imprisoned for a time, and then released (Heb. 13:23). In his letters, Paul refers to Timothy as "my beloved and faithful son" (1 Cor. 4:17) and "my child whom I love" (2 Tim. 1:2). Paul appointed him Bishop of Ephesus (1 Tim. 1:3), and addressed two letters to him. Timothy is said to have been martyred in 97, under Nerva (emperor 96–98).

Titus, perhaps a native of Antioch (today's Antakya, Turkey), may have been a convert of Paul's, and he is first mentioned in the New Testament when he accompanies Paul to Jerusalem (in 49 or 50), to attend a council (Gal. 2:1). In his letters, Paul refers to Titus as his "traveling companion" (2 Cor. 8:16) and "my own true child in one common faith" (Tit. 1:4). Paul placed him in charge of the collection in Corinth for the Jerusalem community (2 Cor. 8:6). With Paul, he went to Crete and was left there to organize the Church (Tit. 1:5); he is thus considered the first Bishop of Crete. Paul sent him to Dalmatia (now part of Croatia) for a time (2 Tim. 4:10); he then returned to Crete, where he died at an advanced age, perhaps in his late nineties. It is appropriate that the memorial of St. Paul's two closest collaborators, SS. Timothy and Titus, be liturgically celebrated on the day following the commemoration of St. Paul's conversion. Today's Mass offers a choice of first readings; the first is taken from the beginning of Paul's second letter to Timothy (1:1–8), and the second is the opening verses of Paul's letter to Titus (1:1–5).

✝ JANUARY 27
St. Angela Merici, Virgin

St. Angela Merici was born in Desenzano, Italy, probably on March 21, 1474. As a young lady, she occupied herself in doing good works in her native town. But in 1506, when she was thirty-two years old, she had a vision in which she learned that she would "found a society of virgins at Brescia." Ten years later, she was invited (1516) to Brescia to stay with Catherine Patengola, a widow, who had just lost two sons by death. While living in Brescia, Angela noticed that the city's poor girls were without schooling, and so she began catechetical work among them. In 1531, she organized a group of twelve girls to help her in her work; then in 1535, when the group numbered twenty-eight, she formed them into the Company of St. Ursula. This was the first religious congregation founded for the education and training of young girls. Angela was convinced that the society of her time needed to be re-Christianized, and to accomplish this, she had to begin by educating girls, the wives and mothers of tomorrow. Angela died in Brescia on January 27, 1540, and was canonized by Pope Pius VII in 1807. The opening prayer today speaks of St. Angela's charity and wisdom, a wisdom that saw the needs of her time and a charity that led her to respond to them.

✝ JANUARY 28 ✍ *Memorial*
St. Thomas Aquinas, Priest and Doctor of the Church

St. Thomas Aquinas is perhaps the greatest theologian that the Catholic Church has ever had. He was born in Roccasecca, near Monte Cassino, Italy, in about 1225, and was the son of Landulf of Aquino, lord of Roccasecca. After his fifth birthday, Thomas's parents placed (1231) him in the Benedictine monastery at Monte Cassino as an oblate; that is, with a view of his eventually becoming a monk. There he studied until 1239, when he transferred to the University of Naples. In April 1244, rather than entering the Benedictine Order, Thomas chose the Order of Friars Preachers (Dominicans), and when his parents heard what their son had done, they physically carried him home. The following year, however, he was permitted to return to the Dominicans. He then studied in Paris (1245–48) and Cologne (1248–52)— under the tutelage of St. Albert the Great (see November 15) in both cities— and back to Paris where he lectured (1252–56) on the *Sentences* of Peter the Lombard. He was subsequently professor (1256–59) at the University of Paris and returned to Italy, teaching at the Dominican *Studium generale* in Orvieto (1261–65) and then to Rome (1265–67). He again taught in Paris (1269–72), but after three years he was once more in Naples. In 1274, Thomas was invited to attend the Second Council of Lyon, but shortly after leaving Naples, and as he was on his way, he became ill and requested to be taken to the nearby Cistercian Abbey of Fossanova. There he died on March 7, 1274. He was canonized by Pope John XXII in 1323, and in 1567 Pope Pius V declared him a doctor of the Church. St. Thomas's many writings in philosophy and theology established him as one of the Church's greatest thinkers. His *Summary of Sacred Theology* has been used as a text since the time it was first written. His memorial is liturgically celebrated on January 28, the date when his relics were transferred (1369) from Italy to the Dominican monastery in Toulouse, France.

✠ JANUARY 31   ✐ *Memorial*
St. John Bosco, Priest

St. John Bosco was born at Castelnuovo d'Asti, near Turin, on August 16, 1815. Because his father had died when John was only two, the family knew poverty. With the encouragement of St. Joseph Cafasso (1811–60), John entered (1835) the diocesan seminary and was ordained a priest in 1841. Soon after his ordination, he gathered several young apprentices from Turin's poorest sections and taught them their catechism. He then opened a hospice for orphan boys, and in time added (1853) workshops, such as shoemaking, tailoring, printing, and bookbinding. Don Bosco, as he was known to everyone, encouraged the young men to learn a trade so that they could not only earn a living and raise families, but also be profitable members of society. When the number of boys under his care grew, Don Bosco trained (1850) others to assist in teaching the boys, and later (1854) these teachers placed themselves under the patronage of St. Francis de Sales (see January 24). Then, in 1859, Don Bosco formed this group into a religious congregation, the Society of St. Francis de Sales, commonly known as Salesians. In 1872, he helped St. Maria Mazzarello (1837–81) found the Daughters of Mary, Help of Christians, who did similar work among girls. Don Bosco died on January 31, 1888, in Turin, and he was canonized by Pope Pius XI in 1934. When today's opening prayer affirms that St. John Bosco was a teacher and father to the young, this is a reference to his work among Italy's poor youth, which is now continued by the two religious congregations he founded.

FEBRUARY

FEBRUARY 2   🌿   *Feast*
Presentation of the Lord

Our Lord's being presented in the Temple of Jerusalem was the fulfillment of two Mosaic laws: that every first-born male was to be consecrated to the Lord (Ex. 13:2), and that the mother of the newborn son was to be purified in the Temple on the fortieth day after the birth (Lv. 12:2–8). This feast, which first originated in the Jerusalem Church, was called Hypapante, or "Encounter," because of the meeting of Jesus with the aged Simeon, which is narrated in today's Gospel (Luke 2:22–40). The feast came to be celebrated in Rome during the seventh century, but by the tenth, because of the emphasis given to Mary's purification, it became known as the Purification of Our Lady. In 1969, the feast was given its original title, the Presentation of the Lord. The procession on this day dates back to the early centuries, and candles are blessed because of Simeon's prophecy that Christ will be "a revealing light to the Gentiles." The prayer at the blessing of the candles echoes that prophecy. Because blessed candles are carried in the procession, this feast is also known as Candlemas Day.

FEBRUARY 3
St. Blaise, Bishop and Martyr

St. Blaise was born in Sebaste, Armenia (today's Sivas, Turkey), became bishop of that city, and was martyred under Licinius (emperor 308–24) in about 316. Not much more is known about Blaise. Tradition has it that when persecution came to Sebaste, he was forced to hide in a cave but was discovered by animal hunters. He was subsequently tortured and beheaded on the orders of the pagan governor Agricolaus. By the sixth century, Blaise was invoked in the East for ailments of the throat; this is based on a story that while in prison he healed a young boy, who was choking because of a fish bone lodged in his throat. Devotion to St. Blaise took root in the West about the ninth century, and by the Middle Ages he was numbered among the saints commonly referred to as the Fourteen Holy Helpers. The blessing of throats with candles began in the sixteenth century, when devotion to St. Blaise was at its highest.

FEBRUARY 3
St. Ansgar, Bishop

Because St. Ansgar was the first missionary to Denmark and Sweden, he is often referred to as the "Apostle of the North." Ansgar was born near Corbie, in northern France, in about 801. He was educated by the Benedictines at Corbie and then entered (about 814) the Benedictine Order. He was later assigned (822) to

the new monastery at Korvey, Westphalia, Germany,
and in about 826, after King Harold of Denmark had
been converted to Christianity at the Frankish court of
Emperor Louis the Pious, Ansgar accompanied him to
Denmark as a missionary. Because he had little success
in Denmark, he left (829) and accepted the invitation to
pursue missionary work in Sweden. After a year and a
half in Sweden, he was recalled by Emperor Louis and
was subsequently appointed (831) bishop of Hamburg.
Ansgar worked in Hamburg for thirteen years, until
the Northmen invaded (845) the land, burned the city,
and razed it to the ground. In 847, he became bishop
of Bremen and assigned missionaries to evangelize the
northern countries. He himself went again to Denmark and converted Eric, king of Jutland; he returned
to Sweden (852–53), and there King Olaf became a
Christian. Ansgar returned to Bremen and died there
on February 3, 865. Because he was revered as a saint by
the faithful in Germany, Pope Nicholas I (858–67) confirmed his cult. Today's prayer reminds us that through
St. Ansgar's missionary efforts he brought the light of
Christ to many nations.

✝ *FEBRUARY 4   ✐ *Memorial*
Jesuit Martyrs of the Missions

Five Jesuit saints and forty-one Jesuit blessed are liturgically commemorated today. All are martyrs and all
have died in what were missionary lands: India, Japan,
Madagascar, and China.

St. John de Brito was born (March 1, 1647) in Lisbon
and martyred in the Madura Mission, India, on Feb-

ruary 4, 1693. He was canonized by Pope Pius XII in 1947.

St. Leon Mangin (b. July 30, 1857) and three Jesuit companions—SS. Paul Denn (b. April 1, 1847), Rémy Isoré (b. January 22, 1852), and Modeste Andlauer (b. May 22, 1847)—all Frenchmen, were missionaries in China and gave their lives (June 19–20, 1900) for the faith during the Boxer Rebellion. They were canonized by Pope John Paul II in 2000.

Bl. Rudolph Acquaviva (b. October 2, 1550) and his four companions also died in India, but on the Salsette peninsula. They met their martyrdom on July 25, 1583, and were beatified by Pope Leo XIII in 1893.

BB. Francis Pacheco (d. June 20, 1626), Charles Spinola (d. September 10, 1622), and thirty-three Jesuit companions died for the faith between 1617 and 1632 while doing missionary work in Japan. They were beatified by Pope Pius IX in 1867.

Bl. James Berthieu, a Frenchman (b. November 28, 1838), went as a missionary to Madagascar and was martyred there on June 8, 1896. He was beatified by Pope Paul VI in 1965.

Today's opening prayer speaks of these martyrs as missionaries who were fearless in proclaiming the Word of the Lord.

✝ FEBRUARY 5 ✄ *Memorial*
St. Agatha, Virgin and Martyr

St. Agatha was probably born in Catania, Sicily, during the first half of the third century, and was martyred there during the persecution of Decius (emperor 249–

51) in about 251. As in the case of other early martyrs, details of Agatha's life are lacking and only legends remain. Accordingly, she was sent to a brothel to force her to deny her faith. Because she remained steadfast in her resolve, her breasts were cut off, but she was subsequently healed when St. Peter appeared to her in prison. A few days later, she underwent further tortures, and as a result of these, she died. The early martyrologies agree in assigning February 5 as the date of her death. Devotion to St. Agatha spread very quickly throughout Sicily and into Italy, and Pope Symmachus (498–514) erected a church in her honor on Rome's Via Aurelia. Her popularity is evidenced by the fact that her name was added to the Roman Canon, probably by Pope Gregory I (590–604). The opening prayer of today's Mass states that Agatha found favor with God because of her chastity and her courage in professing the faith.

✝ FEBRUARY 6   🌿   Memorial

SS. Paul Miki, Religious and Martyr, and His Companions, Martyrs

Christianity first came to Japan in 1548, and with the preaching of St. Francis Xavier (see December 3), the faith finally took a firm foothold. The Church prospered until the ascendancy of Shogun Toyotomi Hideyoshi, who issued an edict in 1597 directed against the Spanish Franciscans, who had come a few years previously from the Philippines. Hideyoshi's fear was that the Spaniards in Japan were attempting to subdue his country as they had the Philippines. Thus he ordered all Spanish Franciscans to be arrested. In the roundup, which took place in December 1596, a total of twenty-four were apprehended: six Franciscans (three priests and three brothers), three Japanese Jesuits (two scholastics and one brother), and sixteen native-born Franciscan tertiaries, who assisted the missionaries as catechists or interpreters.

Paul Miki was born in Setsu no Kuni, near Osaka, in 1564, and his family became Christian when he was about four or five years of age. As a youth, Paul attended the Jesuit seminary in Azuchi, and then in 1586 he entered the Society of Jesus. Though still studying for the priesthood at the time of his death, he had already gained a reputation as a distinguished preacher and excellent disputant with Buddhist leaders. On January 3, 1597, the twenty-four prisoners, now united in a prison in Miyako (today's Kyoto) were sentenced to death by crucifixion. On the following day, with hands tied behind them, they began their long and arduous walk to Nagasaki. Along the road, two more Japanese Christians were added to their number—they had attempted to comfort the prisoners. When the twenty-six future martyrs arrived at the hill of execution, now known as the Hill of Martyrs, and saw crosses awaiting them, their hearts burst into song. They rushed to the crosses and waited for the executioners to fasten the ropes. From his cross, Paul Miki preached his final sermon: He invited the onlookers to accept Christianity, said he was joyfully giving his life for Christ, and finally he forgave his executioners. At a prearranged signal, the soldiers standing by each cross thrust lances into each martyr's breast. The two other Jesuits to die with

Paul were the scholastic John de Goto (b. 1578), and the coadjutor brother James Kisai (b. 1533). All twenty-six martyrs were canonized by Pope Pius IX in 1862. The prayer in today's Mass refers to the manner in which these martyrs entered into the joy of eternal life.

✝ FEBRUARY 8
St. Jerome Emiliani, Priest

St. Jerome Emiliani spent his entire priestly life in caring for orphans and abandoned children, and so it is not surprising that Pope Pius XI declared him their heavenly patron in 1928. St. Jerome was born in Venice in 1486. His father was of senatorial rank, and he himself was educated and trained to follow in his father's footsteps. In early 1511, he enlisted in the Venetian army, and he was captured the following August. While in prison, he underwent a conversion and promised to dedicate himself to the Lord, if released. He, in fact, was freed on September 27 of that year—he merely walked out of prison without anyone taking any notice of him. He returned to his family and thought about how he could better serve God. He was ordained a priest in 1518. In 1527, when a plague broke out in Venice, he worked in the hospitals for the incurables. Then, because of the number of orphans roaming the city streets, he established (1528) a home for them, taught them catechism, and gave them vocational training. His orphanage proved successful, and he extended his work to Brescia and Bergamo. In 1532, he and his two priest fellow-workers formed the Society of the Servants of the Poor and devoted their time and efforts to caring for orphans and abandoned children. St. Jerome died in the town of Somasca, near Bergamo, on February 8, 1537, caring for victims of the plague. About thirty years later (1568), his society became a religious congregation with the name Clerks Regular Somaschi. He was canonized by Pope Clement XIII in 1767. The prayer of the Mass today recalls that St. Jerome was a father and a friend of orphans.

✝ FEBRUARY 8
St. Josephine Bakhita, Virgin

St. Josephine Bakhita was born in the small southwestern Sudanese village of Algoznei in about 1869. One day, when she was about seven years of age and walking outside the confines of her village, she was kidnapped and then sold to a slave merchant. It was at that time that her Muslim owner gave her the name Bakhita, an Arabic word meaning "lucky" or "fortunate." After a month's detention, she managed to escape, but she was again kidnapped and again sold to another slave merchant. She was then taken to El Obeid, in central Sudan, and there given to the Arab chieftain. After serving the chieftain's family, she was sold (1881) to a Turkish general. For seven years, she endured the harshness of slavery under different masters—these were years of cruelty and even torture. Then one day in 1883, when the Italian vice consul was visiting the general, he noticed Bakhita, who was serving them, and arranged to purchase her with the intention of setting her free.

Bakhita lived with the vice consul's family in Khartoum for two years, until he was recalled to Italy. Bakhita traveled with them, and when they arrived (1885) in Italy, the vice consul handed her over to another family. She now became the nursemaid for this family's young daughter, residing in Mirano Veneto. Her years with this family were happy and joyful. In 1889, Bakhita and the daughter were sent to a boarding school operated by the Daughters of Charity (more commonly known in Italy as the Canossian Sisters, after their founder, Magdalene of Canossa). There, under the sisters' tutelage, Bakhita was instructed in the Catholic faith, and on January 9, 1890, the Cardinal Patriarch of Venice baptized her, giving her the names Josephine Bakhita.

Rejoicing in her new faith, Josephine Bakhita entered the Canossian novitiate in 1893 and two years later pronounced her vows. In 1902, she was transferred from Venice to the convent in Schio, near Vicenza, and there she spent her years serving the community in various humble household tasks, such as in the kitchen, sacristy, and as a porter. Because Josephine Bakhita's background was unusual and heroic, her superior at Schio asked her in 1910 to write the story of her life. Because of failing health, she spent her final years in prayer and died at Schio on February 8, 1947. Throughout her years in religion, Josephine Bakhita was known for her docility and meekness, and she never expressed resentment against her kidnappers or past masters. Rather, she viewed all those trials and tribulations as part of God's providence in leading her to know him and the Catholic faith. She became the first Sudanese saint when she was canonized by Pope John Paul II in 2000, at which time he called her "our universal sister."

St. Scholastica, Virgin

St. Scholastica was the sister, perhaps the twin sister, of St. Benedict (see July 11), the founder of monasticism in the West. She was born in Norcia, Italy, in about 480. At first, she lived a contemplative form of life at home, but when companions asked to join her, she founded a monastery at Plombariola, a few miles south of Monte Cassino. Because her brother had already established his monastery there, he undertook the spiritual direction of Scholastica's group. St. Gregory the Great (see September 3) writes in his *Dialogues* that Benedict and Scholastica used to meet once a year to pray and engage in a spiritual colloquy. At their last meeting, because Scholastica had a premonition that she would never see her brother again, she asked him to remain that night so that they could prolong their conversation. Benedict, however, appealed to his *Rule*, saying that he was obliged to return to the monastery. Scholastica then lowered her head in silent prayer and immediately a thunderstorm broke out—one so violent that Benedict was unable to leave. When he accused her of bringing this about, she merely responded: "I asked you a favor and you refused it; I asked it of God and he granted it." Gregory also relates that Scholastica died three days after this meeting (about February 547) and that at the moment of her death Benedict, seeing a dove ascend into Heaven, knew that his sister had departed this world. St. Scholastica is acknowledged as the founder of the women's branch of the Benedictine Order, and from as early as the eighth century her memorial was celebrated at Monte Cassino on February 10.

Our Lady of Lourdes

It was on February 11, 1858, that Bernadette Soubirous (1844–79), a young girl of fourteen years, and two other young girls left their small village, in the parish of Lourdes in southeastern France, to gather kindling wood for the fires at home. When Bernadette was alone on the shores of the River Gave, near the grotto of Massabielle, our Lady unexpectedly appeared to her. The apparitions (eighteen) continued until July 16, but in the beginning Bernadette was never certain who "the beautiful Lady in white" really was. On March 25, the feast of the Annunciation, Bernadette asked her: "Would you please tell me who you are?" The answer she heard was: "I am the Immaculate Conception." Only four years previously, Pope Pius IX had defined (December 8, 1854) Mary's Immaculate Conception. From the time of our Lady's apparitions in that grotto, Lourdes has become the most famous Marian shrine in Western Europe. Countless pilgrims go there each year, and miracles are frequent—for physical healing as well as spiritual. In 1890, Pope Leo XIII permitted the local Diocese of Tarbes, in which Lourdes is located, to celebrate this feast; then Pope Pius X extended (1907) it to the universal Church. When today's prayer refers to Mary as the sinless Mother of God, it reiterates the name that our Lady gave herself when she said "I am the Immaculate Conception." Bernadette, who had entered (1866) the Sisters of Charity and Christian Instruction of Nevers, died in 1879. She was canonized by Pope Pius XI in 1933.

FEBRUARY 14 ✎ *Memorial*
✝ SS. Cyril and Methodius, Bishops

SS. Cyril and Methodius were blood brothers and were born in Thessalonica (modern Salonika), Greece. Cyril, whose true name was Constantine, was born in 827, and Methodius, whose name was Michael, was born about 815. They received the names Cyril and Methodius when they became monks. Though both brothers spoke Greek, they also knew the Slavonic language because many Macedonian Slavs lived in their area. After studies at Constantinople (today's Istanbul), Methodius accepted a government position in a Slavonic-speaking area, and Cyril taught philosophy. Methodius then entered a monastery on Mount Olympus, and in about 855 Cyril joined him. In 862, when Ratislav, the Duke of Greater Moravia (now part of the Czech Republic), requested missionaries capable of instructing the Slavs in their own language, Cyril, who had been ordained a priest, and Methodius were chosen for the task. In preparation for their mission, Cyril invented an alphabet (Glagolithic script) and translated the Gospels and the liturgical books into what is now known as Old Church Slavonic. Because the brothers used Slavonic and not Latin in the liturgy, they ran into difficulty with the Bavarian priests in that same area, but when the brothers went to Rome (867 or 868), Pope Hadrian II (867–72) approved their use of the Slavonic liturgy. Cyril died in Rome on February 14, 869. Methodius was then consecrated archbishop of Sirmium (today's Sremska Mitrovica, Yugoslavia), and he returned to Moravia to continue his missionary work. He died at

Velehrad (in today's Czech Republic) on April 6, 884. SS. Cyril and Methodius are honored as the Apostles of the Slavs, and in 1980 Pope John Paul II proclaimed them co-patrons of Europe. They are also acknowledged as the fathers of Slavonic literature, because of their invention of the Slavonic alphabet and their translation of parts of the Bible.

✝ *FEBRUARY 15 ✄ *Memorial*
  St. Claude La Colombière, Priest

St. Claude La Colombière was born in Saint-Symphorien d'Ozon in southern France on February 2, 1641. He entered the Society of Jesus in 1658, and after ordination was assigned (1675) to the Jesuit residence in Paray-le-Monial. In the Visitation Convent of Paray, but unknown to Fr. Claude, our Lord was revealing the treasures of his Sacred Heart to Sister Margaret Mary Alacoque (see October 16), and our Lord had told her "I will send you my faithful servant and perfect friend." Shortly after his arrival in Paray, Fr. Claude visited the convent, and on that occasion Sr. Margaret Mary heard an interior voice say: "This is he whom I have sent to you." She told him of her revelations, and from that time onward, both he and she worked to have the feast of the Sacred Heart established in the Church. After eighteen months in Paray, Fr. Claude was assigned (1676) to be preacher to the Duchess of York in London. England still had laws against Catholic priests, and in November 1678, he was unjustly accused and arrested for traitorous speech. While he was imprisoned in a damp dungeon, his health deteriorated so rapidly that he was released (January 1679) and sent back to France. He never regained his health, and in August 1681 he returned to Paray-le-Monial, where he died on February 15, 1682. He was canonized by Pope John Paul II in 1992. The prayer of today's Mass speaks of St. Claude as being our Lord's faithful servant and a witness to the riches of his love.

✝ FEBRUARY 17
Seven Founders of the Order of Servites, Religious

In thirteenth-century Florence, seven laymen—all prominent merchants and members of a confraternity known as the Brothers of Penance—decided (about 1233) to abandon their homes, their careers, and their wealth and retire to a place outside the city where they could live a life of prayer, poverty, and penance. The leader of the group was Bonfilius Monaldo, and the others were Bartholomew Amidei, Benedict dell'Antella, John Bonagiunta, Alexis Falconieri, Gerard Sostegni, and Ricovero Uguccione. Two were married, two were widowers, and three were single. They chose the unfrequented slopes of Mount Senario as their place of habitation, and there they built a small chapel and hermitages. Several years later, they returned to Florence and at the bishop's suggestion formed a religious order, calling themselves the Servants of Mary, or Servites. The first superior was Bonfilius (d. 1261), and under him the order grew in numbers and spread to other Italian cities. The last of the seven founders to die was Alexis Falconieri, who always remained a coadjutor brother. He died on February 17, 1310, at 110 years of age. The seven founders were canonized by Pope Leo XIII in 1888. Their memorial is celebrated today, the anniversary of the death of St. Alexis Falconieri. Today's prayer recalls their coming together and forming a religious congregation under the patronage of our Lady, and thereby leading other souls to heaven.

✝ FEBRUARY 21
St. Peter Damian, Bishop and Doctor of the Church

St. Peter Damian was born in Ravenna in 1007. He taught school for a time in his native city, then was ordained a priest, and when he was about twenty-eight years of age he became (1035) a hermit at the Benedictine monastery at Fonte Avellana in northern Italy. He was subsequently chosen (1043) prior of the monastery, and he became known for his austere penitential practices and for revitalizing the monastic spirit among his monks. During this period, he wrote ascetical treatises for his community of monks, as well as several treatises advocating reform within the Church. His ascetical writings were especially appreciated for their practicality—they gave many examples and anecdotes—rather than for overlong explanations of theoretical principles. In the area of reform, he wrote vigorously against simony and clerical marriage. Because of his reform writings, Pope Stephen IX made (1057) him, though unwilling, Cardinal Bishop of Ostia. For the next fifteen years, Peter Damian worked very closely with Pope Stephen and two successive popes (Nicholas

II, 1058–61; and Alexander II, 1061–73) on reform matters. He likewise served them on several special diplomatic missions to France and Germany. In 1072, he revisited Ravenna to effect a reconciliation between that city and Pope Alexander. On his return to Rome, he died at the Benedictine Monastery of Santa Maria in Faenza on the night of February 22–23, 1072. Peter Damian was immediately venerated by his monks as a saint. In 1828, Pope Leo XII approved his cult, extended its celebration to the universal Church, and declared him a doctor of the Church.

✝ FEBRUARY 22 ✍ *Feast*
Chair of St. Peter, Apostle

Today we commemorate Christ's granting of the primacy in the Church to the Apostle Peter, and the Gospel (Matt. 16:13–19) of today's Mass relates how Christ gave Simon the name Peter, telling him: "you are 'Rock' and on this rock I will build my Church" (Matt. 16:18). The office or task that Peter was given was that of universal teacher and pastor of the faithful, and the symbol of that office is the cathedra, or chair; hence, today's celebration is the feast of the Chair of St. Peter. Therefore, on this day, we acknowledge Peter's pontifical authority as well as the pontifical authority invested in Peter's successor, our present pope. The prayers of the Mass speak of a unity in faith and love, a unity which is symbolized by Peter, on whom Christ chose to build his Church. A unity in faith and love with the pope is a unity in faith and love with Peter, and ultimately with Christ our Lord.

✝ FEBRUARY 23   ✎   *Memorial*
St. Polycarp, Bishop and Martyr

Only few details are known about the life of St. Polycarp. He was born in about 69 or 70, was a disciple of St. John the Apostle, and was appointed Bishop of Smyrna (modern Izmir, Turkey), perhaps by St. John. Polycarp paid a visit to Rome (about 155), representing the churches of Asia Minor, to discuss with Pope Anicetus the date when the feast of Easter should be celebrated. The result of their meeting was that the Eastern and Western Churches were to continue to follow their respective systems for computing the date of Easter. Shortly after Polycarp's return to Smyrna, he was arrested by the Roman governor, L. Statius Quadratus, during a public festival, and when urged to betray his Lord and God, Polycarp responded: "For eighty-six years I have been his servant and he has done me no wrong. How can I blaspheme against my king and savior?" Polycarp was consequently sentenced to be burned alive in the stadium in Smyrna, but because the flames did not harm him, he was killed by the sword on February 23, 156 or 157. The story of his arrest and death are described in *Martyrium Polycarpi*, the earliest known Christian document of this genre. His Letter to the Philippians is important because Polycarp is the first to cite passages from the Gospels of Matthew and Luke, as well as from the Acts of the Apostles and from the letters of Peter and John.

MARCH

✝ MARCH 3
St. Katharine Drexel, Virgin

St. Katharine Drexel was born into a prosperous and wealthy banking family in Philadelphia on November 26, 1858. Her education was with private tutors and governesses. Upon the death of her parents, Katharine and her two sisters inherited a sizable fortune. But the Drexel sisters were not ones to squander money; they used it philanthropically. Katharine first became interested in the plight of Native Americans when members of the Bureau of Catholic Indian Missions approached her for help. She responded by building schools, churches, and convents. What the Indian missions needed, according to her friend Bishop James O'Connor of Omaha, were priests. So during a visit (1886) with Pope Leo XIII, she pleaded for missionaries for the Indian missions. But the pope responded: "Why not, my child, yourself become a missionary?" Thereafter, Katharine decided to enter religion, but unable to find a congregation that worked specifically with Indians and blacks, she decided to establish her own. After two years of novitiate training with the Sisters of Mercy in Pittsburgh, she and a few companions founded (1891) the Sisters of the Blessed Sacrament for Indians and Colored People. Throughout her life, she continued to disburse the income from her inheritance by building and maintaining schools among Indians in the Northwest and among blacks in the South. The schools, once built, were then staffed by members of her own congregation. In 1915, she established Xavier University in New Orleans, a university for blacks. Annually, she traveled the country to inspect her foundations. It was on one such tour that she suffered (1935) a severe heart attack; as a result, she had to curtail her travel and work. She then retired to the mother house and spent her time in prayer. She died at Cornwells Heights on March 3, 1955, at the age of ninety-seven years. Though born a millionaire, she chose to live in poverty so that she could help others in need. St. Katharine Drexel was canonized by Pope John Paul II in 2000.

✝ MARCH 4
St. Casimir

St. Casimir was born in Cracow on October 3, 1458, the third son of Casimir IV, the King of Poland and Grand Duke of Lithuania, and of Elizabeth of Austria. As a youth, Casimir joined his father in his travels and campaigns, and when the king went to Lithuania for reasons of state (1481–83), Casimir ruled as regent in Poland. He was especially known for his piety, his generosity toward the poor, and his devotion to the Blessed Sacrament and to the Blessed Virgin Mary. When marriage was suggested, he rejected the idea because he would not renounce his freely chosen chastity. During an official visit to Lithuania, he fell ill, and he died of tuberculosis at the royal castle in Grodno on March 4, 1484, and was buried in the cathedral of SS. Peter and Paul in Vilnius. He was only twenty-five years of age. Casimir was canonized in 1521 by Pope Leo X, and he is the patron of Poland and Lithuania. The prayer of today's Mass reminds us that to serve God is to reign. St. Casimir preferred to serve his eternal King rather than that he himself should be a temporal king.

✝ MARCH 7   ✎   *Memorial*
SS. Perpetua and Felicity, Martyrs

St. Perpetua was a twenty-two-year-old noble lady living in Carthage (in modern Tunis), and St. Felicity was a slave. Perpetua was a mother, still nursing her infant son at the time of her arrest, and Felicity was pregnant. Both were catechumens, and because they refused—during the persecution of Septimius Severus (emperor 193–211)—to pay divine worship to the emperor, they were arrested and eventually condemned to be thrown to wild beasts. Perpetua's non-Christian father, because of his love for his daughter, had several times tried to get her to apostatize. But her reply was: "I am a Christian; I cannot be called anything else." Both ladies were baptized in prison, and there Felicity gave birth to a daughter. When it came time for them to be led to the amphitheater and to death, Perpetua and Felicity walked with so graceful a bearing that it seemed that they were entering heaven. After one of the beasts had attacked them but did not kill them, they were beheaded by a gladiator. Their martyrdom took place on

March 7, 202. The details of their imprisonment and martyrdom are found in *Passion of Saints Perpetua and Felicity*, one of the most ancient and reliable histories of these martyrs. Part of it is said to be in Perpetua's own words. A basilica was built over their tombs in ancient Carthage, and because of their popularity in the early Church, both their names were added to the Roman Canon.

MARCH 8
St. John of God, Religious

John Ciudad was born in Montemor-o-Novo, Portugal, on March 8, 1495. He was taken to Spain as a child, and there he became a shepherd in Castile. When he was twenty-seven years of age, he joined (1522) the Count of Oropesa's forces in fighting the French. He later fought against the Turks in Vienna. When he was forty, he gave up the military life and returned to Spain. John, disturbed and saddened about his former dissolute life, entered upon a life of penance. In Granada, he opened a small religious goods store and began caring for the sick poor. He eventually rented a house to take care of the abandoned sick, and later he founded a hospital for them in Granada. Soon other similar-minded individuals joined him, and because of John's heroic charity the people began calling him "John of God." His little group of helpers expanded, and eventually they formed the religious congregation of Brothers Hospitallers, which still cares for those sick in body and in spirit. After years of tireless service, John fell ill and died on March 8, 1550, his fifty-fifth birthday. He was canonized by Pope Alexander VIII in 1690. Pope Leo XIII proclaimed (1886) him and St. Camillus de Lellis (see July 18) patrons of hospitals and the sick, and in 1930 Pope Pius XI declared St. John of God the heavenly patron of nurses. The opening prayer of today's Mass recalls his love and compassion for others.

✠ MARCH 9
St. Frances of Rome, Religious

St. Frances, a member of the noble and illustrious Busso family, was born in Rome in 1384. Because she was obedient to her parents' wishes, she was married at a very early age to Lorenzo dei Ponziani, a wealthy landowner in Rome's Trastevere quarter. During her years of married life, she bore three children and was an exemplary mother and wife. Those were also difficult years for Rome, as war, famine, and plague ravaged the city. With her husband's consent, Frances devoted herself to works of mercy: helping the poor, caring for the sick in their homes, and visiting hospitals. In 1425, she and several other ladies united to form a group of oblates dedicated to works of charity. In 1433, these ladies began to live in community in the building known as Tor de' Specchi in the center of Rome. But Frances continued to live at home with her husband. Her reputation for charity became widespread, and the people simply referred to her as "Frances of Rome." After the death of her husband (1435), she also went (March 21, 1436) to live in the community she had founded. She died in Rome on March 9, 1440, and was canonized by Pope Paul V in 1608. Her group, the Oblates of Tor de' Specchi, still exists today. The prayer in today's Mass speaks of Frances as a unique example of love in marriage as well as in religious life.

✠ MARCH 17
St. Patrick, Bishop

St. Patrick, the apostle and patron of Ireland, was born in Roman Britain (perhaps today's Scotland?) in about 389. When he was sixteen years of age (405), he was seized by Irish raiders, taken to Ireland, and sold as a slave. After six years of shepherding, he escaped and returned to his homeland. Yet the thought of some day returning to Ireland to convert the pagans living there impelled him to go to Gaul (modern France) to study for the priesthood. In about 432, Pope Celestine I (422–32) had Patrick consecrated a bishop and sent him to Ireland to succeed Bishop Palladius. Patrick traveled throughout the island and tirelessly preached the Gospel to eager ears. He made countless converts, established the Catholic Church, recruited clergy from Gaul and Britain, and founded many monastic communities. He is also said to have established (about 444) the primatial see of Ireland at Armagh. After nearly thirty years of fruitful evangelizing, he died in about 461. Since the seventh century, March 17 has been given as the date of St. Patrick's death.

✠
St. Cyril of Jerusalem, Bishop and
Doctor of the Church

St. Cyril was born of Christian parents in about 315, in or near Jerusalem. He was ordained a priest about 345 and was placed in charge of preparing catechumens for baptism. The twenty-four sermons that he preached to them during Lent 348 or 349 are known today as the *Catechetical Instructions*; of these, nineteen were pre-baptismal and given in Jerusalem's Church of the Holy Cross, while the remaining five were post-baptismal and given in the city's Church of the Resurrection. As a unit, they form a complete explanation of the Catholic faith. Cyril became bishop of Jerusalem in about 350 or 351, at a time when the East was still troubled by the Arian heresy, which held that Christ is a mere creature and not the Son of God. Because Cyril maintained the Nicene faith, that is, that Christ is the true Son of God and is of the same nature as the Father, he was banished three times from his see by the Arians. He later played an important role at the Second Ecumenical Council, which was held in Constantinople in 381. He died in Jerusalem on March 18, 386, having been a bishop for about thirty-five years, sixteen of which had been spent in exile. Because of his writings explaining the faith, Pope Leo XIII declared (1882) him a doctor of the Church.

✠ MARCH 19 ✐ Solemnity
St. Joseph, Husband of
the Blessed Virgin Mary

The only facts that we know of St. Joseph's life are those that we have in the Gospels: He was a carpenter, the husband of Mary, the foster-father of our Lord, and the protector of the Holy Family. There is a choice of Gospel readings for this solemnity. The first is from Matthew (1:16, 18–21, 24a) in which, having learned that Mary, his betrothed, is with child, Joseph debates within himself whether he should divorce her or not. However, the angel of the Lord appears to him and informs him that the child is "through the Holy Spirit" and so he should not "be afraid to take Mary your wife into your home." The second is from Luke (2:41–51a) and relates the incident when the twelve-year-old Jesus remains behind in Jerusalem at the time of the Passover. As early as the ninth century, German martyrologies gave the date of St. Joseph's death as March 19, but none gave the reason why this date had been chosen. By the fourteenth century, the Franciscan and Servite Orders liturgically celebrated a feast honoring St. Joseph, but devotion to him did not become widespread until after the preaching of St. Bernardine of Siena (see May 20) and the writings of St. Teresa of Jesus (see October 15). In 1479, the Franciscan pope, Sixtus IV, introduced St. Joseph's feast in Rome, and by 1621 it was inserted into the Church's universal calendar. In 1870, Pope Pius IX proclaimed Joseph the patron of the universal Church, and in 1962 Pope John XXIII added his name to the Roman Canon.

✝ MARCH 23
St. Toribio de Mogrovejo, Bishop

St. Toribio de Mogrovejo was born in Mayorga, near Valladolid, Spain, in November 1538. He studied at Valladolid and Salamanca. He then taught law in Salamanca until 1574, when he was named inquisitor of Granada. In 1580, Pope Gregory XIII named him archbishop of Lima, but because he was not yet ordained a priest—he had only received tonsure—he at first humbly declined, but then obeyed, the pope's wishes. He was ordained a bishop in Seville in August 1580, and in September he sailed for the New World, arriving in Lima in May 1581. In Peru, Archbishop Toribio was a tireless missionary. During his twenty-five years there, he visited his vast diocese three times and held thirteen diocesan and three provincial synods. He saw to the reform of the clergy and ordered that catechisms be published in the languages of the native Indians; the two most widely used languages were Aymara and Quechua. He introduced the Franciscans, Dominicans, and Jesuits into Peru, established the first seminary in the New World, and encouraged Indians to study for the priesthood. That the Catholic Church was firmly established in Peru is due to his missionary zeal. He fell ill while visiting his diocese and died at Saña on March 23, 1606. He was canonized by Pope Benedict XIII in 1726.

✝ MARCH 25 ❧ *Solemnity*
Annunciation of the Lord

Today we liturgically celebrate the Incarnation of God's Son, when the Word entered our human sphere and took unto himself a human nature, joining his divine nature to our human mortality. The day's Gospel is from Luke (1:26–38) and relates the angel Gabriel's unexpected visit to the humble Mary of Nazareth, informing her that God has chosen her to be the mother of his Son. She is told that "the power of the Most High will overshadow" her, and that he who will be born of her "will be called the Son of the Most High ... and of his Kingdom there will be no end." Her acquiescence to the divine will is in her response: "I am the handmaid of the Lord. May it be done to me according to your word." From that moment onward, God was living among us. Nine months from this date, we celebrate Jesus's birth in Bethlehem. In the early Church, it was commonly believed that Christ was not only conceived on March 25, but that he likewise died on that date. St. Augustine (see August 28) states this in his book *On the Trinity* (iv, 5) when he says: "The VIII Kalends of April [March 25] is both the day of his conception and his passion." This feast of the Annunciation of the Lord was most probably first liturgically celebrated in the Church of Constantinople during the first half of the fifth century, but by the seventh century it was already widespread in the West.

EASTER SUNDAY ✿ *Solemnity*
Resurrection of the Lord

Today we commemorate our Lord's Resurrection from the dead, just as he had foretold it (Mark 10:33–34). In its liturgical calendar, the Church celebrates many feasts, but this one is by far the greatest and the most important. On the first day of the week, after our Lord's crucifixion, death, and burial, the holy women went to anoint his body. But they found the tomb empty. When Peter and John arrived, they also found it empty. But it was only when they had entered the tomb and had seen that all was in order that they remembered that this had been foretold to them (see John 20:1–9). There were no human witnesses to the actual event of Christ's resurrection, but later that evening the apostles and disciples did encounter the risen Lord; they saw the wounds in his hands, feet, and side, spoke with him, and enjoyed his company. That the Lord was risen was to them an indubitable fact. St. Paul tells us: "If Christ is not risen, then your faith is in vain" (1 Cor. 15:17). If Christ is not risen, then he remains dead and his teaching and life have been a deliberate deception, and those who had believed in him were deplorably duped. But the disciples have unanimously agreed: "We have seen the Lord." Christ's resurrection is the key to understanding his entire life; without it, his life would have been a failure. But because the resurrection did take place, it becomes the pledge of our own future resurrection into glory. Christ's resurrection from the dead is the ultimate and definitive proof of his divinity.

APRIL

✝ *St. Francis of Paola, Hermit*

St. Francis was born in Paola, in Calabria, southern Italy, on March 27, 1416. At the age of twelve years, he was placed in the Conventual Franciscan Friary of San Marco in fulfillment of a promise his parents had made to St. Francis of Assisi. After a year at the friary, he and his parents made pilgrimages to Rome, Assisi, Loreto, etc. Returning to Calabria, Francis, who was now going on fourteen, left home and became a hermit. Other young men in time joined him, and they formed (1436) a group known as the Hermits of Saint Francis. Francis's reputation for holiness and as a miracle worker spread throughout Italy and into France, and when King Louis XI (reigned 1461–83) was dying, he asked Francis to come and cure him. The holy hermit was disinclined to make the long trip, but when Pope Sixtus IV urged (1483) him to go, he obeyed. Rather than restoring the king to health, Francis prepared him for death. Francis then remained in France, and in 1492 he changed the name of his group to the Order of Minims to emphasize that they were "the least" in God's family. He died on Good Friday, April 2, 1507, at the age of ninety-one, at Plessis-les-Tours, near Tours, and was canonized by Pope Leo X in 1519. Because many of his miracles were associated with the sea, Pius XII, in 1943, declared him patron of seafarers.

✝ APRIL 4
St. Isidore, Bishop and Doctor of the Church

St. Isidore was most probably born in Seville in about 565. He attended the monastic school where his older brother Leander was a monk, and who, it appears, supervised his education. Isidore himself later became a monk. When Leander died (about 600), Isidore succeeded him as archbishop of Seville. During his years as archbishop, Isidore strengthened the Catholic Church in Spain by calling several synods, both provincial and national. He also presided over the important Fourth Council of Toledo (633), which established liturgical uniformity (the Mozarabic Rite) throughout Spain, and decreed a cathedral school in every diocese. Though his efforts and accomplishments were important and had lasting influence on the Spanish Church, nevertheless, he is better known today for his writings. His many biblical, theological, and historical works enjoyed great prestige throughout Europe, and because they were always deemed significant, they have all survived. Medieval scholars were unanimous in considering Isidore the most learned man of his time, and thus they gave him the title *magister egregius* (preeminent master). Isidore especially deserves this title because of his *Etymologies*, a total of twenty books that formed a general encyclopedia and was a summary of all religious and secular learning up to his time. Isidore died in Seville on April 4, 636. Toledo always looked upon its archbishop as a saint, but widespread devotion to him only began in 1063, when his remains were translated to León, Spain. His cult was officially approved by Pope Clement VIII in 1598, and in 1722 Pope Innocent XIII declared him a doctor of the Church.

✝ **APRIL 5**
St. Vincent Ferrer, Priest

St. Vincent Ferrer was born in Valencia on January 23, 1350, and he entered the Order of Preachers (Dominicans) in 1367, when he was seventeen years of age. As a young Dominican scholastic, he studied at the Dominican *studium generale* in Barcelona. After ordination in 1374, he continued his theological studies in Toulouse. On his return to Spain, he became (1379) prior of the Dominican convent in Valencia, and there he also taught theology at that city's cathedral school. Vincent's most distinguished work, however, was accomplished during the years of the Western Schism (1378–1417), when there were three rival popes, each claiming the allegiance of Catholics. So confusing and complicated was the period that the Catholics of the world had no way of knowing who was the true pope. Vincent himself opted for Pope Clement VII (actually an antipope), then living in Avignon. When the Spanish Cardinal Pedro de Luna (c. 1328–1423) was elected (1394) Pope Benedict XIII to succeed Clement VII, Vincent moved to Avignon and was appointed master of the sacred palace. He eventually came to suspect that Benedict had no desire to heal the wound in the Church, and when he saw that Benedict was, in fact, hindering all moves toward unity, Vincent finally realized that Benedict could not be the true pope. Thus he left Avignon in 1399 and began a preaching apostolate. He spent the next twenty years traveling thoughout Spain, northern Italy, Switzerland, France, and the Low Countries preaching the need for repentance and the coming of the judgment. So forceful and fiery were his sermons—they sometimes lasted three hours—that he became known as the Angel of the Judgment. Vincent lived to see the end of the Western Schism with the election of Pope Martin V (1417–31). Vincent died two years later at Vannes, in Brittany, on April 5, 1419, and was canonized by Pope Callistus III in 1455. The prayer in today's Mass recalls St. Vincent's preaching the gospel of the last judgment.

✝ APRIL 7 ✐ *Memorial*
St. John Baptist de la Salle, Priest

St. John Baptist de la Salle was the founder of the Institute of the Brothers of the Christian Schools, better known as the Christian Brothers. He was born in Reims on April 30, 1651. In 1667, at the age of sixteen years, he was appointed canon at the city's cathedral chapter. He subsequently studied in Paris at the Seminary of Saint Sulpice and at the Sorbonne, and he was ordained to the priesthood in 1678. He then continued studies in theology at Reims, and there earned a doctorate in 1680. During his early years as a priest, he perceived the need for free schools for poor boys, in which they would be given a basic education and would also be taught religion and be trained to be good Christians. He opened his first school in Reims, having been encouraged to do so by Adrien Nyel, who had opened four such schools in Rouen. To ensure that his teachers were properly prepared, John Baptist took upon himself the task of training them. In May 1684, he and his twelve teachers formed a religious congregation and chose to be known as Brothers of the Christian Schools. John Baptist was an innovator in the area of pedagogy: He replaced individual instruction with class instruction, stressed the need for a thorough knowledge of the vernacular, made religious instruction the center of the school day, and established (1686) the first normal school or training college for young men. As the Brothers' new schools opened, their reputation spread, and during the founder's lifetime the Brothers operated schools in many of France's major cities. St. John Baptist died at Rouen on April 7, 1719, and was canonized by Pope Leo XIII in 1900. In 1950, Pope Pius XII named him patron of teachers. Today's prayer in the Mass recalls his dedication in offering a Christian education to the young.

✝ APRIL 11 ✒ *Memorial*
St. Stanislaus, Bishop and Martyr

St. Stanislaus, the patron of Poland, was born at Szczepanów in the Diocese of Cracow in about 1030. His early education was at the cathedral school in Gniezno, and later at Liège (in today's Belgium). After his return to

Poland and his ordination to the priesthood, he became a canon and preacher at Cracow Cathedral. Upon the death of Bishop Lambert, Pope Alexander II in 1072 appointed Stanislaus to succeed him as bishop of Cracow. At first, the new bishop was on friendly terms with King Boleslaus II "the Bold," but because of the king's injustices, cruelties, and dissolute manner of life, Stanislaus found it necessary to excommunicate him. Boleslaus viewed this action as treasonable and sought a way to kill him. While Stanislaus was celebrating Mass on April 11, 1079, in the Church of St. Michael in Cracow, the king with his henchmen entered the church and murdered the bishop. Stanislaus was immediately regarded as a martyr, and because Boleslaus was no longer in favor in his own country, he left to live with relatives in Hungary. He is said to have spent the remainder of his life as a penitent in the Benedictine monastery in Osiak. Nine years after Stanislaus's martyrdom, his body was transferred (1088) to Cracow Cathedral, where his tomb became a center of pilgrimage. He was canonized by Pope Innocent IV in 1253.

✝ APRIL 13
St. Martin I, Pope and Martyr

St. Martin was born in Todi, Italy, on an unrecorded date, and may have been a deacon in Rome when he was chosen pope on July 5, 649. At the time of his election, the Eastern Church was in the throes of a crisis caused by the Monothelites, who claimed that there was but one will in Christ, namely the divine will, for Christ's divine nature had completely overwhelmed and subdued his human nature. In 648, the Monothelite-leaning Emperor Constans II (641–68) issued a decree forbidding all further discussion on Christ's wills. Martin was familiar with this heretical teaching as well as the imperial decree, because before his election he had served as *apocrisiarius*, or representative, of Pope Theodore I (687) in Constantinople (modern Istanbul). Hence, as soon as he was elected to succeed Theodore, he called a synod to meet in Rome in October 649. The synod affirmed the Catholic teaching that there are two wills in Christ, divine and human, and condemned the heretical Monothelite teaching. Because Martin's Roman synod went directly contrary to Constans's decree, the emperor had the pope, though ill and bedridden, arrested (June 17, 653) and taken to Constantinople, where he arrived on September 17, 654. The journey was long and arduous, lasting more than a year due to frequent stops at various islands in the Aegean and a prolonged sojourn at Naxos. When the ailing pope finally arrived in Constantinople, he was, following Constans's orders, brutally maltreated, publicly humiliated, and stripped of his episcopal robes. He was then flogged, placed in chains, and condemned to exile. The pope was subsequently taken (March 26, 655) to Chersonesus in the Crimea, near Sevastopol (in modern Ukraine), where, after many hardships (famine, cold, and abusive treatment), he died on September 16, 655 (or, according to other sources, on April 13, 656). Inasmuch as Martin had been deposed by Constans, a successor, Eugene I, was elected in Rome on August 10, 654. When Martin's death became known in the West, he was immediately honored as a martyr.

His memorial is celebrated on April 13, the date that it has always been celebrated in the East. The prayer of today's Mass speaks of the hardship, pain, and threats of death that never weakened St. Martin's faith and trust in God.

✟ APRIL 21
St. Anselm, Bishop and Doctor of the Church

St. Anselm was born in Aosta in northern Italy in about 1033. He studied in France and there became a Benedictine monk at the Abbey of Bec in Normandy in 1060. Three years later, he was appointed prior, and in 1078 he was elected abbot. Under his supervision, the monastic school at Bec became a renowned center of learning. In 1093, he was named Archbishop of Canterbury, but because of conflicts with William II (Rufus), the King of England, over the spiritual rights of the Church (the problem of lay investiture), Anselm went (1097) into voluntary exile to Italy to seek support. With the death of William (1100), Anselm returned to Canterbury, but the same problems occurred with Henry I (reigned 1100–35), and thus in 1103 Anselm went into exile rather than take an oath of allegiance to the king. When Henry finally agreed to respect the Church's independence in appointing bishops, Anselm also agreed to return to his see, which he did in 1107. He died on April 21, 1109, and his cult was approved by Pope Alexander VI (1492–1503). In 1720, Pope Clement XI declared him a doctor of the Church. St. Anselm was the foremost theologian of his age. His most famous theological work is *Why God Became Man*, in which he opposes the then-current opinion that as a result of original sin the devil had a claim on our nature, and that nature could only be ransomed by Christ's death. In its place, Anselm proposes a doctrine of satisfaction, which holds that because sin is infinite it demands infinite atonement, which only the God-Man was capable of offering. Anselm also often spoke about "faith seeking understanding" to emphasize the harmony between faith and human reason. The prayer in today's Mass adopts St. Anselm's expression when it asks that God's gift of faith come to the aid of our understanding.

✝ *APRIL 22 ✐ Feast*
Blessed Virgin Mary, Mother of the Society of Jesus

On this day, the Society of Jesus celebrates our Lady's motherly care over the Society. At all important junctures in the life of St. Ignatius of Loyola (see July 31), our Lady had an important role to play. But April 22 is special to Jesuits because it was on that date in 1541 that Ignatius and companions pronounced their first Jesuit vows. Early on the morning of April 22, which was the Friday of Easter Week, Ignatius and companions made a pilgrimage to the seven Churches of Rome. When they finally arrived at St. Paul's Outside-the-Walls, Ignatius, the newly elected general, celebrated Mass at our Lady's altar. Immediately before receiving Holy Communion, they all pronounced their vows in the newly formed Society of Jesus. Ignatius chose our

Lady's altar as the place most suitable for the first Jesuits to take their first vows; he knew that he and his companions, and those who were to follow them, would need our Lady's continued maternal protection. The opening prayer of today's Mass alludes to this event when it says that the Society of Jesus consecrated itself to God's glory in the presence of Mary.

✚ APRIL 23
St. George, Martyr

Very little is known about St. George. Tradition claims that he was a soldier, who was martyred (about 303) at Lydda (Lod in modern Israel), during the time of Diocletian (emperor 284–305). By the sixth century, his cult had become immensely popular in the East, and his tomb in Lydda was a favorite place of pilgrimage. Because the faithful commonly referred to him as "the Great Martyr," legends soon began to take hold; for example, his slaying of the dragon. When the crusaders of the eleventh century returned home, they brought with them devotion to St. George, whom they had adopted as their patron because he was usually depicted as a knight or a soldier. As a result, devotion to St. George soon became widespread in the West as well. In 1222, a synod held at Oxford, England, ordered his feast to be celebrated, and in 1347 King Edward III named him patron of England. St. George is likewise the patron of other nations, for example, Portugal, Lithuania, and Ethiopia. His memorial is kept on April 23, the date it has always been celebrated in the East.

St. Adalbert, Bishop and Martyr

St. Adalbert, whose baptismal name was Wojciech, was probably born in 956 in the family's castle in Libice, Bohemia (part of today's Czech Republic). His family belonged to the princely Slavnik line. His early education was under the supervision of St. Adalbert (981), the archbishop of Magdeburg, who, when he confirmed (972) the youth, gave him his own name. On his return to Prague, Adalbert was ordained to the priesthood (981), and when Thietmar, the first bishop of Prague, died (982), Adalbert—though only twenty-six years of age—was chosen (983) to succeed him. In his personal life, he was austere and mortified. As shepherd of the diocese, he sought to spread the Christian faith throughout his territory. To accomplish this, he extirpated whatever pagan customs remained among his people, strove to raise their moral standards, and initiated reform among the clergy. These measures, however, aroused the enmity of some, including Boleslaus II, the Duke of Bohemia, who forced Adalbert to leave the diocese. He subsequently went (990) to Rome, where he entered the Benedictine Abbey of SS. Boniface and Alexis. He returned to Prague in 993, but realizing that he was still unwelcome in his diocese, he again left for Rome, where he was elected prior of his abbey. Being aware that he could never return to his see, he requested Pope John XV (985–96) for permission to be released from his episcopal duties and asked to be appointed an itinerant missionary. At the invitation of Duke Boleslaus Chrobry of Poland, Adalbert settled in that land and began evangelizing non-Christians. In 996, he took his mission to the non-Christian Prussian peoples on the Baltic coast. He traveled as far as Gdansk, but there he encountered great opposition and because he refused to give up his evangelizing mission. He was martyred on April 23, 997. His body was first buried at Gniezno, Poland, and then in 1039 it was translated to Prague.

✝ APRIL 24
St. Fidelis of Sigmaringen, Priest and Martyr

St. Fidelis was born in Sigmaringen, Germany, in October 1578. His true name, however, was Mark Roy. He earned a degree in philosophy from Freiburg-im-Breisgau in 1603, and then he spent several years (1604–10) as a tutor for the sons of German nobility, taking them on educational tours of France, Italy, and Spain. He resumed his studies in 1610 and earned a law degree in 1611. He practiced law in Ensisheim until 1612, when he decided to become a priest. He subsequently entered (October 4, 1612) the Franciscan Capuchin Order; it was then that he received the name Fidelis. In 1617, he initiated his career as a preacher, and in 1622 he was put in charge of the Capuchin mission in the Rhaetian Alps (Switzerland), which was then under the care of the Congregation for the Propagation of the Faith. His preaching among the Grisons, an area which had become Protestant in 1608, was favorably received, and several prominent civic leaders were brought back to the Church. He then decided to preach in Seewis, where he was attacked in church and slain on April 24, 1622. St. Fidelis was the first martyr of the Propagation of the Faith and was canonized by Pope Benedict XIV in 1746.

✝ APRIL 25   ✿   Feast
St. Mark, Evangelist

St. Mark is the author of the second Gospel and was a member of the first Christian community in Jerusalem. His mother, Mary, owned the house where the Jerusalem Christians met for prayer and where Peter stayed after he had been miraculously liberated from prison (Acts 12:12–17). Mark accompanied Paul and Barnabas on their first missionary journey (Acts 12:25) to Antioch (today's Antakya, Turkey). He was likewise with Paul in Rome (Col. 4:10; Phlm. 24) and was associated with Peter in that same city (1 Pt. 5:13). It was most probably in Rome that Mark wrote his Gospel sometime after Peter's death (about 64) and before the year 70, basing it on Peter's preaching. Tradition has it that Mark subsequently went to Alexandria, where he was bishop and where he was martyred toward the end of the first century. His relics were taken (828)—supposedly to keep them from being profaned by unbelievers—by two Venetian merchants to Venice. His feast has been celebrated on April 25 from earliest times.

✝ *APRIL 27 ✎ *Memorial*
St. Peter Canisius, Priest and Doctor of the Church

St. Peter Canisius was a Dutchman, born in Nijmegen, on May 8, 1521. In 1536, he went to study in Cologne, and there he met Blessed Peter Faber (see August 2), one of St. Ignatius of Loyola's (see July 31) first companions. Peter became a Jesuit in 1543, then went to Rome, and from there he was assigned to the Jesuit college in Messina, Sicily. In September 1549, Pope Paul III asked him to return to Germany to defend the Catholic Church against the attacks of the Reformers. He taught at the university in Ingolstadt (Germany), and from the pulpit explained to the faithful the basic teachings of Catholicism. In this way, he brought many Catholics back to the faith. He then went to Vienna (1552), and there did what he had done in Ingolstadt. He wrote a *Catechism*, which proved to be so popular that it was in use until the nineteenth century. During his years in Germany and Austria, he founded eighteen colleges and wrote thirty-eight books, but it was especially through his preaching that he helped restore Catholicism in those countries. He died on December 21, 1597, and was canonized by Pope Pius XI in 1925. In recognition of his writings defending the faith, he was also declared a doctor of the Church. The opening prayer of today's Mass summarizes his apostolate when it prays for men like Peter Canisius to proclaim God's message in the cities of the world so that the people may turn to him.

St. Peter Chanel, Priest and Martyr

St. Peter Chanel was born in the small village of La Potière, near Cuet, France, on July 12, 1803. His early education was under the guidance of his parish priest, and later he attended the seminary in Belley. After his ordination in 1827 as a diocesan priest, he spent three years as pastor of a small parish in Crozet. Ever since seminary days, he had thought of becoming a foreign missionary, and with this in mind he entered the Society of Mary (Marist Fathers) in 1831. He left France in December 1836 for Western Oceania and arrived on Futuna Island in November 1837. During Peter's three and a half years on the island, he struggled with the native language, suffered privation and, finally, was persecuted by local chiefs. As a missionary, he had little success and gained only a few converts to the Church. On April 28, 1841, a group of men came to his hut, and presuming that they wanted to ask him a question, he invited them in. Once in the hut, the men clubbed him to the ground and then killed him with an axe. St. Peter Chanel, Oceania's first martyr, was canonized by Pope Pius XII in 1954.

St. Louis Mary de Montfort, Priest

St. Louis Mary de Montfort, known for his devotion to our Lady, was born at Montfort-la-Canne, France, on January 31, 1673. The family name was actually Grignion, but in his adult life he dropped it and chose

Montfort. His early education was with the Jesuits at Rennes (1685–93), and he then attended the Seminary of Saint-Sulpice (1693–1700) in Paris. Two years after ordination, while serving as chaplain at a hospital in Poitiers, he organized (1702) several of the women working there—teaching orphans and nursing the sick—into a religious congregation, which eventually came to be known as the Daughters of Wisdom. While in Poitiers, he began giving missions, thus hoping to educate the faithful in their Catholic beliefs. Then, in 1705, he founded a men's congregation called the Company of Mary (more commonly known as Montfort Fathers). In 1706, he visited Rome, and there Pope Clement XI appointed him missionary apostolic, an itinerant missionary with western France as his field of evangelization. He spent the next ten years giving missions, almost always in rural areas. When not preaching, he was writing, and among his books are *The Secret of Mary* and the well-known *True Devotion to the Blessed Virgin Mary*, in which he teaches that the best means of achieving union with Christ is by having devotion to his Mother. St. Louis died at Saint-Laurent-sur-Sèvres, in the Vendée, on April 28, 1716, and was canonized by Pope Pius XII in 1947.

✝ APRIL 29 ✐ *Memorial*
St. Catherine of Siena, Virgin and Doctor of the Church

St. Catherine Benincasa was born in Siena in about 1347. From her earliest years, she enjoyed visions and lived a life of penance. When she was about seventeen years of age, she joined (1365) the Third Order of St. Dominic, and because of her reputation for holiness, a group of followers soon formed around her. At the request of the city of Florence, she traveled (1376) to Avignon, where Pope Gregory XI was then residing, to negotiate peace between the pope and the Florentines. While there, she pleaded with the pope to return to Rome, which he did in January 1377. After Pope Gregory's death (March 27, 1378) and the election (April 8, 1378) of Pope Urban VI and that of the Antipope Clement VII (September 20, 1378)—which initiated the Western Schism—Catherine went to Rome and worked to restore the Church's unity. She is also known for her writings, especially her *Dialogues*, which places her among the Church's great spiritual writers and mystics. Catherine died in Rome, at the age of thirty-three, on April 29, 1380. She was canonized by Pope Pius II in 1461, and in 1970 Pope Paul VI declared her a doctor of the Church. Today's prayer mentions Catherine's serving the Church, a reference to her influence in convincing the pope to leave Avignon and return to Rome.

✝ APRIL 30
St. Pius V, Pope and Religious

St. Pius was born Anthony Ghislieri in Bosco Marengo, near Alessandria, northern Italy, on January 17, 1504. He entered the Order of Preachers (Dominicans) in Voghera when he was fourteen years of age and took the name Michael. After his ordination to the priesthood (1528) in Genoa, he taught theology at the Dominican scholasticate in Pavia. In 1551, Pope Julius III appointed him commissary general of the Roman Inquisition, and later (1566) he became bishop of Sutri. In 1567, Pope Paul IV made him a cardinal, and in 1558 he became the Church's Inquisitor General. Upon the death of Pope Pius IV (1559–65), he was elected pope on January 7, 1566, and he chose the name of Pius. As pontiff, he was as ascetical in his daily life as he was in appearance. He was wholeheartedly devoted to reform and determined to preserve the integrity of the Catholic faith against the onslaughts of the Reformers. He revised the *Roman Breviary* (1568) as well as the *Roman Missal* (1570), both of which continued in use until the revisions ordered by Vatican Council II. He died on May 1, 1572, and was canonized by Pope Clement XI in 1712. When the prayer in today's Mass speaks of St. Pius as being chosen by God to protect the faith and to give him more fitting worship, this is an allusion to Pius's determination to keep the faith unadulterated and to his revision of the Church's liturgical books.

MAY

✝
St. Joseph the Worker

Pope Pius XII instituted the feast of St. Joseph the Worker in 1955 and fixed its celebration for May 1. In many European countries, May 1 (May Day) is a civil holiday honoring the worker and had its origin in communist countries. The celebrations on that day, rather than emphasizing the dignity of the laborer, turned the day into political and military propaganda. Because human labor was being exploited by atheistic governments, Pius XII felt the need to remind the world of labor's proper role and God-given dignity. Thus the pope dedicated May 1 to St. Joseph the Worker, the carpenter of Nazareth and foster-father of our Lord. It was by the daily work of his hands that Joseph provided for Jesus and Mary. Joseph personifies all workers and reminds us that there is honor in labor; there is a joy coming from our accomplishments and from our ability to support those we love, our families. As Joseph worked to provide for his family, in a similar fashion we also work to provide for our families. By taking a secular celebration and dedicating it to St. Joseph the Worker, Pius XII emphasized the dignity inherent in human labor.

✝ MAY 2 ✐ *Memorial*
St. Athanasius, Bishop and Doctor of the Church

St. Athanasius was born of Christian parents in Alexandria in about 295. After his ordination as a deacon (318), he became secretary to Bishop Alexander of Alexandria, and with him attended the Church's First Ecumenical Council at Nicaea (325). Upon Bishop Alexander's death, Athanasius was chosen (328) as his successor. During his forty-five years as bishop of Alexandria, Athanasius was five times exiled from his see because he valiantly refused to accept the heretical doctrines of Arianism. He vigorously championed the faith as formulated at Nicaea and fearlessly supported the Church's teaching about the divinity of Christ. Athanasius was a prolific writer; many of his books were written during his seventeen years of exile. His writings, especially his *Discourses against the Arians* (composed about 358), are important for their explanation and defense of the Catholic faith; it is principally because of these that he is honored as a doctor of the Church. He died in Alexandria on May 2, 373, and a few years later, when St. Gregory of Nazianzen (see January 2) was delivering (about 379) a panegyric on the anniversary of Athanasius's death, he referred to him as "a pillar of the Church" and as "the Father of orthodoxy." Today's prayer reminds us that St. Athanasius was an outstanding defender of the truth of Christ's divinity.

✚ MAY 3   ✎   *Feast*
SS. Philip and James, Apostles

SS. Philip and James have shared a common feast in the Church since the time when their relics were placed under the altar of the Roman Church dedicated to them on May 1, 1570. The Church is now more commonly known as the Church of the Twelve Apostles. Philip, a native of Bethsaida in Galilee, was among Christ's first disciples (John 1:43–44). At the miracle of the multiplication of the loaves, it was he who remarked that "not even with two hundred days' wages could we buy enough loaves to give each one a mouthful" (John 6:7). It was also he who served as intermediary when some Hellenistic Jews had asked to be introduced to Jesus (John 12:21–22). After Pentecost, he preached the gospel in Phrygia in Asia Minor (today's Turkey) and was martyred in Hierapolis. Tradition has it that he was crucified head downward during the persecution of Domitian (emperor 81–96).

James was the son of Alphaeus (Matt. 10:3) and a relative of our Lord (Matt. 13:55). He is frequently referred to as "James the Less," perhaps to indicate that he was younger than the other apostle named James (see July 25). He is usually identified with the James who became Bishop of Jerusalem (Acts 15), and he is presumed to be the author of one of the New Testament epistles. He also was martyred, but in Jerusalem, in about 62. He was thrown from a pinnacle of the temple, and then stoned and clubbed to death. The first reading (1 Cor. 15:1–8) in today's Mass recalls the appearance of the Risen Christ to James, and the Gospel reading (John 14:6–14) is Christ's answer to Philip's request: "Lord, show us the Father."

✝ *MAY 4
St. Joseph Mary Rubio, Priest

St. Joseph Mary Rubio was born on July 22, 1864, at Dalías, in southern Spain. He was ordained (1887) a diocesan priest, and after three years of parish work was called to Madrid (1890) to teach in the seminary. Fr. Rubio was always drawn to the Jesuits and had often thought of entering the Society of Jesus, but because of an obligation of gratitude he felt toward an elderly retired priest, who lived with him, he was prevented from fulfilling that desire. Upon that priest's death in 1906, Fr. Rubio, at age forty-two years, finally entered the Society. When his Jesuit formation was over in Granada, he returned (1911) to Madrid and spent the remaining eighteen years of his life there doing pastoral work. He had great appeal in the pulpit—his sermons were simple and sincere, but they always touched people's hearts. He was Madrid's favorite confessor—he spent hours each day guiding individuals along the way of perfection. He also promoted vocations and organized groups of women, who made altar linens and vestments for poor parishes in the outlying villages. Nor did he forget the city's slums—he regularly visited them and preached to the poor. Because no part of Madrid escaped his influence, he came to be known as the "Apostle of Madrid." He died on May 2, 1929, and Pope John Paul II canonized him in 2003. St. Joseph Rubio's apostolate in the confessional and to the city's marginalized are referred to in today's opening prayer, where he is called minister of reconciliation and a father of the poor.

✝ MAY 10
Bl. Damien Joseph de Veuster of Moloka'i, Priest

Bl. Damien de Veuster was born at Tremeloo, Belgium, on January 3, 1840. His baptismal name was Joseph, but Damien was the name he received when he entered (1859) the Congregation of the Sacred Hearts of Jesus and Mary (commonly known as the Picpus Fathers). His brother Auguste (Pamphile in religion) had entered the same congregation two years previously, and two of his sisters also had religious vocations. In 1863— because his brother, who had been chosen to go to the congregation's mission in the Hawaiian Islands, contracted typhus and was too ill to travel—Damien, still a theological student, volunteered to take his place. He arrived at Honolulu in March 1864 and was ordained the following May. For the next nine years, he worked at two of his congregation's mission stations.

Then, in 1873, the bishop asked his priests for volunteers to work on Moloka'i, an island of the archipelago used as a leper colony. The priests going to the island would rotate every three weeks. Damien offered his services and arrived on the island on May 10. After only a few days there, he wrote to the bishop expressing his desire to remain permanently. There were at that time about 800 lepers on the island, but because of deaths and new arrivals, the number fluctuated weekly. Officially, Damien was to act only as pastor for the Catholics, but after seeing the conditions in which the lepers lived—poor housing, nonexistent sanitation, no medical care—he realized that he had to take on other tasks as well. Thus, in the beginning he was both their physician and nurse. He built their houses and solved the island's sanitation problem, and when necessary he also acted as gravedigger and undertaker. In time, he built a hospital and two orphanages. His entire life was devoted to his charges, even to sharing meals with them. After working and living among them for eleven years, he himself contracted (1884) leprosy. During his final years, others—hearing of his selfless charity—came to assist him. Bl. Damien remained active until one month before his death, on April 15, 1889. He was beatified by Pope John Paul II in 1995. His memorial is celebrated today because it was on this day that he arrived on Moloka'i.

✝ MAY 12
SS. Nereus and Achilleus, Martyrs

Very little is actually known about the two Roman soldiers, Nereus and Achilleus, who may have been blood brothers. They are thought to have been martyred about 304, during the persecution of Diocletian (emperor 284–305). Tradition has them attached to the household of the matron Flavia Domitilla, and when she was banished from Rome for being a Christian, Nereus and Achilleus, also Christians, accompanied her to the island of Terracina. Because the three persevered in their profession of Christ, the brothers were beheaded and Flavia Domitilla was burned. Nereus and Achilleus were buried on the Ardeatine Way. Pope Damasus (366–84) (see December 11) placed a marble inscription over their tomb, and in 390 Pope Siricius built a church over it. Their memorial is celebrated on this date, as given in the Hieronymian Martyrology (about 450).

✝ MAY 12
St. Pancras, Martyr

St. Pancras, a fourteen-year-old youth, died a martyr's death in Rome, about 304, during the persecution of Diocletian (emperor 284–305). He was beheaded on the Aurelian Way, about two miles outside the city; his body was then claimed by the Roman matron Ottavilla and was buried near the site where he had been martyred. Because devotion to young Pancras was so popular in Rome, Pope Symmachus transformed (505) the original small oratory over the tomb into a large church, which still stands today. Accounts of Pancras's martyrdom—written many years later and therefore somewhat less reliable—claim that he was born in Phrygia in Asia Minor (now in modern Turkey) and that with an uncle he had come to Rome, where they became Christians. During the Diocletian persecution, rather than deny his newly adopted faith, the youthful Pancras chose death. The fifth-century Hieronymian Martyrology gives May 12 as the date of his martyrdom.

✝ MAY 13
Our Lady of Fatima

It was on this date in 1917 that our Lady first appeared to three shepherd children in the tiny village of Fatima, Portugal. It was a Sunday, and after the children—Lucia dos Santos (b. 1907) and her cousins Francisco (b. 1908) and Jacinta (b. 1910) Marto—had returned from Mass, they took their flocks to the nearby Cova da Iria to graze. When noon came, they heard what they thought was thunder and found themselves surrounded by a strong, almost blinding light. Looking toward a little holm tree—an evergreen oak—they saw, as they said, a beautiful lady standing on a cloud over the tree. The lady first spoke to the children, assuring them not to be afraid. When Lucia asked who she was, her response was "I come from Heaven." She then asked the children to return to that place on the thirteenth of the following five months, and she encouraged the children to pray the rosary daily and to offer their sufferings in reparation for sins. She also informed them that she would identify herself in October.

There were a total of six apparitions from May 13 to October 13. During the June apparition, our Lady also urged devotion to her Immaculate Heart. In July, she promised that a "great miracle" would take place in October. The August apparition occurred on the nineteenth at Valinhos, because the children had been kidnapped and held for two days (August 13 and 14) by unbelieving town officials. There followed apparitions in September and finally in October, when the Lady identified herself as Our Lady of the Rosary. When this final apparition was over, there occurred the celestial prodigy known as the Miracle of the Sun, witnessed by about 50,000 bystanders. For approximately ten minutes, the sun turned in the heavens as if it were a wheel of fire, sending forth rays in all directions; at one point, it appeared as if it had left the heavens and were falling to earth. Our Lady's constant message during these apparitions was to recite the rosary daily, pray for sinners, make reparation for sin, and to honor her Immaculate Heart. After years of investigation (1922–29), the bishop of Leiria declared (October 13, 1930) that visions at the Cova were worthy of credence and thereby authorized public devotion to Our Lady of Fatima. In 1942, Pope Pius XII consecrated both the Church and the entire human race to the Immaculate Heart of Mary.

Francisco and Jacinta fell victim to the 1918 influenza epidemic; the former died at Fatima on April 4, 1919, and the latter from tuberculosis in Lisbon on February 20, 1920. Both were beatified by Pope John Paul II on May 13, 2000. Lucia entered the Sisters of St. Dorothy in 1925, and in 1948 transferred to the Carmelites at Coimbra.

✝ MAY 14 ✎ *Feast*
St. Matthias, Apostle

St. Matthias was not one of the original Twelve Apostles, but after Judas's betrayal and death, and before the Holy Spirit's descent upon the Church at Pentecost, Peter gathered the disciples to choose someone to take Judas Iscariot's place among the Twelve. Two candidates were proposed, as today's first reading (Acts 1:15–17, 20–26) narrates. "The choice fell to Matthias" (Acts 1:26), and thus he was numbered among the apostles. Other than this single incident in Acts, nothing else is known about him. Some early writers say that he preached the gospel in Palestine, and others maintain that he evangelized Cappadocia (in today's Turkey) or Ethiopia. He is revered as a martyr, but neither the date nor the manner of his martyrdom is known with certainty. May 14 has been selected for his feast so that it approaches the time of the Ascension and precedes Pentecost, the period when Matthias was chosen to be an apostle.

✝ MAY 15
St. Isidore

The St. Isidore of today's memorial is distinguished from St. Isidore, Archbishop of Seville (see April 4), by referring to him as Isidore "the Laborer" or "the Farmer." He was born in Madrid in about 1080. Because his parents were extremely poor, as soon as he was old enough, he was employed as a day laborer working on the large estate of a Madrid landowner. He remained in that job for the rest of his life. Isidore took his Christian upbringing seriously. Before going to work each morning, he went to Mass, and then throughout the day he continued his prayers, whether he was plowing the fields or sowing seed. He was always thoughtful of others and was ever ready to help them; he was likewise generous to the poor and often shared his meals with them. What was exceptional about Isidore was that people noticed that he did marvelous things—he performed miracles. He died in 1130, and after his death miracles continued to occur and in greater number. Even the kings of Spain were the beneficiaries of his intercession, and thus his cause was officially introduced. His cult was confirmed by Pope Paul V in 1619, and at that time May 15 was established as his feast day. He was subsequently canonized by Pope Gregory XV in 1622. St. Isidore the Farmer was later made patron of Madrid, and because he is the patron of farmers, he was named (1947) patron of the U.S. National Catholic Rural Life Conference.

✝ *MAY 16 ✐ *Memorial*
St. Andrew Bobola, Priest and Martyr

St. Andrew Bobola, one of the patrons of Poland, was born in the Palatinate of Sandomir in 1591 and entered (1611) the Society of Jesus when he was twenty years of age. His priestly life was mostly spent in preaching and pastoral work. In both Vilnius and Warsaw, he gained a reputation as a preacher. He was also an exemplary pastor, and when assigned to parishes in Eastern Poland his main concern was to recall to the Catholic Church those who had left it because of an earlier lack of Catholic priests in those areas. Through his preaching, two entire villages returned to the Catholic faith. His enemies nicknamed him "soul-hunter" and grew to despise him more and more. Whenever he walked through town, adults urged street ruffians to throw mud and stones at him. Such annoyances did not deter him from doing the Lord's work. In May 1657, Cossacks invaded the Pinsk region where he was evangelizing, and—unable to persuade him to renounce his Catholicism—they dragged him to nearby Janów, where they subjected him to one of the cruelest torments that any of Christ's martyrs ever had to suffer. With God's grace, he endured it without any sign of weakness, and after two hours of brutal torture a saber's blow brought his passion to an end. He died on May 16, 1657, and was canonized by Pope Pius XI in 1938.

✝ MAY 18
St. John I, Pope, Martyr

St. John was born in Tuscany. He was a senior deacon in Rome at the time of his election, and he was consecrated pope on August 13, 523. Shortly before John's election, Emperor Justin I (518–27) passed oppressive measures with regard to the Arians in Constantinople (today's Istanbul); he seized their churches and forced them to become Catholics. Because Theodoric, Ostrogoth King of Italy (493–526), was an Arian, he looked for a way to get Justin to repeal his anti-Arian laws. Theodoric summoned Pope John to his palace in Ravenna and compelled him to go to Constantinople and order Justin to cease his harsh treatment of the Arians. Pope John arrived in Constantinople in October or November 525 and was fittingly received as the successor of St. Peter. He informed Justin of Theodoric's wishes, and though Justin agreed to return the seized churches to the Arians, he would not allow the converted Arians to revert to Arianism. When the pope returned to Ravenna in early May 526, Theodoric—infuriated because he did not get from Justin all that he demanded—imprisoned the pope. Because Pope John was then ill and worn out from the voyage, he died shortly afterward on May 18, 526, perhaps from maltreatment. He was immediately honored as a martyr and his body was taken to Rome and buried in St. Peter's basilica.

✝ MAY 20
St. Bernardine of Siena, Priest

St. Bernardine, whose family name was Albizzeschi, was born at Massa Marittima, near Siena, on September 8, 1380. After his studies at the University of Siena, he entered (1402) the Franciscans. He was ordained in 1404, but it was not until 1417 that he became an itinerant preacher, a ministry he continued until his death twenty-seven years later. Bernardine was the best known preacher in the Italy of his day. He crisscrossed northern and central Italy, and wherever he preached he drew such crowds that the churches were often too small. During the course of his sermons, he preached on living honestly and doing penance, against gambling and worldly ostentation, and always included a sermon or two on reverencing the Holy Name of Jesus. At the conclusion of these sermons, he always displayed a tablet with the trigram IHS surrounded by rays emanating from the Holy Name. It was because of Bernardine's preaching on the Holy Name that that particular devotion gained a foothold in Italy and then spread throughout the world. In 1444, while on his way to preach in Naples, and traveling through the mountainous Abruzzi area of central Italy, he became ill with a fever and was taken to nearby Aquila, where he died on May 20, 1444. During his lifetime, he was offered three bishoprics—of Siena, Ferrara, and Urbino—but declined them all. He was canonized by Pope Nicholas V in 1450, six years after his death. The prayer in today's Mass makes particular mention of St. Bernardine's special love of the Holy Name of Jesus.

✝ MAY 21
St. Cristopher Magallanes,
Priest and Martyr,
and His Companions, Martyrs

Between 1915 and 1929, the Catholic Church in Mexico experienced one of its most difficult periods. On February 5, 1917, the country's new Constitution went into effect, and because it was both anticlerical and antireligious, Catholic priests were its main target. St. Christopher Magallanes and his twenty-four companions were victims of this persecution, all of whom were martyred in hatred of the Catholic faith. Among these martyrs, there were twenty-two priests and three young laymen; seventeen of the martyrs were from the Archdiocese of Guadalajara, and the remaining eight came from five other dioceses. All were assassinated by the state authorities without any trial, and many were tortured and executed at the very place where they had been apprehended. These arrests and assassinations took place at night, for fear of any reaction on the part of the faithful.

Fr. Christopher Magallanes was born on July 30, 1869, in San Rafael Totatiche, Jalisco. He had been pastor in his hometown area, where he exercised great zeal toward his parishioners and also did missionary work among the indigenous people, the Huicholes. He was arrested on May 25, 1927, with another priest, Fr. Augustine Caloca (b. May 5, 1898), and minutes before being shot at Colotlán, he said to his companion: "Be at peace, my son; it takes but one moment, then it will be Heaven." He then turned to his executioners and said: "I die innocent. I pray to God that my blood serves the unity of my Mexican brethren." Despite the persecution that threatened these twenty-five martyrs, they never yielded to fear; instead, it emboldened them to continue their ministry, which they did with heroic courage and dedication. All freely and calmly accepted their martyrdom, and at their last moment, while giving their final witness to the Catholic faith, they likewise forgave their executioners.

✝ *St. Rita of Cascia, Religious*

Very little is known about St. Rita's early life. Her parents were peasants living at Roccaporena, near Cascia, Umbria, and there Rita was born, most probably in 1381. In her youth, she was quiet and contemplative by nature, so much so that her only desire was to give her life to God by entering the convent. Rita, however, was a dutiful child and had been brought up to be obedient, so when her parents insisted that she marry, she set aside her personal desire to obey them. The young man she married is described in the sources as "brutal and violent." Her married life was not a happy one; she endured her husband's maltreatment and never complained. She always treated him with kindness and gentleness, even when he yielded to abusive anger. Her constant goodness toward him eventually won him over, and in time he grew mellow and even came to love his wife. Tragedy, however, then struck the family. Her husband was murdered, supposedly in retaliation for some deed of his done many years previously.

Within a year after she became a widow, Rita's two young sons also died. Because she now found herself without a family, she decided to do what she had always wanted to do. On three occasions, she sought admission at the Augustinian convent of S. Maria Maddalena in Cascia, but each time she was refused—the reason always given was that though she was now a widow, nevertheless, she had been married. On her fourth attempt in 1407, she gained admittance.

Rita spent the next forty years of her life in that convent, where she became known for her dedication to prayer, charity toward her sisters, and observance of the rule. Her preferred subject for meditation was the Passion of Christ, and one day while at prayer before a crucifix, she felt a thorn from Christ's own crown being plunged into her forehead, producing a deep wound. She bore this wound for fifteen years, and because it never healed but at times became purulent and emitted a fetid smell, she was sometimes forced to separate herself from her community. Worn out by penance and fasting, she died on May 22, 1447. Within ten years after her death, the citizenry of Cascia called her their "saint." In 1627, Pope Urban VIII approved a Mass in her honor, and in 1900 Pope Leo XIII canonized her and called her "the precious pearl of Umbria."

✝ *MAY 24
Our Lady of the Way

Jesuits have a special devotion to Our Lady of the Way because the Roman church that bore that name was the Society's first church and it was there that St. Ignatius of Loyola (see July 31) and the early Jesuits focused their apostolate. When Ignatius and his companions settled (1538) in Rome, they celebrated Mass, heard confessions, preached, and taught the catechism to children in that church. When the pastor of the church witnessed the good that the Jesuits were accomplishing, he too entered the Society and asked the pope to place the church under the Society's care (1542). All the early Jesuits prayed before the image of our Lady in that church, and it was at her altar that many of them pronounced their religious vows. When the church was replaced by the larger Church of the Gesù, the image of our Lady was placed in the new church in a special chapel, which is still a favorite shrine for Jesuits and Romans. In today's opening prayer, we ask that through Mary's intercession, and through our following of Jesus, who is the way, the truth, and the life, we be led to the Father in Heaven.

✝ MAY 25
*St. Bede the Venerable, Priest
and Doctor of the Church*

St. Bede was born in northern England, in the Kingdom of Northumbria, in about 672 or 673. At the age of seven years, he was entrusted to the Benedictine monasteries at Wearmouth and was educated there as well as at Jarrow. After his studies, he became a monk and taught in the monastery school; he was not ordained until he was thirty. He spent much time doing research in the monastery's library and in writing. He produced many theological and exegetical books, but the most outstanding is his *Ecclesiastical History of the English People*, which he completed in about 731. This is the most important historical work of that period and is the only source today for the early history of England and of the Church in England. It is because of this invaluable record that he is known as the Father of English History. He died at the monastery at Jarrow on May 25, 735, and in recognition of his erudition he was immediately referred to as the "Venerable" and revered as a saint. In

1899, Pope Leo XIII named him a doctor of the Church. Today's prayer recalls St. Bede's erudition when it affirms that God has enlightened the Church with the learning of St. Bede and prays that we may learn from his wisdom and benefit from his prayers.

✝ MAY 25
St. Gregory VII, Pope, Religious

Before becoming pope, St. Gregory worked closely with five other popes. His name was Hildebrand, and he was born in Tuscany in about 1021. He then went to Rome, where he became a monk, probably at Santa Maria on the Aventine. When Pope Gregory VI (1045–46) was forced into exile (1046), Hildebrand accompanied him to Germany. When Pope Leo IX (1049–54) was elected, he called Hildebrand to Rome and made him treasurer of the Roman Church. Pope Leo and his successor Pope Victor II (1055–57) both used Hildebrand for special papal missions. Hildebrand subsequently worked closely with Pope Nicholas II (1058–61) and Pope Alexander II (1061–73), and after Alexander's death, he himself was elected pope on April 22, 1073, by popular acclaim. Pope Gregory was a man of exceptional ability and sought to promote reform within the Church by renewing decrees against clerical marriage and simony, and to abolish lay investiture, that is, secular control over the appointment of bishops and abbots. When Emperor Henry IV of Germany (reigned 1056–1106) ignored the pope's orders and appointed bishops, Gregory excommunicated (1076) him and forbade him to exercise royal powers. Gregory rec-

onciled him to the Church only after the emperor had
submitted at Canossa (January 1077). When Henry
later (March 1084) seized Rome, Gregory was forced to
go south to Salerno, where he died on May 25, 1085. Today's prayer speaks of the courage and the love of justice that distinguished Pope Gregory, and thus it recalls
what are said to be the pope's final words: "I have loved
justice and despised iniquity, and because of this I die
in exile."

✝ MAY 25
St. Mary Magdalene de' Pazzi, Virgin

St. Mary Magdalene de' Pazzi was born Catherine de'
Pazzi in Florence on April 2, 1566. Hers was an ancient
and noble family. She received the name Mary Magdalene when she entered the Carmelite convent of Santa
Maria degli Angeli in Florence in 1582. There she lived
a contemplative life of prayer and penance, and in return God favored her with supernatural gifts, visions,
and ecstasies. In obedience to her confessor's wishes,
she dictated her supernatural experiences to secre-
taries; these accounts are still extant. She became mistress of novices in 1598, and then in 1604 subprioress of
the community. About three years before her death,
she became ill and then bedridden. Though she suffered greatly, her constant prayer was: "Lord, let me
live on that I may suffer more!" She died in Florence on
May 25, 1607, and was canonized by Pope Clement IX in
1669. The opening prayer of the Mass today recalls her
extraordinary mystical graces when it says that God
filled her with heavenly gifts and the fire of his love.

✝ MAY 26 *ø* *Memorial*
St. Philip Neri, Priest

St. Philip Neri, a lawyer's son, was born in Florence on July 21, 1515. When he was seventeen years of age, he went (1532) to live with an uncle, a merchant, to learn how to become a man of business. But business was not to Philip's liking; he preferred to serve God, and after a year with his uncle, he went (1533) to Rome. There he began his studies in philosophy and theology; but after a couple of years, he gave them up to spend his time in prayer and in helping the poor, sick, and homeless. In 1548, with some like-minded individuals, he formed the Confraternity of the Most Holy Trinity to see to the needs of Rome's poor and to care for sick pilgrims in Rome. Realizing that he could do more by becoming a priest, he was ordained in 1551. To his regular apostolic work, Philip now added celebrating Mass, hearing confessions, teaching catechism, and offering counsel. Then, with his priest friends, he founded (1575) the Congregation of the Oratory. Philip was very popular in Rome—there was no one who did not recognize him—and he did so much good and had helped so many that he was called the "Apostle of Rome." After a full apostolic life, he died at the age of eighty, on May 26, 1595, and was canonized by Pope Gregory XV in 1622.

✝ MAY 27
St. Augustine of Canterbury, Bishop

St. Augustine of Canterbury is referred to as the "Apostle of England." He was prior of the monastery of St. Andrew on Rome's Coelian Hill when Pope St. Gregory the Great sent (596) him and about thirty monks to evangelize the Anglo-Saxons. Augustine and his monks landed in Kent during the summer of 597. Because Bertha, the wife of Ethelbert, the king of Kent, had been a Christian before her marriage, the king readily permitted the missionaries to preach in his kingdom. The king likewise gave the monks a house and a church in Canterbury. Through Augustine's preaching, Ethelbert became a Catholic (597) as did many of his subjects. Augustine established his see at Canterbury—the only Christian Anglo-Saxon kingdom on that island—built the first cathedral there, and sent missionaries and bishops to other parts of England. Augustine's ministry in England lasted only seven years; he died on May 26, 604 or 605. Because he planted the seeds of the Catholic Church in England, St. Augustine is also known as the Father of the Church in England.

✝ MAY 31 ✒ *Feast*
Visitation of the Blessed Virgin Mary

Immediately after the angel Gabriel announced to Mary that she was to become the Mother of God, the angel likewise told her that her "kinswoman has conceived a son in her old age" (Luke 1:36). Upon hearing this news, Mary set out to visit her cousin Elizabeth. Today we commemorate that visit, and the Gospel for today's Mass describes what happened when the cousins met (Luke 1:39–56). The feast of the Visitation first originated within the Franciscan Order, as early as 1263. The feast then spread throughout Europe. It was extended to the universal Church by Pope Urban VI in 1389, to obtain Mary's intercession in bringing an end to the Western Schism, which had begun in 1378. In 1969, the date of the feast was changed from July 2 to May 31, so that the feast may precede the feast of the Birth of John the Baptist, celebrated on June 24, and thus better conform to the New Testament account.

✠ *Ascension of the Lord* ✒ Solemnity

Forty days after our Lord's resurrection, and after accomplishing his mission on earth, he gathered his disciples on a mount outside Jerusalem and, after a final discourse, departed from them, ascending body and soul into Heaven. Mark describes this event in the fewest of words: "After speaking to them, the Lord Jesus was taken up into Heaven and took his seat at God's right hand" (16:19). This mystery embraces three moments: (1) Christ's leaving his disciples, who are to continue his mission on earth; (2) his triumphant entrance into Heaven, whence he had come; and finally (3) his sitting at the Father's right hand in glory. This departure of Christ in his humanity was to be the inauguration of a new presence, one more profound and fruitful, for he had said: "If I do not go, the Advocate will not come to you; but if I go, I will send him to you" (John 16:7). This promise was fulfilled ten days later with the descent of the Holy Spirit. This feast of Christ's Ascension nourishes and increases our hope of attaining Heaven, for he ascended there to prepare a place for us (see John 14:2).

✝ *Pentecost Sunday* ✐ Solemnity

This feast, whose name comes from the Greek *pente-chostos*, meaning fiftieth, commemorates the descent of the Holy Spirit on the Virgin Mary, the apostles, and the infant Church. Immediately before our Lord's Ascension into Heaven, during his last instruction to his disciples, he promised them the gift of the Spirit: "You shall receive power when the Holy Spirit has come upon you, and you shall be my witnesses" (Acts 1:7–8). This promise was fulfilled ten days later, when they were all gathered in one place: "Suddenly a sound came from heaven . . . and it filled the house where they were sitting. Tongues as of fire appeared, which parted and rested on each of them. All were filled with the Holy Spirit" (Acts 2:2–4). Immediately afterward, the apostles went out and gave witness to Christ, with Peter's first public discourse being preserved in Acts 2:14–41. This outpouring of the Holy Spirit on the infant Church marks the beginning of the Church's recognizable existence on earth and reveals whence the Church draws her power for her evangelizing mission. The same Holy Spirit is also the guarantor of the Church's growth throughout the world. With the Spirit's descent, the Father, the Son, and the Holy Spirit now dwell in a new way in the Christian. This feast is sometimes called Whitsunday—that is, White Sunday—because of the white baptismal robes that the newly baptized were accustomed to wear at this day's liturgical celebration.

JUNE

✝ JUNE 1 🖉 *Memorial*
St. Justin, Martyr

St. Justin was born of Greek parents in Flavia Neapolis (ancient Shechem, Samaria; today's Nablus, Jordan) in about 100. He was trained in Greek Platonic philosophy and became (130) a Christian after an old man, whom he had met on the seashore, spoke to him about the prophets of the Old Testament and about Christianity. Justin saw Christianity as the fulfillment of Plato's highest aspirations. After Justin's conversion, he taught Christian philosophy at Ephesus, and in 135 left for Rome, where he opened his own Christian school. In about 165, during the reign of Marcus Aurelius (emperor 161–80), Justin was delated to the city prefect, Rusticus, for being a Christian, and when he refused to sacrifice to idols, he was scourged and beheaded with six other Christians. The *Acts* of his martyrdom are extant, and their importance lies in the fact that they are a contemporary record. The date of his martyrdom is unknown, but his memorial has always been celebrated in the East on June 1. Justin was the Church's first great apologist, and he was the first Christian thinker to try to reconcile the teachings of faith with reason.

His two *Apologies* are invaluable for their description of the Church's early liturgy. The prayer in today's Mass hints that by setting aside his pagan philosophy St. Justin rejected falsehood and chose the sublime wisdom of Jesus Christ.

✝ JUNE 2
SS. Marcellinus and Peter, Martyrs

SS. Marcellinus and Peter were Romans. The former was a priest and the later an exorcist, and both were martyred in about 303 or 304, during the persecution under Diocletian (emperor 284–305). The tradition with regard to their martyrdom is as follows: Marcellinus and Peter were taken to a wood outside Rome, called Silva Negra—so that their place of burial would remain unknown—and were beheaded after they had dug their own graves. Later, when their executioner had become a Christian, he revealed the burial site, and the bodies of the martyrs were subsequently placed in a crypt on Rome's Via Labicana. Constantine (emperor 306–37) then erected a church over the crypt, and Pope Vigilius (537–55) added their names to the Roman Canon. The Hieronymian Martyrology (about 450) gives June 2 as the date of their martyrdom.

✝ JUNE 3 ✒ *Memorial*
*SS. Charles Lwanga
and Companions, Martyrs*

Today we commemorate the twenty-two canonized martyrs of Uganda, who died between 1885 and 1887.

Charles Lwanga was born in Buddu County, Uganda, in about 1860. Having learned about the Catholic faith from converts—Cardinal Lavigerie's White Fathers had opened a mission in that region in 1879—he also began taking instructions. While still a catechumen, Charles was given a position (1884) in the household of Mutesa, Kabaka (king) of Buganda (now part of modern Uganda), as assistant to Joseph Mkasa, who was in charge of the boy pages. Months after Mwanga had succeeded (October 1884) his father Mutesa, Mwanga's attitude toward Catholics changed. He feared that the foreigners would eventually take over his country and was loathe to see his people abandon their old religious rites and customs. When Mwanga sought sexual favors from the young pages, Mkasa, who was a Catholic and a catechist, berated him for his licentiousness. He was subsequently arrested on trumped-up charges and beheaded on November 15, 1885. Charles now had to protect his pages from the ruler's perverted demands. Aware that death might come to them at any moment, Charles, who himself had only recently been baptized (November 1885), baptized the youths whom he had been instructing in the faith. On May 26, 1886, Mwanga initiated a persecution against "those who pray," that is, Christians, and that same day Charles and his Christian pages were arrested, condemned to death, and forced to march to Namugongo, about thirty miles distant. There they were martyred by slow fire on June 3, 1886. Charles Lwanga, his twelve pages, and nine others who met death before or after June 3 were canonized by Pope Paul VI in 1964. In today's Mass, the prayer over the gifts recalls the courage that St. Charles Lwanga and companions showed in choosing death rather than yielding to sin.

✠ JUNE 5   ✍   *Memorial*
St. Boniface, Bishop and Martyr

St. Boniface is the great Apostle of Germany. His baptismal name was Winfrid, and he is said to have been born at Crediton, Devonshire, England, in about 675. As a youth, he was educated by the Benedictines at Exeter and then at Nursling. He entered the Benedictines at Nursling, and after ordination was appointed director of the monastery school. In 716, he went as a missionary to Frisia (part of today's Netherlands), but because that country was not ready for missionaries, he returned to Nursling. In 717, he was elected abbot, but resigned the following year to go to Rome to ask the pope for a mission assignment. On May 15, 719, Pope Gregory II assigned him to evangelize the pagan tribes of Germany, and at the same time the pope changed his name from Winfrid to Boniface. Boniface began his evangelizing mission in Thuringia. He was later consecrated a bishop in Rome in 722 and immediately returned to his mission—he now had jurisdiction over all of Germany. His thirty-two years as bishop were very successful, especially after he felled the Oak of Thor at Geismar— conversions were numerous, the number of churches increased, new monasteries and dioceses were established, and new bishops were appointed. In about 747, Pope Zacharias made Boniface Archbishop of Mainz and Primate of Germany. In about 754, he resigned his see and returned to the mission in Frisia. While he was preparing to administer confirmation at Dokkum (June 5, 754), the town was attacked by pagans, who massacred the archbishop and fifty-three others. Both Germany and England immediately acknowledged Boniface as a saint, and in 1874 Pius IX extended his feast to the universal Church.

✝ JUNE 6
St. Norbert, Bishop

St. Norbert was born into a noble family in Xanten, Germany, in 1080. Though a canon in Xanten, he led a rather worldly life at the archbishop's court in Cologne and at that of Emperor Henry V (reigned 1099–1125). In 1115, a bolt of lightning threw him from his horse; he interpreted this as God's way of telling him to change his manner of life. He retired to a quiet place near Xanten, and there he lived (1115–18) a life of penance and recollection. It was during this period that he was ordained (December 1115) a priest. After three years, he left (1118) his solitude and met Pope Gelasius II at Saint-Gilles in Languedoc, France, where the pope authorized him to preach wherever he chose. Norbert began his mission as an itinerant preacher in 1119 and traveled through France and parts of today's Belgium and Germany. In 1121, he established a monastery near Laon (France), in the isolated valley of Prémontré; hence, his religious community came to be known as the Premonstratensians. Because of Norbert's renown as a preacher, the cathedral chapter at Magdeburg, Germany, elected

(1126) him that city's archbishop. He remained in Magdeburg for eight years, but his zeal in reforming the German clergy brought him enemies. He died there on June 6, 1134. In 1582, Pope Gregory XIII approved his cult and permitted a liturgical celebration in his honor among the Premonstratensians. Pope Clement X then extended (1672) it to the universal Church.

✝ JUNE 9
St. Ephrem, Deacon and Doctor of the Church

St. Ephrem is said to have been born of a Christian mother and pagan father in Nisibis, Mesopotamia (modern Nusaybin, Turkey), in about 306. He was baptized a Christian when he was a young man of eighteen and became a teacher in his native city. After the cession of Nisibis to Persia in 363, he moved to Edessa, Greece, where he continued to teach. He remained a deacon all his life, and to escape episcopal consecration he is supposed to have feigned madness. His writings, written in Syriac, include biblical exegesis and dogmatic treatises, as well as ascetical works. The Syrian Church refers to him as the Harp of the Holy Spirit, not only because of his many hymns, which are still sung in the Syrian liturgy, but also because many of his other works were written in verse. Ephrem had singular devotion to the Virgin Mary, and in his writings he so emphasized her perfect sinlessness that he is now numbered among the earliest Fathers of the Church to teach Mary's Immaculate Conception. Ephrem died in Edessa on June 9, 373, and in 1920 Pope Benedict XV

gave him the title of doctor of the Church—the only
Syrian Father to be so honored. The opening prayer of
the Mass today hints at St. Ephrem's poetical talent
when it says that the Holy Spirit inspired the deacon
Ephrem to sing the praise of God's mysteries.

✝ *JUNE 9
Bl. Joseph de Anchieta, Priest

Bl. Joseph de Anchieta is Brazil's most famous missionary. He was born on March 19, 1534, at San Cristóbal de
la Laguna on Tenerife in the Canary Islands. Two years
after he entered the Society of Jesus, he was sent (1553)
to the missions in Brazil, where for forty-four years
he preached God's word to the native population and
helped them to better their way of life. From his tiny
mission at São Paulo, today's great metropolis developed, and the great city of Rio de Janeiro grew out of
the small settlement he founded. He was proficient in
the language of the Tupi Indians, and because he wrote
plays in Tupi and Portuguese for the students in the Jesuit schools in Brazil to perform, he is honored as the
Father of Brazilian Literature. Throughout his missionary life, he had but one principle of action: "Nothing is too arduous that has for its purpose the honor of
God and the salvation of souls." Worn out working for
the Lord, he died at Reritiba (now named Anchieta) on
June 9, 1597. He was beatified by Pope John Paul II in
1980. Today's prayer sums up Bl. Joseph's missionary
life: He identified himself with Brazil's native population so that he could give them God's word and thereby
lead them to Jesus.

✝ JUNE 11 🖉 *Memorial*
St. Barnabas, Apostle

Though St. Barnabas is not listed among the Twelve Apostles, tradition has given him this title because of his commission by the Holy Spirit and his role in the Church's early missionary efforts. Barnabas was a Jew, born in Cyprus; and though his name was Joseph, he is known as Barnabas ("son of encouragement"), the name given him by the other apostles (Acts 4:36). It was Barnabas who first introduced the newly converted Paul to the apostles (Acts 9:27), and it was he whom the Church of Jerusalem sent as official visitor to the Christian community in Antioch (Acts 11:22). Later, Barnabas and Paul were set apart by the Holy Spirit (Acts 13:2) for a special mission to Cyprus, Barnabas's homeland. After attending the Council of Jerusalem (in about 50), Barnabas returned to Cyprus (Acts 15:39), while Paul went to evangelize other lands. Barnabas is traditionally considered to be the founder of the Cypriot Church, and he is said to have met a martyr's death at ancient Salamis in 61. His memorial is celebrated on June 11, the date when he is honored in the East.

✝ JUNE 13 🖉 *Memorial*
St. Anthony of Padua, Priest and Doctor of the Church

St. Anthony, whose baptismal name was Ferdinand, was born in Lisbon in 1195. As a youth of fifteen, he there joined (1210) the Clerks Regular of St. Augustine. Having been moved by the martyrdom of five Franciscans in Morocco, whose relics had been recently returned to Portugal, he was overcome by a desire to be a missionary in Africa. And thus he left the Clerks Regular and entered (1220) the Franciscans, where he received the name Anthony. He then went as a missionary to Morocco, but poor health forced him to return to Europe. The vessel taking him to Portugal was driven off course during a storm, and it eventually found safe harbor in Messina, Sicily. Anthony disembarked and made his way to Assisi, the cradle of the Franciscan Order. Because of his special talent for preaching, he was assigned to preach against the heretics in northern Italy (1222–24) and southern France (1224). St. Francis of Assisi (see October 4) appointed him the order's "lector in theology," the first to hold that position among the Franciscans. Anthony then taught theology to the friars in Montpellier, Bologna, and Padua. He was also superior of various communities, and despite his many duties, he continued his preaching. So active was he that his health weakened, and he died at the age of thirty-six at Arcella, near Padua, on June 13, 1231. Less than a year after his death, he was canonized (May 30, 1232) by Pope Gregory IX. The Franciscans always honored St. Anthony as a doctor of the Church, and Pope Pius XII confirmed them in this belief in 1946. Today's prayer in the Mass mentions St. Anthony's ability in preaching and also calls him a ready helper in time of need—a reference to the popular custom of seeking his intercession whenever something is lost.

✝ JUNE 19
St. Romuald, Abbot

St. Romuald, founder of the Camaldolese Order, was born of the noble Onesti family in Ravenna about 952. After his father had killed a relative in a duel, Romuald went (about 972) to the monastery of St. Apollinare in Classe to do penance for his father's deed. There he became a monk. But seeking a more austere way of life, he left (about 974) the monastery to became a disciple of the hermit Marinus near Venice. In about 978, he and Marinus moved to the Pyrenees and lived as hermits near the Abbey of Cuxa (outside today's Prades, France). Ten years later, Romuald returned to Ravenna. In 998, Otto III (emperor 983–1002) appointed him abbot of St. Apollinare in Classe, but Romuald resigned within the year to return to his eremitical way of life. During his lifetime, he founded various eremitical congregations in northern and central Italy, but the most important was that at Camaldoli (1012) near Arezzo. This monastery later became the motherhouse of the Camaldolese Order. Romuald died at his hermitage in Val di Castro, near Fabriano, Italy, on June 19, 1027, and five years after his death Rome permitted an altar to be erected over his tomb and his feast to be celebrated. The prayer in today's Mass reminds us that through St. Romuald's monasteries he renewed the life of solitude and prayer in the Church.

✝ St. Aloysius Gonzaga, Religious

St. Aloysius Gonzaga, the eldest son of the Marquis of Castiglione, was born in Castiglione delle Stiviere, Italy, on March 9, 1568. Because he was heir to the family title, he was educated as befits a nobleman. In 1577, he and his brother were sent to learn the customs of princely life at the Medici court in Florence. But the empty show of Florentine courtly life was not to his liking. In 1581, he and his family traveled with Empress Maria of Austria, the widow of Emperor Maximilian II and daughter of Charles V, to Madrid, and while in Spain Aloysius decided to become a Jesuit. When the marquis heard of his son's decision, he became enraged, took (1584) him back to Italy, and sent him touring, thus hoping to distract him from his plan. But Aloysius was not one to change his mind, and finally his father consented. Aloysius relinquished his title in favor of his brother Rudolph and entered the Society of Jesus in Rome in 1585. In 1591, when Rome was suffering from a plague, he walked the streets looking for the sick so that he could carry them to hospitals, where he washed them and prepared them for the sacraments. Having caught the plague from someone he had helped, he died in Rome on June 21, 1591. He was canonized by Pope Benedict XIII in 1726, and three years later the same pontiff named him the patron of youth, which Pope Pius XI reaffirmed in 1926. The opening prayer of today's Mass recalls St. Aloysius's setting aside of honors, wealth, and the world so that he might seek only God's glory.

✝ JUNE 22
St. Paulinus of Nola, Bishop

St. Paulinus was born Pontius Meropius Anicius Paulinus at Bordeaux, France, in about 353. He came from a
wealthy family, was well educated, had been governor
(about 381) of Campania, Italy, and had married a
wealthy Spanish lady. After a successful career, he retired from public life and was baptized (about 389) at
Bordeaux. Then, in 390, he and his wife settled near
Barcelona. Upon the death, shortly after birth, of their
only child, Paulinus and his wife agreed to adopt an ascetical way of life and distributed all their goods to the
poor. In 395, at the insistence of the people, Paulinus
was ordained a priest; the following year, he and his
wife went to Nola (near Naples), where he devoted his
time to promoting the cult of St. Felix of Nola, a holy
confessor who at one time had Paulinus under his care.
In about 409, Paulinus was chosen bishop of Nola, and
as bishop he sought to help pilgrims and alleviate the
needs of the poor. He died in Nola on June 22, 431. It is
said that he was the first to introduce (about 420) the
use of bells in Christian worship. During his life, he
was in correspondence with the leading churchmen of
his time, and his extant poetry indicates that he was
among the better Christian poets of the fifth century.
The opening prayer of today's Mass mentions Paulinus's love of poverty and concern for his people.

JUNE 22
SS. John Fisher, Bishop and Martyr, and Thomas More, Martyr

St. John Fisher, Cardinal Bishop of Rochester, and St. Thomas More, former lord chancellor of England, were both martyred in 1535. John Fisher was born in Beverley, Yorkshire, in 1469. He was university educated and had earned a doctor of divinity degree in 1501. In 1504, he was chosen chancellor of Cambridge University, and there he arranged for scholarships in Greek and Hebrew, expanded the library's holdings, and invited Erasmus of Rotterdam to lecture there. Likewise, in 1504, King Henry VII named him Bishop of Rochester. When King Henry VIII (reigned 1509–47) asked his opinion with regard to the king's desired divorce from Catherine of Aragon, the bishop maintained that the marriage was valid. This response earned him the king's displeasure, and when Henry attempted to make himself the supreme head of the Church in England, Bishop Fisher publicly spoke out (1531) against it. Royal displeasure was now converted into wrath.

Sir Thomas More also earned the king's displeasure. He was born in London on February 7, 1477, and after studies at Oxford, he did law in London. He was married (1505) and had four children. Because Thomas was a brilliant lawyer, King Henry VIII took him into his service (1518); he knighted him in 1521, and in 1529 made him Lord Chancellor of England. But when it came to the question of King Henry's divorce, Sir Thomas was unable to support his king. The day after the English clergy had yielded to the king's demands, Sir Thomas resigned (May 16, 1532) as chancellor and retired from public life.

Because Bishop Fisher and Sir Thomas refused (April 13, 1534) to take the oath to the new Act of Succession, they were both taken (April 17, 1534) to the Tower of London. When Pope Paul III heard that Bishop Fisher had been imprisoned for his fidelity to the Church's teaching, he raised (May 20, 1535) him to the Cardinalate. Cardinal Fisher was convicted of treason on June 17, 1535, and executed on June 22. Sir Thomas was convicted of the same on July 1, 1535, and was executed on July 6. Both martyrs were canonized by Pope Pius XI in 1935.

✠ JUNE 24 ✐ *Solemnity*
Nativity of St. John the Baptist

Our Mass today commemorates the nativity of St. John the Baptist, the precursor of our Lord. John, the son of Elizabeth, a relative of our Lady, and of Zechariah, a priest, was born six months before our Lord. The series of miraculous events connected with John's birth indicated that his was to be no ordinary vocation. The angel Gabriel, having been sent by God, appeared to Zechariah, while fulfilling his priestly duties in the Temple, to inform him that his wife Elizabeth, who was both barren and well along in years, was to have a son. When Zechariah expressed his doubt, he suddenly became mute (Luke 1:1–25). Later, when Mary visited Elizabeth, the unborn child in Elizabeth's womb leaped with joy in the presence of his Lord (Luke 1:39–41). And as today's Gospel reading (Luke 1:56–66, 80) narrates, at the child's circumcision, Zechariah suddenly regained his voice, when he insisted that the child's name was John, the name given him by the angel. John was to be no ordinary saint; he was chosen by God to have a very special place in the role of redemption—it was his task to preach repentance and prepare the people for Christ's coming. It is infrequent that the Church in her liturgical calendar celebrates a birthday; there are only three such, that of Christ (December 25), that of our Lady (September 8), and today's, that of John the Baptist. For all other saints, we regularly celebrate the day they died, that is, their birthday in Heaven. The three prayers of today's Mass underline St. John's unique role of precursor—he was chosen to prepare the world for the coming of Christ.

✝ JUNE 27
St. Cyril of Alexandria, Bishop and Doctor of the Church

St. Cyril was born in Alexandria in about 382. Little is known about his early life, except that he studied in Alexandria and was there ordained a priest. When his uncle Theophilus, Patriarch of Alexandria, died, Cyril was chosen to succeed (412) him. Cyril's years as bishop were uneventful, until Nestorius (d. about 451) became Patriarch of Constantinople (today's Istanbul) in 428. Nestorius refused to use the word Theotokos ("God-bearer") with reference to the Virgin Mary; he denied that she was the Mother of God and said that she was merely the mother of the human Christ, that is, Christotokos. But against Nestorius, Cyril maintained:

"If Christ is God, and Mary is his mother, then how is she not the mother of God?" Cyril began writing and preaching against Nestorius's teaching, and because this heresy so disturbed the Church in the East, a general council of bishops was called by Theodosius II (emperor 408–50) to meet at Ephesus (now in Turkey) in June 431. Cyril presided over that council—he represented Pope Celestine I (422–32)—and there Nestorius's heretical teaching was condemned and Nestorius himself deposed. Cyril then returned to his see, where he died on June 27, 444. Cyril was the foremost theologian of his day, and his writings on Christ and on Mary's divine maternity remain as valuable today as when first written. Because of his writings and his championing of the faith, he has always been acknowledged as a doctor of the Church. The opening prayer of today's Mass mentions that St. Cyril courageously taught that Mary was the Mother of God.

✝ JUNE 28 ✿ *Memorial*
St. Irenaeus, Bishop and Martyr

St. Irenaeus was the first great theologian of the Church. He was born perhaps between 130 and 140, and possibly in Smyrna (modern Izmir, Turkey). He was a disciple of St. Polycarp (see February 23) in Smyrna, and he later studied at Rome under Justin Martyr (see June 1). He subsequently went to Gaul (modern France) and was ordained a priest in Lyon. As the representative of the Church of Lyon, he visited (about 177) Pope Eleutherius in Rome with regard to the Montanist controversy, but while he was in Rome persecution broke out in Lyon and Pothinus, the local bishop, was martyred. Upon Irenaeus's return (about 178) to Lyon, he was chosen to succeed him. As bishop, Irenaeus sent missionaries to different parts of Gaul and opposed the teachings of the Gnostics; his most famous work, *Against Heresies*, was specifically directed against them. Another work of his is the *Demonstration of the Apostolic Tradition*, an apologetical treatise defending the fundamental teachings of the Catholic Church as being identical with those of the apostles. In these, he likewise makes use of Old Testament prophecies to prove the truth of Christian revelation. The tradition in the Church is that Irenaeus died a martyr on June 28, in about 202 or 203. When the opening prayer of today's Mass says that St. Irenaeus upheld God's truth, this is a reference to his writings, through which he sought to foster unity and peace in the Church.

✝ JUNE 29　✄　*Solemnity*
SS. Peter and Paul, Apostles

SS. Peter and Paul enjoy a joint liturgical celebration because both are considered the founders of the Church in Rome. It was to Peter that our Lord gave the duty of caring for his flock, when he said: "Feed my sheep!" (John 21:15–17). After Pentecost, Peter was the undisputed leader in the Church (see Acts 2:14–39), and because he was so prominent among the Christians, he was arrested. But he was also miraculously released, as today's first reading tells (Acts 12:1–11). He then departed Jerusalem (Acts 12:17), probably for Antioch (see Gal. 2:11–14), and sometime after 50 went to Rome, where he was martyred (between 64 and 67) during the reign of Nero (emperor 54–68). Tradition has it that Peter was crucified upside down (see John 21:18–19) in the Circus of Nero and that he was buried on Vatican Hill, not far from the place where he had died. Recent archeological research confirms that Peter's tomb is beneath the present St. Peter's in Rome.

Paul, known as the "Apostle of the Gentiles," was undoubtedly the Church's greatest missionary. After his three extensive missionary journeys, covering 47 to 58, he was arrested (Acts 22:24–25) in Jerusalem in about 58 and taken to Caesarea, where he was confined for two years (Acts 23:27). When Governor Festus was about to transfer him to Jerusalem for trial, Paul exercised his right as a Roman citizen and appealed to Caesar (Acts 25:11); that is, he requested that his trial be in Rome. He was subsequently sent to Rome during the winter of 60–61. Though under house arrest (Acts 28:16) during his two years (61–63) in Rome, he was still able to receive visitors and preach to them (Acts 28:30–31). He was then set free, and he may have returned to some of his former missions. He was arrested a second time, again taken to Rome, and was martyred, also during the reign of Nero, sometime between 64 and 67. Tradition maintains that Paul was beheaded about three miles from Rome; his body was then buried on the Ostian Way.

When the Christians feared that the tombs of Peter and Paul might be violated during the persecution of Valerian (emperor 253–59), they secretly moved (June 29, 258) these sacred relics to "the Catacombs," known today as the Catacombs of St. Sebastian. When peace was restored and when the relics were returned to their original tombs, Constantine (emperor 306–37) built (324) basilicas over each of them. Today, the magnificent Basilica of St. Peter stands over that of the Prince of the Apostles, and the inspiring Basilica of St. Paul Outside-the-Walls stands over that of the Apostle of the Gentiles.

✝ JUNE 30
*First Holy Martyrs of the
Holy Roman Church*

On the day following the commemoration of SS. Peter and Paul, both of whom had died in the persecution under Nero (emperor 54–68), we commemorate the many others who died for the faith (by crucifixion, fire, or exposure to wild beasts) during the same persecution. Because the number and the names of all these are known to God alone, we remember them today as the First Martyrs of the Church of Rome. A large part of Rome—some sources say two-thirds of the city—had been destroyed by fire (July 18–24, 64) and the Roman historian Tacitus tells us (*Annales* 15, 44, 3) that Nero tried to blame the Christians. He thus initiated a persecution, the first such by a Roman emperor, accusing the Christians of being incendiaries and of being filled with "hatred for the human race." A martyr is a witness, not an ordinary witness, but one who testifies to the faith in blood. The mere shedding of blood does not make martyrs; it is the reason why the blood is shed. This blood is the martyr's testimony preferring death to separation from God.

† SUNDAY AFTER
PENTECOST *✎* *Solemnity*
Most Holy Trinity

Having completed the commemoration of the mysteries of our salvation, from Christ's birth to the descent of the Holy Spirit, we now contemplate the central mystery of our faith, that is, the Most Holy Trinity—one God in three persons, the Father, the Son, and the Holy Spirit. Although the Old Testament proclaims that God is one, the New Testament explicitly mentions three distinct persons in the Godhead. In our Lord's final instruction to his disciples, before his Ascension, he commanded them: "Go, therefore, make disciples of all nations, baptizing them in the name of the Father, and of the Son, and of the Holy Spirit" (Matt. 28:19). When Paul writes to his beloved Corinthian Christians, he ends his letter with the blessing: "The grace of the Lord Jesus Christ, and the love of God, and the fellowship of the Holy Spirit be with you all" (2 Cor. 13:13). We have been baptized in the name of these same three persons, and we profess that though they are distinct, nevertheless, they are undivided in splendor and are equal in glory and majesty (as expressed in today's Preface). At the same time, these three persons are but one Lord, one God. The earliest reference to a feast honoring the Blessed Trinity is in Tours, in 796. The feast was later introduced at Cluny in 1091, and St. Thomas Becket adopted it at Canterbury in 1162. Pope John XXII (1316–34) approved the feast for the universal Church in 1331.

✝ SUNDAY AFTER
TRINITY SUNDAY ✿ *Solemnity*
Most Holy Body and Blood of Christ

Today we honor the mystery of the Holy Eucharist, that is, the real presence of Christ's most holy body and blood in the Blessed Sacrament. This feast differs from that of Holy Thursday, for then we celebrate the institution of the Eucharist on the eve of Christ's passion and death, whereas here we do not have sorrowful overtones; rather, we prayerfully reflect on Christ's loving decision to remain among us by means of this Holy Sacrament. This feast, known until recently as that of Corpus Christi, had its origin in the thirteenth century. In 1209, in the Diocese of Liège, Belgium, the nun Juliana of Mont-Cornillon (1192–1258) enjoyed visions and discovered that among the Church's many feasts there was none honoring the Blessed Sacrament. Her request for such a feast was passed on to the archdeacon of Liège, Jacques Pantaléon, and in 1246 that diocese established a feast honoring the Blessed Sacrament. Within a few years, the feast spread to other dioceses, and when Pantaléon became Pope Urban IV (1261–64), he extended (1264) the feast to the entire Church. It was also Urban who commissioned St. Thomas Aquinas (see January 28), then teaching in Orvieto, to write the Mass and Office for the feast. Within a short period, the feast spread throughout the Church, and by the end of the thirteenth century, a solemn procession, first within the Church and later throughout the town, was initiated (1279) in Cologne.

† FRIDAY FOLLOWING
SECOND SUNDAY
AFTER PENTECOST   *Solemnity*
Most Sacred Heart of Jesus

In the early Middle Ages, devotion to the Heart of Jesus was connected with devotion to his Passion—his Heart being the symbol of his redemptive love. Though the devotion was known for centuries, it only became widespread in France through the zealous preaching and admirable writings of St. John Eudes (see August 19). It was, however, first to St. Margaret Mary Alacoque (see October 16) that Christ revealed the treasures of his Sacred Heart and asked that a feast be celebrated in its honor. When these revelations became public, the devotion became popular, for it now took on specific devotional practices, such as that of the First Fridays and reparation to the Sacred Heart. St. Claude La Colombière (see February 15) worked with St. Margaret Mary in trying to have such a feast approved in the Church. It was in 1765 that Pope Clement XIII first allowed such a feast to be celebrated in Poland and at the Archconfraternity of the Sacred Heart in Rome. Pope Pius IX then ordered (1856) it to be celebrated throughout the world on the Friday following the Second Sunday after Pentecost, when it is still celebrated. In 1899, Pope Leo XIII consecrated the human race to the Sacred Heart of Jesus.

✝ SATURDAY AFTER
THE SECOND SUNDAY
AFTER PENTECOST ✐ *Memorial*

Immaculate Heart of the Blessed Virgin Mary

Devotion to the Immaculate Heart of Mary has its roots in the writings of St. John Eudes (see August 19), who was a staunch promoter of the devotion to the Sacred Hearts of Jesus and Mary. By the beginning of the nineteenth century, devotion to Mary's Immaculate Heart was sufficiently widespread in Europe for Pope Pius VII to allow (1805) a feast in its honor, in those dioceses that chose to celebrate it. Then, when the world was being torn apart by World War II, Pope Pius XII consecrated (December 8, 1942) the human race to the Immaculate Heart of Mary, and in 1944 the same pontiff extended the feast to the universal Church and fixed its celebration as August 22. Because August 22 is now the feast of the Queenship of Mary, the memorial honoring her Immaculate Heart is appropriately celebrated on the day following the Solemnity of the Most Sacred Heart of Jesus.

JULY

Bl. Junípero Serra, Priest

Bl. Junípero Serra is the founder of the Franciscan missions in California. He was born at Petra, Mallorca, on November 24, 1713; his baptismal name was Miguel José, but when he became a Franciscan in 1730, he received the name Junípero. After ordination (1738), and earning a degree in theology (1742), he taught (1743–40) at the Lullian University in Palma de Mallorca. He then sailed (1749) for Mexico, and for the next nineteen years worked in that country, first among the native population in outlying mission stations, then in Mexico City itself, and later in the Spanish missions of Lower California. When Spain began (1769) to move northward into Upper California (the present-day State of California), Fr. Serra accompanied the expedition. On July 1, 1769, he arrived in the area now known as San Diego, and on a hill overlooking the bay he founded (July 16, 1769) his first mission, San Diego de Alcalá. The following year, he founded (June 3, 1770) the mission of San Carlos Borromeo at Carmel and made that his headquarters. In all, he established nine missions, from San Diego to San Francisco (founded

June 29, 1776), and during his fifteen years in California, he five times traversed the full length (almost 1,000 miles) of the missions, despite his injured leg. He died, beloved by Indians and Spaniards, at Carmel on August 28, 1784, and was buried in the mission church. Fr. Serra was beatified by Pope John Paul II in 1988. His memorial is celebrated on July 1 because this was the day when he first arrived in what is now San Diego. The Franciscan missions of California stand today as Bl. Junípero's monument.

✝ *JULY 2 ✿ Memorial
SS. John Francis Regis, Bernardine Realino, Francis Jerome, and BB. Julian Maunoir and Anthony Baldinucci, Priests

The three Jesuit saints and the two Jesuit blessed we commemorate today spent most of their priestly lives traveling through various parts of Italy and France, preaching parish missions to the faithful. The inspiration and content of these missions came from the *Spiritual Exercises* of St. Ignatius of Loyola (see July 31).

St. John Francis Regis was a Frenchman, born at Font-couverte, on January 31, 1597. His mission area was southern France. He died at La Louvesc on December 31, 1640, and was canonized by Pope Clement XII in 1737.

St. Bernardine Realino was an Italian, born at Carpi on December 1, 1530. He mainly worked in and around Lecce, in Apulia. He died there on July 2, 1616, and was canonized by Pope Pius XII in 1947.

St. Francis Jerome, also an Italian, was born at Grottaglie, near Taranto, on December 17, 1642. Naples was his mission area for forty years. He died there on May 11, 1716, and was canonized by Pope Gregory XVI in 1839.

Bl. Julian Maunoir did missionary work in Brittany for forty-three years. He was born at Saint-Georges-de-Reintembault, near Rennes, on October 1, 1606, and died at Plévin on January 28, 1683. He was beatified by Pope Pius XII in 1951.

Bl. Anthony Baldinucci, was born in Florence on June 19, 1665, and for twenty years preached his missions in the cities and towns surrounding Rome. He died at Pofi on November 7, 1717, and was beatified by Pope Leo XIII in 1893.

The prayer of the Mass today recalls the journeys that these itinerant preachers made to proclaim to towns and villages the gospel of peace.

✝ JULY 3　✎ Feast
　 St. Thomas, Apostle

St. Thomas was one of our Lord's Twelve Apostles (Matt. 10:3). The name Thomas means "twin," as John twice tells us in his Gospel (11:16; 20:24). It seems that the Gospels only identify him by this nickname, but later writings, known as apocryphal, call him Judas Thomas, or Judas the Twin. That Thomas was courageous in his following of Christ is well brought out in his remark when Jesus talked about his returning to Judea: "Let us go along with him and die with him" (John 11:16). But Thomas is better remembered for the incident related in today's Gospel (John 20:24–29). He may have once been a "doubting" Thomas, but he was transformed into a "believing" Thomas, and it was this "believing" Thomas who, after Pentecost, became a missionary and evangelized the lands between the Caspian Sea and the Persian Gulf. There is a tradition that he traveled as far as India, where he preached and died a martyr's death. He is said to have been buried at Mylapore, near Madras, in 72. The Syriac St. Thomas Christians along India's Malabar Coast claim him as the founder of their Church. His feast is celebrated on July 3 so that we may join with the Malabar Christians in honoring the apostle. The prayer after Communion today echoes St. Thomas's unforgettable confession of Christ's divinity when he saw the Risen Lord for the first time.

✝ JULY 4
St. Elizabeth of Portugal

St. Elizabeth, the daughter of Peter III, the King of Aragon, was probably born in Saragossa, Spain, in about 1270; at her baptism, she was given the name of her great aunt, St. Elizabeth of Hungary (see November 17), who had been canonized thirty-five years previously. As a young girl, Elizabeth was married (1282) to Denis, the King of Portugal, and though she bore him two children, the marriage was not a happy one. With great patience, she endured her husband's infidelities, and with great love she raised his illegitimate children as her own. As queen of Portugal, she was devoted to her people's welfare and was most generous to the poor; she likewise founded hospitals and convents. She was also a peacemaker: She reconciled her husband to their rebellious son Alfonso, and on two occasions she averted war between the kings of Aragon and Castile. After her husband's death in 1325, she sold her jewels and possessions, gave the money to the poor, and became a Franciscan tertiary, living near the convent of the Poor Clares in Coimbra. She died at the royal castle in Estremoz, Portugal, on July 4, 1336, while attempting to make peace between her son, now Alfonso IV of Portugal, and her nephew, Alfonso XI of Castile. St. Elizabeth was canonized by Pope Urban VIII in 1626. Today's prayer recalls her peacemaking measures when it affirms that God, the Father of peace and love, gave St. Elizabeth the gift of reconciling enemies.

✝ JULY 5
St. Anthony Mary Zaccaria, Priest

St. Anthony Zaccaria was born in Cremona, Italy, in 1502. He studied medicine and graduated from the University of Padua in 1524. He then returned to Cremona and soon gave up practicing medicine to devote his life to the religious apostolate. Thereupon, he taught catechism in a church near his home and studied for the priesthood; he was ordained in 1528. Two years later (1530), he was sent to Milan to be chaplain to Countess Luisa Torelli of Guastalla, and while in Milan he joined the Oratory of Eternal Wisdom. Soon, he and two friends began laying the foundations for a new congregation of priests, the Clerks Regular of St. Paul, more commonly known as Barnabites, because their church in Milan was that of St. Barnabas. The purpose of this new congregation was to reform sixteenth-century society by preaching, practicing penance, and giving parish missions. St. Anthony himself traveled through Lombardy and the Veneto preaching missions among the people. While on a visit to his mother in Cremona, he died on July 5, 1539, the result of overwork. He was canonized by Pope Leo XIII in 1897. The opening prayer in the Mass today tells us that when St. Anthony Zaccaria founded his congregation to preach Christ's message of salvation, he was following in the spirit of St. Paul, after whom he had named his religious family.

✝ JULY 6
St. Maria Goretti, Virgin and Martyr

When St. Maria Goretti died a martyr's death to preserve her purity, she was not yet twelve years of age. She was born at Corinaldo, near Ancona, Italy, on October 16, 1890. Because her father was unable to find suitable employment, the family twice moved, the last time in 1899 to Ferriere di Conca, about six miles from Nettuno, where her father became a tenant farmer. Because the family was extremely poor, Maria never went to school. Her father died in 1900, and while her mother spent her days working in the fields, Maria cared for the house and looked after her five brothers and sisters. A young lad, in his late teens, who lived next door, became interested in Maria and twice tried to seduce her. But Maria declined his advances, and to make sure that she would not speak of this to his or her mother, he threatened to kill her. Then, on July 5, 1902, while Maria's mother was at work, the youth, carrying a dagger, entered the Goretti house. Maria, who had just made her First Communion six weeks before, again repulsed him saying: "No, God does not want it. If you do this, you will go to Hell for it." The angry youth then stabbed her a dozen times. Maria died in the hospital at Nettuno the following day. She was canonized by Pope Pius XII in 1950.

✝ JULY 9
St. Augustine Zhao Rong,
Priest and Martyr, and
His Companions, Martyrs

On October 1, 2000, Pope John Paul II canonized 120 martyrs who, over a period of nearly 300 years (1648–1930), gave their lives in fidelity to Jesus Christ and the Catholic Church on Chinese soil. At different times during these years and in various places, persecutions broke out against the Catholic Church. Of these martyrs, one died in the seventeenth century, the Spanish Dominican priest, Francis Fernández de Capillas. In 1648, the Manchu Tartars invaded the region of Fujian and because of their hostility to the Christian religion, they arrested him, tortured him, and finally beheaded him on January 15, 1648. The Chinese Church looks upon him as her protomartyr. Of these new saints, five were then martyred during the eighteenth century, and twenty-five in the nineteenth.

Among the martyrs of the nineteenth century is Augustine Zhao Rong. At one time, he had been a soldier in the emperor's service, and when the French missionary Bishop Gabriel Dufresse was arrested, Augustine was assigned to the military detail that escorted him to prison. Augustine witnessed the bishop's patience and charity throughout his ordeal, and he was so moved by the bishop's Christian demeanor that he decided to become a Catholic. He was subsequently baptized, and he was then sent to a seminary and was ordained a priest. Eventually, he too was apprehended, cruelly tortured, and martyred in 1815.

The majority of these martyrs—eighty-six—died in 1900 at the hands of the Boxers, a quasi-religious movement to which the English gave this name because of their strenuous gymnastic training. The Boxers were especially antagonistic toward Catholics and had initiated a systematic campaign to destroy them. Of these eighty-six martyrs, four were French Jesuit priests and the remainder native Chinese. Of the thousands of Christians actually killed by the Boxers, only eighty-two were included in the cause for canonization because for these some definite or specific information was available, whereas in the case of the others there was either insufficient information or their names were not even known. The two youngest to die in this group were two lads, Paul and Andrew, each nine years of age. Finally, three martyrs died in 1930.

Of the 120 martyrs, 87 were Chinese (4 priests, 7 seminarians, 12 catechists, and 64 lay faithful) and 33 were foreign missionaries (6 bishops, 19 priests, 7 sisters, and 1 brother). By canonizing these martyrs, the Church recognizes them as models of courage and constancy, and at the same time gives honor to the noble Chinese people.

† JULY 11   *Memorial*
St. Benedict, Abbot

St. Benedict is the patriarch of Western Monasticism. He was born in Norcia, Italy, about 480, and because his family was a distinguished one, he studied in Rome. The worldly ways of Rome, however, did not appeal to him, and thus he donned (about 500) a monastic habit and went to live as a hermit in a grotto near Subiaco. After several years, disciples joined him, and not long afterward he built twelve monasteries, each for ten monks, in the vicinity. Because of friction from the local clergy, Benedict and many of his monks left that area (about 525), and they went further south to Monte Cassino, where they built a new monastery among the woods and groves. It was at Monte Cassino that Benedict wrote the *Rule* for his monks, and it was there that he is said to have died on March 21, 547, just a few weeks after his sister Scholastica (see February 10), next to whom he was buried. By the eighth century, the Benedictines kept their founder's feast on July 11. In 1964, Pope Paul VI proclaimed Benedict patron of Europe. When the opening prayer of today's Mass speaks of preferring God's love to everything else, it echoes St. Benedict's *Rule*, in which he tells his monks "to put nothing before the love of Christ" (chap. 4, 21).

✝
St. Henry

St. Henry is known in history as Henry II. He was born near Hildesheim on May 6, 973, the son of Henry "the Wrangler," Duke of Bavaria. He was educated at Hildesheim and in 995 succeeded his father. Then, in 998, he married Kunegunde, daughter of the Count of Luxembourg. Upon the death of Otto III (emperor 983–1002), Henry was elected (1002) King of Germany, and throughout his years he worked to secure a lasting peace in his realm. In about 1007, he founded the see of Bamberg and, with his wife, richly endowed it. Henry, who had a devout disposition, had great love for the Church, and thus he desired that only suitable and capable bishops be appointed, and that the clergy and monks live up to their calling. During his second visit to Rome, when he intervened to quell a disturbance in that city, Pope Benedict VIII crowned (February 14, 1014) him emperor. He died at Grona, near Göttingen, on July 13, 1024, and was buried in the cathedral at Bamberg. During life and after death, he was revered for his piety and ascetical life. He was canonized by Pope Eugene III in 1146, and his wife Kunegunde was canonized by Pope Innocent III in 1200. During the Middle Ages, St. Henry was looked upon as the ideal Christian ruler.

Bl. Kateri Tekakwitha, Virgin

Bl. Kateri, the daughter of a Christian Algonquin mother, who had been taken captive by the Mohawk Indians, and of a pagan Mohawk father, was born at Ossernenon (today's Auriesville, New York) in April 1656. Because she was born at sunrise, she was given the name Ioragade ("Sunshine"). As a result of a smallpox epidemic (1659), she lost her parents, and she was subsequently brought up by an aunt. Because Kateri's vision had been weakened by the disease, and because she walked with her hands extended in front of her, her uncle gave her the name Tekakwitha ("who stretches out her hands"). Kateri remembered the rudiments of the Catholic faith that her mother had instilled in her, and when Jesuit missionaries visited the camp in 1667, she hesitated, in her shyness, to ask about the God whom her mother had worshiped. It was only in 1675 that she asked the missionary, who then resided at the camp, about becoming a Christian. She was baptized on Easter Sunday, April 5, 1676, and was given the name Kateri (Catherine). Because she had been harshly treated by her aunt and uncle since her conversion, the missionary suggested that she secretly go to the Indian settlement at Caughnawaga, near Montreal, where other Catholic Mohawks were then living. She arrived there in October 1677 and made her First Communion that Christmas. Her three years there were years of peace; she prayed and cared for the sick and elderly. Due to excessive acts of penance, her health failed, and she died at Caughnawaga on April 17, 1680. She was beatified by Pope John Paul II in 1980. The monument, which marks the site of her original tomb, bears the inscription: "the most beautiful flower that blossomed."

✝ JULY 15 🌶 *Memorial*
St. Bonaventure, Bishop and Doctor of the Church

St. Bonaventure's baptismal name was John, but he received the name Bonaventure when he became a Franciscan. He was born at Bagnoreggio, near Viterbo, Italy, about 1221. He studied in Paris, and having become acquainted with the Franciscans there, he entered (about 1243) their Paris monastery. He subsequently received his degree from the University of Paris and taught (1248–55) there. In 1257, he was elected Minister General of the Franciscans, and the remaining years of his life were spent writing and traveling on behalf of his order. In May 1273, Pope Gregory X named him Cardinal Bishop of Albano, and because the Second Council of Lyon, which Pope Gregory had convoked, was soon to begin, Bonaventure traveled with the pope to Lyon, where they arrived in early November. On about November 11, the pope ordained Bonaventure a bishop, and afterward they worked closely together preparing for the council (May 7–July 17, 1274). Bonaventure played a prominent role at the council, especially with reference to the union of the Greek and Latin Churches. He died at Lyon on July 15, 1274, two days before the council ended. He was canonized by Pope Sixtus IV in 1482. In 1588, Pope Sixtus V declared him a doctor of the Church. St. Bonaventure was the outstanding

Franciscan theologian during the Middle Ages, and he is especially celebrated for his treatises on mystical theology.

✝ JULY 16
Our Lady of Mount Carmel

The feast of Our Lady of Mount Carmel was instituted by the Order of Friars of the Blessed Virgin Mary of Mount Carmel, more commonly known as the Carmelites, between 1376 and 1386 to celebrate Pope Honorius III's approbation of the order in 1226. The Carmelites chose to celebrate the feast on July 16, the traditional date, when our Lady appeared (1251) in a vision to St. Simon Stock (1165–1265), the sixth general of the order, and gave him the Carmelite scapular. At that time, our Lady also directed him to start a confraternity and promised that anyone wearing the scapular would enjoy her special protection. When the use of the scapular became popular in Europe, Pope Benedict XIII added (1726) the feast to the Roman calendar.

✝ JULY 18
St. Camillus de Lellis, Priest

St. Camillus de Lellis was born at Bucchianico, Italy, on May 25, 1550. As a young man, he thought of enrolling in the military, but an ulcer on his right foot kept him from fulfilling that desire. He went (1571) to Rome's Hospital of San Giacomo for treatment, and after the wound healed, he found employment at the hospital as a servant. His service, however, did not last long because he was dismissed for gambling. He then served in the Venetian army for four years (1571–74), and when he gambled away all that he owned he got a job as a laborer at a Capuchin monastery in Manfredonia. Repenting his past life and undergoing a conversion, he joined (1575) the Capuchins as a coadjutor brother. Because the wound on his foot again became ulcerated, he left the Capuchins and returned to the hospital in Rome. Once healed, he remained at the hospital for almost three years working with the sick. He then reentered (1579) the Capuchins, but again his wound opened and he was forced to leave.

Camillus now decided to dedicate his life to the sick. He returned to San Giacomo, and there they asked him to serve as the hospital's superintendent. Coming under the influence of St. Philip Neri (see May 26), Camillus began studies for the priesthood and was ordained in 1584. He gathered others about him who also wanted to share his work; they called themselves Servants of the Sick. They daily visited Rome's Santo Spirito Hospital, and there they nursed the sick, offering them both physical and spiritual assistance, especially in cases near death. Camillus, who was renowned for his charity, died in Rome on July 14, 1614, and was canonized by Pope Benedict XIV in 1746. The congregation he founded is called the Order of the Servants of the Sick, but its members are more commonly known as Camillians. In 1886, Pope Leo XIII named St. Camillus de Lellis and St. John of God (see March 8) patrons of the sick and of hospitals; and in 1930, Pope Pius XI named St. Camillus patron of nurses. Today's Mass prayer also mentions St. Camillus's special love for the sick.

✝ St. Apollinaris, Bishop and Martyr

Very little is known with certainty about the life of St. Apollinaris, the first Bishop of Ravenna. St. Peter Chrysologus (see July 30), who was Bishop of Ravenna from 431 to 450, once preached a sermon (No. 128) about his predecessor. From this sermon, we learn that Apollinaris was the first bishop of that see, that he had labored there for many years, and on different occasions had suffered much and had often shed his blood, and though his was not a violent death, nevertheless, he should be considered a martyr. There is also the witness of St. Severus, who, as bishop of Ravenna, attended the Council of Sardica (342–43), and at which he mentioned that the first bishop of his see flourished around the middle of the second century.

When historical details are lacking, legend easily fills them in. In the seventh century, there appeared a *Passion of St. Apollinaris*, and according to this historically unreliable document, we are told that Apollinaris came from Antioch (today's Antakya, Turkey), and arrived in Rome with St. Peter (see June 29), who then sent him to evangelize Ravenna. Because of his success in making converts, Apollinaris twice suffered mistreatment at the hands of nonbelievers and was forced to leave the city. He traveled to Corinth, Greece, and then preached in Thrace (part of today's Balkan Peninsula). He once again suffered violence and was forced to leave. He returned to Ravenna at the time when Vespasian's (emperor 69–79) persecution against the Christians was in effect. Apollinaris was subsequently arrested and placed under the care of a centurion. Because that centurion happened to be a Christian, he permitted the bishop to escape. He was then pursued by the raging populace, who attacked and severely wounded him and left him for dead. The bishop was later found by Christians and died seven days later (July 23) as a result of his wounds. Apollinaris had been bishop of Ravenna for about twenty years, and the year of his death is sometimes given as 70. However, the latest edition of the *Martyrologium Romanum* (2001) agrees with St. Severus and gives his death as occurring sometime in the second century. Ursicinus, the Bishop of Ravenna (532–36), began a church in his honor, which was later dedicated by his successor Maximian in 549. It was then that the saint's body was translated there. That church, now known as San Apollinare in Classe, still stands and because of its magnificent sixth-century mosaics is one of the wonders of Ravenna.

✝ JULY 21
St. Lawrence of Brindisi, Priest and Doctor of the Church

St. Lawrence's true name was Julius Caesar Russo. He was born in Brindisi, southern Italy, on July 22, 1559. After his parents' death, he went to Venice and later entered (1575) the Capuchin Order, in which he received the name Lawrence. He studied at Padua and Venice, and during those years his remarkable ability for languages became evident. He was able to speak and preach in at least a half dozen languages. After ordination (1582), he was assigned to preaching, his most characteristic apostolate, and he traveled throughout northern Italy and beyond the Alps evangelizing the people. He likewise spent time (1599–1602, 1606–13) in Bohemia, Germany, Austria, and Hungary working to win back those who had gone over to the Reformation. Within the Capuchin Order, he held many positions of authority, and in 1602 he was chosen superior general. He also engaged in diplomacy; he served as special papal emissary and effected (1614) a peace between Spain and Savoy. Late in his life, the city of Naples, suffering under the oppressive measures of its viceroy, asked him to represent its case before King Philip III of Spain. He met the king in Lisbon and won not only a hearing but also a favorable reply. While in Lisbon, Lawrence fell ill, and he died there on July 22, 1619. He was canonized by Pope Leo XIII in 1881, and Pope John XXIII named him a doctor of the Church in 1959. When today's prayer says that God gave St. Lawrence courage and right judgment, the courage refers to his fearlessness during many years of preaching in non-Catholic lands, and the judgment to his years as a religious superior and his diplomatic missions.

✝ JULY 22 * *Memorial*
St. Mary Magdalene

St. Mary Magdalene was a native of Magdala, formerly a town on the western shore of the Sea of Galilee. Luke introduces her in his Gospel as the one "from whom seven devils had gone out" and as one of those who "were assisting [Jesus and the apostles] out of their means" (Luke 8:2). She witnessed our Lord's crucifixion and valiantly stood beneath his cross (John 19:25), and as today's Gospel reading (John 20:1–2, 11–18) narrates, she was the first to see the empty tomb and the resurrected Lord. Tradition sometimes identifies Mary Magdalene, though it is not absolutely clear in the Gospels nor universally held, with Mary, the sister of Martha (Luke 10:39), or the unnamed sinner who entered the house of Simon the Pharisee and wiped our Lord's feet with her hair (Luke 7:37). Today's Mass formula says nothing about Mary Magdalene having been a sinner (as the Mass formula before the 1969 liturgical changes had done), but it stresses that it was she who first saw the Risen Jesus and was given the commission to be the messenger of Paschal joy to the apostles. The tradition in the East is that she went to Ephesus (in modern Turkey) with St. John and there she died. By the tenth century, her feast was celebrated in Constantinople (modern Istanbul) on July 22. Two texts are proposed for the first reading: the one from the Song of Songs (3:1–4) recalls Mary Magdalene's search for Jesus at the sepulcher, and that from 2 Corinthians (5:14–17) recalls the love that burned within her.

✟ JULY 23
St. Bridget of Sweden, Religious

St. Bridget, patron saint of Sweden, was born into an aristocratic family at Finstad about 1302 or 1303. Her father was the governor of the Province of Uppland.

When she was about fourteen years of age, she was married (1316) to Ulf Gudmarsson, and of that union four sons and four daughters were born. In 1335, she was invited to the court of King Magnus II to serve as principal lady-in-waiting to Queen Blanche, and she remained there for two years. After her husband's death in 1344, she lived as a penitent near the Cistercian monastery at Alvastra, and during this period her visions and revelations, which had begun in her youth, became more frequent, and she began to record them in writing. In about 1346, she made the first plans for a new religious congregation, the Order of the Most Holy Savior, more commonly known as Brigittines, after its founder. The new congregation was established to initiate reform in the monastic life and to promote devotion to Christ's Passion. In 1349, Bridget went to Rome to seek approval of her order, and there she worked for the pope's return from Avignon and cared for the poor and the pilgrims in the city. After a pilgrimage to the Holy Land, she died in Rome on July 23, 1373, and in the following year her daughter, St. Catherine of Sweden, took her body to her homeland. Throughout her life, St. Bridget enjoyed mystical graces and revelations, many of which were connected with our Lord's Passion. These were published in 1492 as *Revelations* and were held in great esteem during the Middle Ages. St. Bridget was canonized by Pope Boniface IX in 1391. The prayer of today's Mass affirms that God revealed the secrets of Heaven to her while she meditated on the suffering and death of our Lord.

✝ *St. Sharbel Makhluf, Priest*

St. Sharbel Makhluf is the first Maronite saint to be included in the Latin Church's calendar. He was born, the youngest of five children, in the tiny mountain village of Bika'Kafra, Lebanon, on May 8, 1828. At his baptism, he was given the name Youssef (Joseph). His family was of peasant stock and were members of the Maronite Church. Young Youssef was brought up in a religiously devout family; his paternal uncle was a deacon in the parish church, and two of his maternal uncles were monks of the Lebanese Maronite Order. Youssef learned to read and write by attending classes held in the town square beneath the large church oak. When not in class, he helped in the fields or watched over the family's small flock. As he grew older, he joined the church choir in singing the office and the liturgy. He made frequent visits to his uncles at the Monastery of St. Anthony at Qozhaya, and there he joined in singing the monastic office. In time, he too thought of becoming a monk, but his mother was of a different opinion. He was needed in the fields, and she did not want to lose her youngest child. But Youssef had a mind of his own and knew what he wanted in life, and thus he awaited his hour.

One Sunday morning in 1851—he was now twenty-three years of age—without revealing his plans to anyone, he rose early, and taking nothing with him quietly left home and walked all day to the Monastery of Our Lady of Mayfuq. No one greeted him on his arrival; he had not notified them of his coming. When he did meet a monk, he merely informed him: "I would like to become a monk." After a short interview, the superior accepted him as a postulant. Eight days later, he received the habit and changed his name to Sharbel, after an early martyr of Antioch. For his second year of noviceship, he was sent to the Monastery of St. Maron at Annaya, a four-hour walk away. There he pronounced his vows in 1853, and subsequently he was sent to study theology, in preparation for the priesthood, at the Monastery of St. Cyprian of Kfifan. There he spent six years and was fortunate in having Fr. Nehmetallah Kassab El Hardini (1808–58) as his spiritual director. Fr. El Hardini was not only an excellent spiritual guide but was also known for his holiness. He was beatified by Pope John Paul II in 1998.

Sharbel was ordained on July 23, 1859, and shortly thereafter returned to the monastery at Annaya. He spent the next sixteen years there. When he was not working, he was praying; he kept prolonged fasts, ate but one meal a day, and preferred silence. He had two favorite books, the Bible and Thomas à Kempis's *Imitation of Christ*. A desire gradually grew within him to give himself more completely to God, and thus he requested to live as a hermit. Permission was granted in 1875, and he moved into the Annaya hermitage, where he spent his remaining twenty-three years. He became a man of ceaseless prayer. He celebrated his last Mass on December 16, 1898, during which he felt a pain in his chest. When he completed the consecration, he suffered a stroke. He died on December 24. During his life, the local people looked upon him as a saint and in this they were not in error, for miracles soon began occurring at his tomb. His fame spread not only among Maronites, but throughout the entire Catholic Church. Pope Paul VI canonized him in 1977.

✝ JULY 25 ✄ *Feast*
St. James, Apostle

St. James was born in Galilee, the son of Zebedee and the brother of John (Matt. 4:21). His mother may have been the Salome mentioned in Mark (15:40) and Matthew (27:56). James was a fisherman, as were his father and brother, and it was while he was preparing his nets that our Lord called him to follow him (Matt. 4:21–22). Our Lord nicknamed the brothers Boanerges, or Sons of Thunder, probably because both had manifested their tempers; when a certain Samaritan village refused to accept Jesus and his teaching, the brothers suggested that they should call down fire from Heaven and destroy it (Luke 9:51–56). Together with Peter and John, he witnessed two important moments in our Lord's life: the transfiguration on Mount Tabor (Mark 9:2–8) and the agony in the Garden of Gethsemane (Mark 14:32–42). Tradition maintains that after Pentecost James evangelized Samaria and Judea, and even traveled as far as Spain. He was arrested and beheaded by order of Herod Agrippa I in 44 (Acts 12:1–2), and supposedly he was buried in Jerusalem. James was the first of the apostles to die for Christ, thereby making good his "We can," when our Lord, in today's Gospel (Matt. 20:20–28), asks him and John: "Can you drink of the cup as I am to drink of?" To distinguish him from the other

James, also an apostle, he is often called "the Greater," to indicate either that he was called by our Lord before the other or that he was the elder.

✝ JULY 26 ✒ *Memorial*
SS. Joachim and Anne, Parents of the Blessed Virgin Mary

Joachim and Anne are the traditional names given to the parents of the Virgin Mary. These names do not appear in the canonical Gospels, but come from the Protoevangelium of James (about 170–80), a second-century apocryphal gospel, without historical value. In this work, Joachim and Anne are portrayed as old and childless, and one day while Anne was at prayer, an angel appeared to inform her that she would bear a child. The angel proclaimed the same message to Joachim as he was in his desert hermitage. Inasmuch as Joachim and Anne were chosen by God to be the parents of the immaculate Mother of God, it is not unreasonable to attribute holiness to them as well. Devotion to St. Anne preceded devotion to St. Joachim. By the middle of the sixth century, a church was dedicated to her in Jerusalem, built on the traditional site of her home, and about the same time a church was dedicated (550) to her in Constantinople (now Istanbul). Her feast was celebrated in Rome by the eighth century, but it became popular in Europe with the return of the crusaders, who brought the devotion back with them. A feast honoring St. Joachim was first introduced in the fifteenth century. The popularity of devotion to SS. Joachim and

Anne is easily explained by their close connection to Mary, and because they were the grandparents of our Lord, they also share in being members of the extended Holy Family.

✝ JULY 29 🖉 *Memorial*
St. Martha

Martha lived together with her sister Mary and brother Lazarus in Bethany, a town about two miles distant from Jerusalem. Our Lord loved these three very dearly (John 11:5) and often visited their home (Luke 10:38), where Martha, perhaps the elder sister, welcomed him with her usual gracious hospitality and ministered to his needs, as the second of today's Gospel readings (Luke 10:38–42) narrates. It was, however, at the time of their beloved Lazarus's death, as the first of today's Gospel readings (John 11:19–27) tells the story, that Martha made her powerful confession of faith in Jesus, a confession very similar to that made by Peter, when he and Christ were near Caesarea Philippi (Matt. 16:16). Our Lord asked Martha whether she believed if he were "the resurrection and the life." " 'Yes, Lord,' she replied, 'I have come to believe that you are the Messiah, the Son of God, who is to come into the world'" (John 11:27). The prayers of the Mass today allude to the service of Christ, a service similar to that which Martha had shown him.

✝ JULY 30
St. Peter Chrysologus, Bishop and Doctor of the Church

St. Peter Chrysologus was born in Imola, Italy, in about 400, and in about 431 he became bishop of Ravenna, at that time the imperial capital of the West. He was an acquaintance of Eutyches (371?–455), the originator of the Monophysite heresy (i.e., that there are not two natures, divine and human, in Christ, but only one, divine). When Eutyches asked Peter to speak out in his favor, Peter wrote to Eutyches insisting that in the matters of faith it is always necessary to adhere to the teaching of the Bishop of Rome. Eutyches's teaching was eventually condemned at the Council of Chalcedon (451). During his life, Peter gained a reputation for being an exceptional preacher, as today's opening Mass prayer affirms. There are 183 extant sermons attributed to him, and many of them deal with Christ's Incarnation. Because of his eloquence, he was given the additional name Chrysologus, or "golden-worded." This epithet first originated in the seventh century and most probably in imitation of the epithet given to St. John Chrysostom (see September 13), that is, "golden-tongued." Peter Chrysologus is thought to have died, perhaps at Imola, on July 31, in about 450. Pope Benedict XIII proclaimed him a doctor of the Church in 1729.

JULY 31   ✐   *Solemnity*

✝ St. Ignatius of Loyola, Priest and Founder of the Society of Jesus

St. Ignatius of Loyola was born in his family's castle, near Azpeitia, in Spain's Basque country, sometime before October 23, 1491. As a youth, he served (1506?–17) as a page to Juan Velázquez de Cuéllar, King Ferdinand V's chief treasurer, and there he learned his courtly manners. In 1517, he entered the service of the Duke of Nájera, Viceroy of Navarre, and while defending the fortress at Pamplona was wounded (May 20, 1521) by a cannon shot. He convalesced at Loyola Castle, and by reading a life of Christ as well as those of the saints, he experienced a conversion and resolved to visit the Holy Land and serve the Lord.

On his way to the Holy Land, he stopped at the Benedictine monastery at Montserrat, and there he made a night's vigil (March 24–25, 1522) before the Black Madonna. He then went to nearby Manresa and spent about eleven months in prayer and penance. After a brief visit to Rome to request papal approval for his pilgrimage, he left Venice and arrived in Jerusalem on September 4, 1523. Less than a month later, he left to return to Venice. He then made his way to Barcelona to begin his studies "in order to help souls." After studies in Barcelona (1524–26), Alcalá (1526–27), and Salamanca (1527), Ignatius went to the University of Paris (1528–35), and there he gathered a group of six like-minded men. On August 15, 1534, in a Montmartre chapel, the small band of seven took a vow to go to Jerusalem within a year after their studies, if this were possible, and work for the conversion of the Turks. After their arrival in Venice (1537), they learned that they could not sail for the Holy Land because of imminent war; hence, they went (November 1537) to Rome and offered (November 18–23, 1538) their services to Pope Paul III.

After Ignatius and his first companions decided to form a new religious congregation, their plan received Paul III's approval (September 27, 1540), and thus the Society of Jesus was born. Ignatius was then elected general and accepted the office on April 19, 1541; on April 22, in a ceremony at St. Paul Outside-the-Walls, the six pronounced their vows as Jesuits. As general of the new order, Ignatius remained in Rome, wrote its Constitutions, and supervised the Society's growth, not only in Italy, but in the other countries of Europe as well. He likewise sent missionaries to India. Because of the excessive acts of penance he had practiced while at Manresa, his health had been severely impaired. St. Ignatius died in Rome on July 31, 1556, and was canonized by Pope Gregory XV on March 12, 1622. His *Spiritual Exercises* had been first approved by Pope Paul III on July 31, 1548, and on July 25, 1922, Pope Pius XI named him heavenly patron of all Spiritual Exercises.

AUGUST

AUGUST 1   🌿   *Memorial*
St. Alphonsus Liguori, Bishop
and Doctor of the Church

St. Alphonsus Liguori was born into a noble Neapolitan family in the small town of Marianella, Italy, on September 27, 1696. His early education was under the care of tutors, and at the age of thirteen years (1708), he began to study law at the University of Naples. He graduated in 1713 with a degree in both canon and civil law. He then practiced law for several years, until October 1723, when he set his practice and the world aside and began to study theology. After ordination in 1726, he devoted his time and efforts to preaching and hearing confessions. In 1732, he founded a group of priests, which eventually came to be known as the Congregation of the Most Holy Redeemer, or more commonly as the Redemptorists. Alphonsus, being aware of the needs of the faithful of his time, directed his congregation toward preaching, giving missions, and instruction. In this way, he hoped to educate the people in the faith and win back those who had become lax in their practice of it. In 1762, he was appointed bishop of Sant'

Agata dei Goti; his interests now included the reform of the clergy and the upgrading of seminaries. As bishop, he put an end to certain abuses, restored churches, fostered good liturgy, and visited the many parishes in his diocese. In 1768, he was stricken with a rheumatic illness that eventually forced him to resign his see in 1775. He spent the rest of his life supervising the growth of his congregation and writing ascetical and theological books. His ascetical writings were the outpouring of his own rich spiritual life; he wrote on the mysteries of Christ's life, the Mass, devotion to the Blessed Sacrament, on Mary, and prayer. In all of these, he opposed the then-current Jansenist teachings. He is especially remembered for his text in moral theology, which was used in seminaries throughout the world. He died at Nocera de' Pagani, near Salerno, on August 1, 1787, and was canonized by Pope Gregory XVI in 1839. In 1871, Pope Pius IX declared St. Alphonsus Liguori a doctor of the Church, and in 1950 Pope Pius XII made him patron of moralists and confessors.

✝ AUGUST 2
St. Eusebius of Vercelli, Bishop

St. Eusebius was born in Sardinia sometime in the early fourth century. After his father's death, his mother took the family to Rome, where he studied and was ordained a priest during the pontificate of Pope Julius I (337–52). He was subsequently appointed the first Bishop of Vercelli, in Piedmont, Italy, in about 345. He and his clergy lived in community, in a manner similar to that later developed by the Canons Regular. Throughout his years as bishop, Eusebius was a strong opponent of the Arians, who denied Christ's divinity, and firmly supported the teachings of St. Athanasius (see May 2) at the Council of Milan (355), at which he served as Pope Liberius's legate. Because of Eusebius's anti-Arian stand, Constantius II (emperor 337–61), who favored the heretics, ordered him sent into exile to Scythopolis in Palestine (today's Bet She'an, Israel). He was released in 362, after Julian "the Apostate" (emperor 361–63) came to power, but only after suffering much maltreatment at the hands of the Arians. He returned to his diocese, where he continued to oppose the Arians and their doctrines. He died at Vercelli on August 1, 371. The Mass prayer today aptly recalls that St. Eusebius affirmed the divinity of Christ in his long conflict with the Arian heretics. He is especially venerated today for his persistence in supporting orthodox teaching.

AUGUST 2
St. Peter Julian Eymard, Priest

St. Peter Julian Eymard was born at La Mure d'Isère, a small town nestled in the French Alps in the Diocese of Grenoble, on February 4, 1811. From his earliest years, he thought of becoming a priest, but because his father did not enjoy the same vision as he, Peter Julian found it necessary to study Latin secretly. After his father's death in 1831, Peter Julian entered the major seminary in Grenoble and was ordained to the diocesan priesthood in 1834. His first assignments were in two small parishes, but because he felt called to the religious life he received his bishop's approval and entered (1839) the newly founded Society of Mary (Marist Fathers). For the next seventeen years, he held positions of authority in that congregation; he was spiritual director at the junior seminary at Belley (1840–44), then provincial superior of the congregation (1844–51) in Lyon, and finally rector (1851–56) of the College of La Seine-sur-Mer. During a visit to the shrine of Our Lady of Fourvière in February 1851, he was deeply inspired to found a religious society devoted principally to promoting devotion to and adoration of the Blessed Sacrament. Aware that no such religious congregation existed in the Church, he felt it his duty to found one. Because he was unable to organize such a group within the Marists— this did not fall within the scope of their apostolate— he approached, with his superior's permission, the Bishop of Paris, and in 1856 founded the Priests of the Most Blessed Sacrament (known as the Blessed Sacrament Fathers), of which he was superior general until his death. In 1857, he founded the Pious Union of Priest Adorers and then in 1858 the Servants of the Blessed Sacrament, a community of cloistered contemplative nuns devoted exclusively to perpetual adoration. He guided these communities until his death in his native town on August 1, 1868. He was canonized by Pope John XXIII on December 9, 1962, and he is acknowledged as the "Priest of the Blessed Sacrament."

✝ *AUGUST 2
Bl. Peter Faber, Priest

Bl. Peter Faber was St. Ignatius of Loyola's first recruit. He was born on April 13, 1506, in Villaret, Savoy, and went (1525) to study at the University of Paris, where his roommate was St. Francis Xavier (see December 3), and later St. Ignatius (see July 31). Under the latter's direction, Peter decided to become a priest. On August 15, 1534, he and six companions vowed poverty, chastity, and to go to the Holy Land to convert the Turks. When they arrived in Venice and learned that it was impossible to advance further because of imminent war with the Turks, Peter and his friends went to Rome and offered (November 1538) their services to Pope Paul III. The pope then appointed Peter to teach Scripture at Rome's Sapienza College, and in 1540 the pope sent him to Worms and Regensburg (Germany) to attend the Catholic–Protestant dialogue. From there, he went (1541) to Spain where, by his sermons and missions, he made the young Society of Jesus known. Responding to a new papal order, he again went to Germany, this time as assistant to the papal nuncio. Then, at the request of King John III of Portugal, he visited that country and prepared the way for the Jesuits to work there. Because Pope Paul III had named Peter one of the papal theologians to assist at the Council of Trent, Peter traveled to Rome to see Ignatius before making his way to the council. While in Rome, he became ill, and he died on August 1, 1546. Pope Pius IX, acknowledging the cult that had been shown to Peter Faber in his native Savoy, declared, on September 5, 1872, that he was among the blessed in heaven.

✝ St. John Mary Vianney, Priest

St. John Mary Vianney is better known as the Curé of Ars. He was born at Dardilly, near Lyon, on May 8, 1786. Because the years of his growing up coincided with those of the French Revolution and its aftermath, he only had a few months of formal schooling. When he was eighteen years of age, despite the disturbed times, he began private studies for the priesthood, but such studies were difficult for one without a proper educational foundation. In 1809, he was called to military service, but due to illness he was unable to join his unit before it departed, and later when it was time to join a subsequent unit, he missed it because he visited a church on the way. While trying to catch up with this second unit, he found another young man in a similar situation and went along with him; but the young man, rather than looking for the unit, sought asylum in a small village, and there they remained until an amnesty was granted in March 1810. John then attended the minor seminary; in 1813 he went to Lyon for theology, but he had to leave the following year (1814) because of his inability to cope with the Latin language. After being tutored privately, he was finally ordained on August 12, 1815. In 1818, he was assigned to Ars, a small parish of 230 individuals, all of whom had become slovenly in the practice of their religion. He cleaned and restored the church, visited the families in the parish, and began catechism classes. Within eight years, what had been a dying parish was now vibrant with life. Fr. Vianney was known for his ability to read hearts and, thus, he became a renowned confessor, with penitents coming to him from all parts of France. He spent an average of twelve to thirteen hours a day in the confessional! He died at Ars on August 4, 1859; he had been there forty-one years. He was canonized by Pope Pius XI in 1925, and in 1929 the same pope made him patron of parish priests.

✝ AUGUST 5
Dedication of the Basilica of St. Mary Major in Rome

Today we commemorate the dedication of the Basilica of St. Mary Major in Rome. This church is sometimes called "Basilica Liberiana" in a desire to identify it with a church built by Pope Liberius (352–66) on Rome's Esquiline Hill. Pope Sixtus III (432–40) is said to have reconstructed Pope Liberius's earlier church, and on August 5, as stated in the Hieronymian Martyrology (about 450), he dedicated (434) it to our Lady. The dedication was in memory of the definition of the Council of Ephesus (431) that Mary was indeed Theotokos, that is, the Mother of God. Sixtus's church may have been the first church dedicated to Mary in Rome. The basilica is now called St. Mary Major, not only because it may be the oldest church honoring our Lady, but because it is the largest and most important of all churches dedicated to her. This feast, which was at first only celebrated in Rome, was at one time also known as that of Our Lady of the Snow. A legend going back to the tenth century states that the Virgin Mary appeared to a Roman patrician in a dream (on August 4) and told him to build a church on the site, where he would find snow the following morning. The next morning, he went to tell Pope Liberius of his dream, but the Virgin had also appeared to the pope on the previous night and told him that he would find snow on the Esquiline Hill, and there he was to outline the dimensions of the new church. The pope found the miraculous snow as our Lady had predicted, and on that very spot he built his basilica.

✠ AUGUST 6 ✒ *Feast*
Transfiguration of the Lord

The feast of our Lord's Transfiguration was celebrated in the East as early as the fourth or fifth century. Though the New Testament accounts of the Transfiguration (Matt. 17:1–9; Mark 9:2–10; Luke 9:28–36) do not mention the mountain where this singular event took place, nevertheless, tradition has taken it to be Mount Tabor, about six miles southeast of Nazareth. In the fourth or fifth century, a church had been erected on that mount, and because that church had been consecrated on August 6, that became the date for the feast's celebration. The feast was then introduced in the West in the eighth century, but it remained for a long time only a local Roman celebration. Then, on August 6, 1456, news arrived in Rome that the Christian army at Belgrade (Yugoslavia), on the previous July 22, had been victorious over the Turks. In memory of this victory, and the fact that the news arrived in Rome on the feast of the Transfiguration, Pope Callistus III added (August 6, 1457) the feast to the universal Roman calendar so that it could be celebrated throughout the Christian world.

SS. Sixtus II, Pope and Martyr, and His Companions, Martyrs

St. Sixtus, who may have been of Greek extraction, was elected pope in August 257. On succeeding Stephen I (254–57), Sixtus became heir to the controversy that had originated during Stephen's pontificate concerning the validity of baptism conferred by heretics. The Churches of Africa and Asia Minor held to their custom of rebaptizing heretics and schismatics, but Sixtus, like Stephen before him, upheld the Roman view that baptism, when properly administered even by heretics, was valid. With regard to this matter, Sixtus succeeded —where Stephen had failed—in restoring good relations with St. Cyprian, Bishop of Carthage (see September 16). The year of Sixtus's election to the papacy was also the year of Valerian's (emperor 253–59) decree against the Christians, in which he did not exactly demand that they renounce their religious beliefs but merely demonstrate their loyalty by offering sacrifice to the gods. Because most Christians remained faithful to their beliefs and practices, the imperial decree turned into a full-scale persecution, with Church leaders as the main target. On August 6, 258, Sixtus, together with his seven deacons, was conducting a service in the cemetery of Praetextatus when imperial police discovered them and beheaded Sixtus and four of the deacons (Januarius, Magnus, Stephen, and Vincent). Two deacons (Felicissimus and Agapitus) were most probably martyred later that day, while the seventh (Lawrence) was martyred four days later (see August 10). The bodies of Sixtus and the four deacons were buried in the cemetery of Callistus on the Appian Way, directly across from the cemetery of Praetextatus. Sixtus was one of the most venerated martyrs of the Roman Church and, thus, his name was added to the Roman Canon. His epitaph was written by Pope Damasus I (see December 11).

✝ AUGUST 7
St. Cajetan, Priest

St. Cajetan, son of Count Gaspare da Theine, was born in Vicenza, northern Italy, in October 1480. He pursued law studies at the University of Padua, and after graduation went (1506) to Rome, where Pope Julius II had given him an appointment as prothonotary apostolic in the Roman Curia. In Rome he joined the Oratory of Divine Love, a group devoted to piety and charity, and helped at the San Giacomo hospital for incurables. He was ordained in 1516 and was back in Vicenza in 1518, engaged in charitable works. In 1520 he went to Venice and there founded (1522) a hospital for incurables. He returned (1523) to Rome and in 1524 he and three companions formed the Congregation of Clerks Regular, priests dedicated to work for the reform of society according to Christian principles. Their congregation is more commonly known today as the Theatines, a name derived from Theate, the Latin name for Chieti, the episcopal see of their first superior, Gianpietro Caraffa (later Pope Paul IV). They were active in Rome until the sack of the city in 1527, when they moved their headquarters to Venice. Later, in 1533, Cajetan became superior of a new foundation in Naples; he labored there until his death, except for the period (1540–43) when he was superior in Venice. While in Naples, he preached against the teachings of Juan de Valdés (c. 1490–1541) and Bernardino Ochino (1487–1564), both of whom had Protestant leanings and were then active in the city. Cajetan died in Naples on August 7, 1547, and he was canonized by Pope Clement X in 1671. When today's prayer affirms that St. Cajetan imitated the apostolic way of life, this is in reference to his founding of a religious congregation intent on seeking the salvation of the neighbor.

✠ AUGUST 8   *✎*   *Memorial*
St. Dominic, Priest

St. Dominic Guzmán was born in Caleruega, Old Castile, Spain, sometime after 1170. On completing his studies in theology at Palencia, he was appointed (about 1196) a canon of the cathedral chapter at Osma, and in 1201 he was chosen prior of that cathedral community. He accompanied Osma's bishop, Diego de Azevedo, on two royal embassies to northern Europe, and during that time he became acquainted with the needs of the Church, especially in the Languedoc region of France, where the Church was severely threatened by the Albigensian heresy. To assist the Church in her present grave need, Dominic and several other priests were commissioned by Pope Innocent III (1198–1216) as itinerant preachers to save the French faithful from the heretics. Dominic preached throughout southern France for a period of about eleven years

(1206–17). In 1214, he conceived the idea of forming a religious community to continue this important work of preaching, so he and his companions went to Toulouse in 1215, and there they formed what eventually came to be known as the Order of Friars Preachers, more commonly called Dominicans. Dominic only had six more years to live, but during that time he saw his order expand into France and Spain, Italy, Germany, and Poland. The cities of Paris and Bologna, both university centers, became the principal bases for the order's growth. In 1221, after participating in the order's second general chapter in Bologna, Dominic became ill and died there on August 6, 1221. He was canonized by Pope Gregory IX in 1234. Today's prayer recalls that during a period of crisis St. Dominic came to the aid of the Church, that is, by his preaching against the heretics and by founding the Order of Friars Preachers.

✝ AUGUST 9
St. Teresa Benedicta of the Cross,
Virgin and Martyr

Edith Stein was born October 12, 1891, in what is now Wrocław, Poland, but which had been Breslau since the Prussian occupation of western Poland in 1741. Edith was the youngest of eleven children. Because her father died when she was very young, her mother, who was a devout Jew, raised the family and saw to its support. Though the mother was meticulous in observing all Jewish holy days and customs, nevertheless, by the time Edith reached her early teen years, she was an avowed atheist. In 1911, she matriculated at the university in her native city; she intended to study German and history, but she became interested in experimental psychology, in the hope that this would help in her search for truth. While at the university, she was introduced to the writings of Edmund Husserl (1859–1938), and because she found them inspiring, she transferred (1913) to Göttingen to be one of his students. While there, she met the philosopher Max Scheler (1874–1928), and it was through him that she had her first contact with Catholicism. When Husserl moved to Freiburg in 1916, Edith went along as his graduate assistant and there received her doctorate. Feeling the beginnings of an interior transformation, Edith now began to read the New Testament.

During the summer of 1921, as a house guest of friends in Bergzabern, she began reading the autobiography of St. Teresa of Jesus (see October 15). She spent the entire night reading, and when she finished it the next morning her remark was, "This is the truth!" Having been moved by what she had read, she then purchased a catechism and a missal, and after studying both, attended her first Mass in Bergzabern. After Mass, she asked the priest to baptize her. She was finally baptized on January 1, 1922, at which time she took the name Teresa. There was also growing within her the desire to be a Carmelite nun. Later, in 1922, she began teaching German at St. Magdalena's School in Speyer. The school was operated by Dominican sisters, and because Edith had taken private vows, her manner of life was similar to that of the sisters. She left Speyer in 1931 and returned home, busying herself in translating philosophical treatises of St. Thomas Aquinas (see January 28). Then, in 1932, she was appointed lecturer at the German Institute for Educational Theory in Münster; but the following year, she was asked to leave because of her Jewish heritage. Adolf Hitler (1889–1945) had recently come (1933) into power, and Germany had launched a large-scale offensive against the Jews. It was now time for her to fulfill her deepest desire.

On October 14, 1933, she entered the Discalced Carmelite convent in Cologne, and when she received her habit in April 1934, she took Teresa Benedicta of the Cross as her name in religion. Then, on November 9, 1938, there occurred Kristallnacht—when synagogues were burned and Jews were driven from their homes. Knowing that her presence could cause difficulties for the nuns, she left her Cologne monastery on December 31, crossed the border into Holland under the cover of darkness, and arrived at the Echt convent the following morning. But when Germany occupied Holland (1940), she knew she was no longer safe even there. On July 26, 1942, the Dutch bishops issued their pastoral letter denouncing the deportation of Jews. The Nazis responded by ordering the arrest of all non-Aryan Catholics in Holland, and on August 2, 1942, Sr. Teresa Benedicta was arrested and taken from her convent. Then, on the morning of August 7, she and about a thousand others were transported to Oswiecim (also known by its German name, Auschwitz), and there, on August 9, 1942, she met her martyrdom in the gas chambers. St. Teresa Benedicta of the Cross was canonized by Pope John Paul II in 1998.

St. Lawrence, Deacon and Martyr

St. Lawrence, one of the seven deacons of the Church of Rome, was in charge of distributing alms to the poor. He was martyred during the persecution of Valerian (emperor 253–59), who in August 258 had ordered the execution of Christian bishops, priests, and deacons. While assisting at a liturgical service in the cemetery of Praetextatus, together with Pope Sixtus II (see August 7) and six other deacons, he was apprehended but was martyred four days later, on August 10, 258. The tradition concerning Lawrence's death is as follows. Because he was in charge of alms, the prefect of Rome, being in need of money, asked him to hand over the Church's treasury. In answer to this request, Lawrence assembled the city's poor, to whom he had distributed whatever money the Church had as alms, and, pointing to them, he said: "This is the treasury of the Church." Thinking he could compel Lawrence to reveal his hiding places, the prefect had him roasted on a gridiron and, thus, Lawrence died a martyr's death. Legend has it that after he had been broiled on one side, he himself suggested to his executioners to turn him over so that the other side could also be done. Lawrence was one of the most popular saints in the early Church, and his name was added to the Roman Canon. During the time of Constantine (emperor 306–37), a chapel was built over his tomb in the cemetery of Cyriaca on the Via Tiburtina. Later, Pope Pelagius II (579–90) built a larger church; it is still in use and is known as St. Lawrence Outside-the-Walls, one of Rome's patriarchal basilicas.

✝ *St. Clare, Virgin*

St. Clare was born in Assisi in 1193 or 1194 and—moved by the example and preaching of Francis of Assisi (see October 4)—she determined (1211) to follow his way of life. She divested herself of her possessions and, against her family's wishes, she went to live in poverty with Francis and his followers. She received the habit from him at the Portiuncula in March 1212, and she set about living a penitential and ascetical life. For a monastery, Francis gave Clare an old house near the Church of San Damiano, a short distance from Assisi. She was soon joined by her younger sister Agnes; then their mother, Ortolana, asked to join them; and finally their sister Beatrice also joined. In 1215, Francis appointed Clare superior of the community. Their way of life was most penitential: sleeping on the ground, not eating meat, wearing only sandals, and speaking only when there was need. From about 1225 until her death, Clare was almost constantly ill, no doubt a condition brought on by her extreme penitential practices. Through her great love for the Blessed Sacrament, she was successful, in 1243, in preserving her convent and the city of Assisi from raiding Saracens. She died on August 11, 1253, and devotion to her became so widespread that she was canonized two years later, on August 15, 1255, by Pope Alexander IV. Today's prayer reminds us that the love of poverty that Clare lived and had in her heart was inspired by God. The religious communities that follow her rule are today known as Poor Clares.

✝ SS. Pontian, Pope and Martyr, and Hippolytus, Priest and Martyr

St. Pontian was a pope and St. Hippolytus an antipope; they became reconciled when both were sent into exile. Hippolytus was born about 170, and his mother tongue was most probably Greek. He came to Rome, and there he was ordained during the days of Pope Victor I (189–198). Hippolytus was a man of great learning and was recognized as the leading intellectual among the Roman clergy. The election of Pope Callistus (see October 14) in 217 did not meet with Hippolytus's approval. He always looked with disdain on this former slave and cemetery-keeper, and now that Callistus was pope, Hippolytus openly disagreed with his penitential discipline. He thought the pope was much too easy with regard to forgiving sinners; hence, Hippolytus had his followers elect (217) him antipope—the first antipope in the history of the Church. Hippolytus remained antipope during the following pontificate of Pope Urban I (223–30) and into that of Pope Pontian. In 235, Maximinus Thrax (emperor 235–38) initiated his persecution by striking against the Church's leaders, and thus he exiled both Pontian and Hippolytus to the salt mines of Sardinia. Hippolytus was one of the more prolific writers of the early Church, and of all his works the *Apostolic Tradition* is perhaps the most famous, because in it he has left us a description of the liturgical practices in use in the early third century.

Pontian was Roman-born and was elected to the papacy on July 21, 230, to succeed Urban I. The early years of his pontificate were years of peace, until Maximinus Thrax was acclaimed emperor in March 235. The Christian religion was no longer tolerated, and its leaders were singled out for attack. Thus Pontian and Hippolytus became the emperor's first victims. Both were arrested and sent to Sardinia. Knowing that his deportation was for life, Pontian, on September 28, 235, abdicated the papacy (the first pope to do so) so that another could succeed him. Either on their way to Sardinia or shortly after arriving there, Pontian and Hippolytus became reconciled. Pontian died in Sardinia in October 235, not long after his arrival, as a result of the harsh treatment to which he had been subjected. Hippolytus died shortly afterward of the same cause. The Christians in Rome immediately revered both as martyrs, and Pope Fabian (236–50) (see January 20) had their bodies brought to Rome. Pontian was the first martyred pope to be solemnly buried (August 13, 236 or 237) in the crypt of the popes in the cemetery of Callistus, and Hippolytus was buried in the cemetery on the Via Tiburtina. Their memorial is celebrated on the anniversary of their burial in Rome.

✝ AUGUST 14   ✒   *Memorial*
St. Maximilian Mary Kolbe, Priest and Martyr

St. Maximilian Mary Kolbe was born at Zdunska-Wola, Poland, on January 8, 1894. His baptismal name was Raymond; Maximilian was the name he received when he entered (1910) the Conventual Franciscan Friars. He did his studies for the priesthood (1912–19) in Rome, where he organized (1917) the Militia of Mary Immaculate, an association dedicated to promoting devotion to the Blessed Virgin Mary. After earning doctorates in theology and philosophy, he returned to Poland in 1919 to teach Church history at the seminary, and there in 1922 he started *Knights of the Immaculata*, a periodical for militia members. Years later, in 1927, he founded the City of the Immaculate (Niepokalanów) on the outskirts of Warsaw. Upon being sent (1930) to Japan, he founded a similar community in Nagasaki, and he planned on establishing others throughout the world. In 1936, he returned to Poland and became superior of Niepokalanów. With the German invasion of Poland in early September 1939, World War II began. Fr. Kolbe was first arrested on September 19 of that year and was transferred to three different concentration camps. After several months, he was unexpectedly released and, thus, he returned to Niepokalanów, where he continued, as best he could, his former apostolate. His second arrest came on February 17, 1941, and having been given No. 16670, he was sent on May 28, without trial or sentencing, to the concentration camp at Oswiecim (more commonly known by its German name, Auschwitz). When he arrived, there were already tens of thousands of prisoners there, and though forbidden, he managed clandestinely to minister to Catholics and at times spent the entire night hearing confessions. Then, one day toward the end of July, because a prisoner had escaped from Fr. Kolbe's block, ten individuals were chosen at random to die in the starvation bunker. Fr. Kolbe was not among the ten. However, when one of the chosen ten sighed: "My poor wife, my poor children!" Fr. Kolbe offered to take his place. The offer was accepted. Two weeks later, when the Germans needed the cell for more victims, the officer in charge opened (August 14, 1941) the bunker and found four victims still alive. Fr. Kolbe was the only one still conscious. The officer then ordered an injection to be given to Fr. Kolbe and the other men, thus hastening their death. On the following day, Fr. Kolbe's body was burned. He was canonized as a martyr of charity by Pope John Paul II in 1982. Today's Mass prayer mentions St. Maximilian's love for Mary Immaculate and his heroic love of neighbor, a love that inspired him to give his life for another.

✝ AUGUST 15 ✿ *Solemnity*
Assumption of the Blessed Virgin Mary

On November 1, 1950, Pope Pius XII issued an Apostolic Constitution, *Munificentissimus Deus*, in which he solemnly defined Mary's bodily assumption into heaven: "We proclaim and define it to be a dogma revealed by God that the immaculate Mother of God, Mary ever Virgin, when the course of her earthly life was finished, was taken up body and soul into the glory of heaven." Though this truth of the faith is not found explicitly in the Gospels, it is nevertheless implicitly present, and it has become more and more explicit in the belief of Catholics as the centuries passed. Mary's corporal assumption is a necessary conclusion from her sinlessness, her fullness of grace, and the fact that she is the Mother of God (see Luke 1:28, 42). Because Mary was conceived without sin, she was also free from the consequences of sin and from its punishments, which include death and bodily corruption. That she did die (as commonly held by theologians) was not due to sin, but to her desire to be conformed to her Son in all things, even in death. There is no way of knowing how long Mary remained on earth after our Lord's Ascension, but because she had been given to John and to the Church as his and our mother (John 19:27), she remained with the apostles as long as the infant Church needed her guidance and motherly care. By the end of the sixth century, the faithful in the East celebrated the feast of the Dormition (or Assumption) of Our Lady, but because it was kept on different dates in different places, it was Emperor Maurice (+ 602) who stipulated that it be everywhere kept on August 15. By the seventh century, the feast was commonly celebrated in Rome and in the West. With the passage of time, the belief in Mary's corporal assumption into heaven became universally held by the Catholic faithful, and in 1950 the pope and the hierarchy of the Roman Church thought the time suitable for its solemn definition.

✝ AUGUST 16
St. Stephen of Hungary

St. Stephen was the first King of Hungary. He was born at Esztergom in about 975, the son of Géza, Duke of Hungary, and he was given the name Vajk. Sometime during his early years (perhaps 985), he and his father converted to Christianity and were baptized; it was then that he received the name Stephen. In 995, he married Gisela, sister of St. Henry II (see July 13). Upon the death of Stephen's father in 997, he succeeded to the throne, and on Christmas 1000, he was crowned king with a crown that Pope Sylvester II (999–1003) had sent him. Since his conversion, Stephen had been a fervent Christian, and as king he set about Christianizing his country. He abolished all pagan customs and ordered severe punishments for theft, murder, and adultery. He built many churches and gradually established ten dioceses throughout his land; he likewise promoted the spread of Benedictine monasteries. During his rule, the people lived in harmony and the nation prospered. He died at Esztergom on August 15, 1038, and was buried in Székesfehérvár in the basilica he had built and had dedicated to Mary. It was in that church that the kings who succeeded him were crowned and buried. Stephen was canonized by Pope Gregory VII in 1083. Hungarian Catholics look upon St. Stephen as the founder of the Hungarian Church and of the Hungarian state.

✝ AUGUST 18
St. Jane Frances de Chantal, Religious

St. Jane Frances de Chantal was the founder of the Order of the Visitation of Holy Mary. She was born Jane Frances Frémyot, in Dijon, France, on January 23, 1572. When she was twenty-one years of age, she married Baron Christophe de Rabutin-Chantal, and the couple had six children (three of whom died at an early age). After seven years of marriage, her husband died as a result of a hunting accident and, consequently, she took it upon herself to raise and educate her remaining son and two daughters. In 1604, she met Bishop Francis de Sales (see January 24), and she soon placed herself under his spiritual direction. Since she had become a widow, she had thought of entering the religious life. In the meantime, however, she continued caring for her children, while following a strict rule of life and visiting the sick and the dying. In 1610, she and Francis founded the Order of the Visitation, whose members would not be cloistered but would be free to assist others in need. Because no one at the time heard of unenclosed sisters, their plan met with such opposition that in the end St. Francis had to agree to enclosure. Under Jane Frances's guidance, the order prospered, and the number of convents grew. At the time of her death in Moulins, France, on December 13, 1641, there were eighty monasteries. St. Jane Frances was canonized by Pope Clement XIII in 1767. The prayer in her Mass today recalls that she fulfilled a double vocation: marriage and religious life.

✝ *AUGUST 18
Bl. Albert Hurtado Cruchaga, Priest

Bl. Albert Hurtado Cruchaga is esteemed throughout his native Chile as the founder of El Hogar de Cristo, shelters that offer, in the name of Christ, assistance to the homeless and the poor. Albert was born in Viña del Mar on January 22, 1901, and he knew poverty from his youth. It was only because of a scholarship that he was able to attend the Jesuit High School in Santiago. During those early years of study, he regularly spent his Sunday afternoons in the city's slum district, helping the poor in any way he could. Upon graduation, he thought of becoming a Jesuit, but his mother and brother needed his assistance, so he found afternoon and evening employment while reserving the mornings to study law at Santiago's Catholic University. Busy as he was, he still spent his Sunday afternoons with the poor. This he would not give up. Then, in 1923, with his law degree in hand, he entered the Jesuit novitiate. In 1927, he was sent to Spain for his philosophical studies, and he completed his theological course at Louvain, where he was ordained (1933).

He returned to Chile in 1936. While teaching pedagogy at the Catholic University, he involved his sodality students in various apostolic endeavors; for example, working with the poor, visiting the sick, and teaching catechism to children. The poor were continually on Fr. Hurtado's mind, especially the homeless. With help from benefactors, he opened his first shelter, which he named El Hogar de Cristo, where he welcomed them as into Christ's home. In time, there were shelters for men, boys, and then for women and girls. While offering assistance, Fr. Hurtado rehabilitated the adults, trained the young in various skills, and instilled Christian values in all. Similar residences were opened in other Chilean cities, and from there they passed to other South American countries. Ever eager to teach and explain the Church's social teaching to the working laity, Fr. Hurtado wrote several books and started the periodical *Mensaje* (Message). In 1951, his health began to fail, and he was diagnosed with pancreatic cancer. He died in Santiago on August 18, 1952, and was beatified by Pope John Paul II in 1994.

✝ AUGUST 19
St. John Eudes, Priest

St. John Eudes was born in Ri, Normandy, France, on November 14, 1601. In 1615, he was sent to study with the Jesuits at Caen, and there he joined (1618) that school's Sodality of Our Lady. In 1620, he received the tonsure and minor orders, but he remained uncertain whether he should become a diocesan priest. While in Caen, he became familiar with the Oratorians—a society of priests living in community that had been established by St. Philip Neri (see May 26)—and in 1623 he entered the Oratory in Paris. He was ordained a priest in 1625. During the plagues of 1627 and 1631, he selflessly worked among the victims in his native Normandy. Then, in 1633, he entered upon his career as a home missioner visiting parishes giving hundreds of missions, some of which lasted four to six weeks. His principal aim was to teach the faithful the fundamentals of the Catholic faith. Thus he traveled throughout Normandy and northern France.

After eight years of such missions, he began (1641) giving conferences to the clergy, but he soon came to realize that the great need was to upgrade the training and education of candidates for the priesthood. With this in mind, he left the Oratorians in 1643 and with several other priests formed the Congregation of Jesus and Mary (more commonly known today as Eudists), whose purpose was to conduct seminaries and work for the continued formation, both spiritual and intellectual, of the clergy. To provide seminarians with matter for prayer, he wrote many devotional books, and he was one of the most widely read spiritual authors of the seventeenth century. Throughout his life, both in his preaching and writing, he promoted devotion to the Sacred Hearts of Jesus and Mary. He was the first to recommend that a feast honoring the Sacred Heart of Jesus be established; such a feast would not be approved until 1765 by Pope Clement XIII. St. John died at Caen on August 19, 1680, and was canonized by Pope Pius XI in 1925. The prayer of the Mass today refers to St. John's deep love for the Sacred Heart and his preaching on that Heart.

✝ AUGUST 20 ✍ *Memorial*
St. Bernard, Abbot and Doctor of the Church

St. Bernard was born into a noble family at Fontaines, near Dijon, France, about 1090. In 1112, with thirty-one other young noblemen—some of whom were his brothers—he entered the Cistercian monastery at Cîteaux, and three years later (1115) the abbot, St. Stephen Harding (1134), appointed Bernard and twelve monks to establish a new monastery at Clairvaux. With Bernard as its abbot, Clairvaux eventually became one of the chief monastic centers in Europe, and he became one of the most influential ecclesiastics in the Church. In 1117, his father, now somewhat advanced in age, and his younger brother Nivard entered his community. During the period when there was both a pope and an antipope, Bernard persuaded the antipope Anacletus II (1130–38) to submit to Innocent II (1130–43) and, thus, he restored peace to the Church. With the election of Pope Eugene III (1145–53)—Bernard's pupil, former monk at Clairvaux, and abbot of the Cistercian monastery of SS. Vincenzo and Anastasio outside Rome—Bernard's influence increased. Eugene commissioned (1146) Bernard to preach the Second Crusade, and Bernard spent 1146 and 1147 traveling through France fulfilling that commission. Within his own Cistercian Order, he was known for his sermons, which were almost always commentaries on Scripture or the liturgy, for example, those on the Song of Songs. In the sphere of theology, there are his *On Loving God* and *On Grace and Free Will*. Bernard's writings show a faith nurtured by a sublime mysticism. It was his saintliness and personality that made him so influential and popular. He died, worn out by austerities and illness, at Clairvaux on August 20, 1153, and was canonized by Pope Alexander III in 1174. In 1830, Pope Pius VIII declared him a doctor of the Church. Each of the prayers in the Mass today has a reference to St. Bernard's life: He is called a radiant light, who strove to bring harmony to the Church and whose teachings can help us to become wise.

✝

AUGUST 21   🌿   *Memorial*
St. Pius X, Pope

St. Pius X is known as the "Pope of the Eucharist." He was born Joseph Melchior Sarto on June 21, 1835, in Riese, northern Italy. He entered the seminary in Padua in 1850, and after studies he was ordained in 1858 for the Diocese of Treviso. For the next nine years, he did pastoral work in small parishes. In 1867, he became archpriest of Salzano, and then in 1875 he was named chancellor of the Treviso Diocese and spiritual director at the major seminary. In 1884, Pope Leo XIII made him Bishop of Mantua, and then in 1893 the same pontiff named him a cardinal and Patriarch of Venice. He was elected pope on August 4, 1903. During his pontificate, which lasted eleven years, he saw to the publication of guidelines for the education and training of priests, and when a diocese could not maintain its own seminary, he encouraged regional seminaries. He supervised the codification of the Church's canon law, reformed Church music by restoring Gregorian chant, and fought against the threats of Modernism (a movement first known as "New Catholicism"). His decree *Lamentabili* (July 3, 1907) contains a list of sixty-five errors taught by the Modernists, and in his subsequent encyclical *Pascendi* (September 8, 1907), he condemns the movement.

Pius likewise promoted devotion to the Holy Eucharist. His decrees on the Eucharist recommended frequent and even daily Communion (1907), and lowered the age for receiving First Communion (1910). He set up a commission to promote biblical studies, which he entrusted to the Benedictines, and he encouraged the daily reading of the Bible. In 1909, he founded the Biblical Institute for scriptural studies in Rome, and this he entrusted to the Jesuits. With the outbreak of World War I, his heart was broken, and he died on August 20, 1914. Throughout his life, whether as parish priest, bishop, or pope, Pius was admired for his simplicity and sincerity. He was canonized by Pope Pius XII in 1954. In today's Mass, the prayers over the gifts and after Communion recall St. Pius X's devotion and love of the Eucharist, and the opening prayer quotes his motto as pope: "to make all things new in Christ" (Eph. 1:10).

✝

AUGUST 22 ✿ Memorial
Queenship of the Blessed Virgin Mary

The memorial of the Queenship of Mary dates from October 11, 1954, the date of its institution by Pope Pius XII. The decree for its liturgical celebration may be recent, but the title of Mary as Queen of Heaven is one of her oldest. Mary is Queen because of her divine motherhood and the excellence of her holiness. Because she is the mother of Christ, who is our Lord and King, then she too is our Lady and Queen. But she is also Queen because she is the holiest of creatures, even from the first moment of her conception. She surpasses all the saints in holiness, and being the finest of our race she now reigns over us as our Queen. This memorial of the Queenship of Mary is fittingly celebrated on the octave of Mary's Assumption, thus linking the two feasts. After our Lady's arrival into Heaven, her Son, who had already granted her other singular privileges, now, in the presence of the angels and saints, gives her a place at his right hand and crowns her Queen of Heaven.

AUGUST 23
St. Rose of Lima, Virgin

St. Rose of Lima is the patron of Peru, South America, and the Philippines. Her name was Isabel de Flores, and she was born in Lima on April 20, 1586. Her father was a

Puerto Rican, who had come to Peru in 1548 with the Spanish conquistadors. She received the name Rose when a housemaid, gazing upon her when she was still an infant, remarked: "She's as lovely as a rose." Her mother decided that Rose would be her daughter's name, and later she was given that name at the time of confirmation. As a young girl growing up, Rose was given to austerities: fasting and mortification. Because her parents denied her permission to enter a convent, and because she preferred not to marry, she endured much misunderstanding from her parents and friends. She continued, however, to remain at home, but she lived a secluded life. To do her share in supporting the family, she did needlework and sold the flowers she cultivated. When she was twenty years of age, she joined the Third Order of St. Dominic and converted a little hut in the backyard into a hermitage, where she often went to pray. She also transformed a room in her parents' house into a sort of infirmary, where she cared for destitute children and elderly people. She died on August 24, 1617, at the age of thirty-one, and she was canonized by Pope Clement X in 1671. St. Rose of Lima is the first saint from the Americas. The Mass prayer today recalls her austerity of life and the fervor of her love of God.

✝ AUGUST 24 ◢ *Feast*
St. Bartholomew, Apostle

St. Bartholomew was one of the Twelve Apostles, as the Gospels tell us (Mark 3:18; Matt. 10:3; Luke 6:14). It is most likely that the Nathanael mentioned in today's Gospel reading (John 1:45–51) is Bartholomew. Why this difference of name? Bartholomew is not a given first name but a patronymic and means "son of Tala-mai" and, therefore, Nathanael could be his given name. It was Philip who brought Nathanael Bartholo-mew to Christ (John 1:45), and at his first meeting with our Lord, Nathanael confessed: "Rabbi, you are the Son of God; you are the king of Israel." Tradition holds that after Pentecost, Bartholomew preached in Greater Armenia, and that it was there, in the city of Albanopolis (today's Derbent, Dagestan), that he was flayed alive and beheaded by order of King Astyages. When today's opening prayer states that St. Bartholomew was ever loyal to Christ, this is but another way of phrasing what Jesus remarked about him: "This man is a true Israelite. There is no guile in him" (John 1:47).

✠ AUGUST 25
St. Louis of France

St. Louis of France is known in history as Louis IX, King of France. He was the son of Louis VIII and was born at Poissy on April 25, 1214. Upon the death of his father in 1226, he became king of France. In 1234, he married Marguerite of Provence, and the royal couple had eleven children—five sons and six daughters. Louis was known for his promotion of justice and peace, at home and abroad, and the nation came to realize that the king's piety and goodness were the source of his strength. During a serious illness in December 1244, Louis vowed to go on a crusade to the Holy Land. The previous October, the Christians of Palestine had been sorely defeated by the Muslims at Gaza. He left for Cyprus in 1248, and he captured (June 1249) the city of Damietta, Egypt. But because of floods and heat, his men were unable to advance, and as a result they were eventually routed at Mansourah (now Al-Mansura, Egypt) on April 5, 1250. Louis himself was taken prisoner. For his freedom and that of his men, Louis surrendered Damietta and paid a heavy ransom. On his release on May 6, Louis went on to Syria, and then he spent the next four years rebuilding the strongholds still in the hands of the Christians. He was back in France in 1254, but on the occasion of another crusade, he left France on July 1, 1270, and sailed to Tunis, and while there he fell ill with dysentery and died on August 25, 1270. Louis embodied the highest and finest ideals of medieval kingship and was a model to his successors. He was canonized by Pope Boniface VIII in 1297.

✝ AUGUST 25
St. Joseph Calasanz, Priest

St. Joseph Calasanz, one of the foremost figures in Catholic education, was born at Petralta de la Sal, Aragon, Spain, on September 11, 1556. He studied at the universities of Lérida and Valencia and then was ordained in 1583. Shortly thereafter, he was appointed vicar general of the Trempe Diocese. He subsequently resigned this post, and in 1592 he went to Rome, where he was tutor to the Colonna family and engaged in charitable works (helping in hospitals and teaching catechism). Being aware that the poor, under present circumstances, had no chance of ever becoming educated, he decided to do something for them. Thus, in November

1597, together with three other priests, he opened the first free school in Rome for poor children. Here the children would learn secular subjects as well as their catechism. There was no problem finding students for such a school, and the schools multiplied in number, not only in Rome but also in other Italian cities. In 1617, his community of teachers received recognition as a religious congregation; they called themselves Clerks Regular of the Pious Schools (more commonly known as Piarists). Too rapid a growth of the congregation created problems for the founder, and the congregation soon suffered from internal friction. A favorable solution was eventually had, but only after the founder's death. St. Joseph Calasanz died in Rome on August 25, 1648, and was canonized by Pope Clement XIII in 1767. In 1948, Pope Pius XII declared him the patron of all Christian schools. St. Joseph Calasanz's special vocation to be a teacher finds mention in the opening prayer of today's Mass.

✝ AUGUST 27 ✒ *Memorial*
St. Monica

St. Monica was probably born in Tagaste, Numidia (today's Souk-Ahras, Algeria), Africa, in about 331. Though a Christian, she was married to a pagan, who was converted before his death (371). The couple had at least three children, and of these St. Augustine (see August 28) was the oldest. As any mother would be, she was interested in her children's careers, but when she saw Augustine living a dissipated and dissolute life, her maternal heart ached. She wept for him and prayed daily for his conversion. After he left (383) Africa to teach in Rome and then in Milan, Monica followed him. In Milan, she witnessed Augustine's conversion and baptism (387), and because her son was now determined to live a different manner of life, they decided to return to North Africa. At the Roman port of Ostia, just days before they were to sail, Monica became ill and died (387). Augustine paints a magnificent portrait of his mother in his *Confessions*. Her cult began to develop in the later Middle Ages, and it became popular when her relics were moved (1430) from Ostia to Rome. Her memorial is now appropriately celebrated on the day before that of her distinguished son. The opening prayer of today's Mass speaks of the tears St. Monica shed in beseeching God to convert her son.

✝ AUGUST 28 ✎ *Memorial*
St. Augustine, Bishop and Doctor of the Church

Aurelius Augustine was born in Tagaste, Numidia (today's, Souk-Ahras, Algeria), Africa, on November 13, 354. His mother was St. Monica (see August 27), and his father was Patricius, a pagan. Augustine was enrolled among the catechumens as a child, and though his baptism was put off, he, nevertheless, had a Christian upbringing. He studied (372–75) rhetoric at Carthage (in modern Tunis), and while there he got into the habit of a disordered and dissolute life. For many years, he lived with a companion who was not his wife; their son Adeodatus ("Given by God") was born in 372. Augustine subsequently opened a school of rhetoric (376–83) in

Carthage; but being attracted by the Manichaeans, he joined them and followed their teachings for nine years. When Manichaeism was unable to answer all his questions, he separated from them. In 383, he went to Rome, where he taught rhetoric for a year, and then he moved (384) on to Milan, because he had won, through a competition, that city's chair of rhetoric. Professional curiosity led him to attend the sermons of Bishop Ambrose (see December 7); he not only found them eloquent but also his heart soon was touched by what Ambrose said. He subsequently dismissed his companion, who returned to Africa, but kept his son with him. With his mother's arrival in Milan, Augustine retired (386) to Cassiacum, near Milan, together with his son, who died shortly thereafter, and his brother Navigius. Augustine there devoted his time to penance and prayer, preparing himself for his new life. He was baptized by Ambrose during the Easter Vigil liturgy of April 24–25, 387.

Upon his return to Tagaste, Augustine freed himself of all his possessions and lived as a monk. He was ordained (391) at the request of the people, and he eventually became (395) bishop of Hippo (today's Annaba, Algeria). Augustine was bishop for thirty-five years, and during that time he courageously fought for the faith against a variety of heresies (Manichaeism, 388–405; Donatism, 394–411; and Pelagianism, 412–30). He died at Hippo on August 28, 430. Augustine was an outstanding preacher, perhaps the Church's greatest; and because he was the most influential theologian in the Western Church, it is but natural that he should be acknowledged as the greatest doctor of the Latin Church. His writings are numerous, and they have been preserved these many centuries because they have always been deemed important. The most famous of all, perhaps, is his *Confessions*, an autobiography in which he delineates God working in his soul. The *Confessions* have never gone out of style, nor out of print. When the opening prayer of today's Mass mentions our thirsting for God alone, this is reminiscent of Augustine's famous remark, "You made us for yourself, and our hearts find no peace until they rest in you" (*Confessions* I, 1).

✝ AUGUST 29 ✎ *Memorial*
Martyrdom of St. John the Baptist

The Nativity of St. John the Baptist is celebrated on June 24, and today we commemorate his martyrdom by beheading. His death is recorded not only in the Gospels, as in today's reading (Mark 6:17–29), but also by the Jewish historian Josephus, who mentions it in his *Antiquities* (15, 8, 2). Though Herod Antipas, tetrarch of Galilee, regarded John as a just man, nevertheless, when John publicly criticized him for his unlawful marriage to Herodias, his brother's wife, as well as for his other misdeeds, he had John imprisoned (Luke 3:19–20). Josephus also informs us that it was in the fortress of Machaerus, on the eastern side of the Dead Sea, where John was detained. Herodias had revenge in her heart and waited for the proper moment; it came when her unnamed daughter danced before Herod and his guests. Thus, to fulfill a royal whim, he, of whom our Lord said: "history has not known a man born of woman greater than John" (Matt. 11:11), gave his life in final witness. This feast was celebrated in Jerusalem as early as the first part of the fifth century, and it seems to have been celebrated in Rome by the sixth century. That the feast should be celebrated on August 29 is probably due to the fact that a church dedicated to St. John in Sebaste (today's Sivas, Turkey), where his tomb was believed to have been, was dedicated on this day.

SEPTEMBER

✝ SEPTEMBER 3 🖋 *Memorial*
*St. Gregory the Great, Pope
and Doctor of the Church*

St. Gregory was born of a patrician family in Rome in
about 540. He was educated in law and entered the Roman civil service, and in about 572 he became prefect of
Rome. Two years later (574), he decided to become a
monk, and so he converted his house on Rome's Coelian Hill into a monastery. In 579, Pope Pelagius II sent
him to Constantinople (today's Istanbul) as his *apocrisiarius* or representative to the imperial Byzantine court.
Gregory was recalled to Rome (about 585 or 586) and
became Pope Pelagius's adviser. On the death of Pope
Pelagius, Gregory was elected his successor and was
consecrated on September 3, 590. As pope, he sent (596)
St. Augustine of Canterbury (see May 27) and about
thirty monks to convert England, and it was he who introduced several changes into the liturgy of the Mass,
for example: the Kyrie and Christe eleison were to be
sung alternately by clergy and laity, the Alleluia was
to be dropped in penitential seasons, and the Lord's
Prayer was to be said after the Canon. He was inter-

ested in Church music and promoted a plainchant that now bears his name. He was the first pope to refer to himself as the "Servant of the Servants of God," a title still in use by the popes today. In his dealing with the Church in Constantinople, he emphasized Rome's primacy, maintaining that all bishops are subject to the Roman see, for the Roman Church has been set over all Churches. He was also a voluminous writer. Many of his homilies have been preserved, but he is best remembered for two works: *Pastoral Care* (about 591), which details the duties of a bishop toward his flock, and *Book of Morals*, a commentary on the Book of Job, which is, at the same time, a summary of dogmatic and moral theology as well as asceticism and mysticism. Gregory died on March 12, 604, but his memorial is celebrated today, the anniversary of his consecration as pope. His writings were so esteemed over the centuries that he was the most frequently quoted ecclesiastical author during the Middle Ages. Pope Boniface VIII declared him a doctor of the Church in 1298. St. Gregory is one of the four great doctors of the Latin Church.

✝ *SEPTEMBER 7   *Memorial*
SS. Stephen Pongrácz and Melchior Grodziecki, Priests and Martyrs, and St. Mark Križevčanin, Canon of Estergom, Martyr

SS. Stephen Pongrácz, Melchior Grodziecki, and Mark Križevčanin met their martyrdom at the hands of Hungarian Calvinists in Košice (in today's Slovakia). Stephen was born about 1582 in the family's Alvincz Castle in Transylvania (now in Romania), and he entered (1602) the Society of Jesus in Moravia (part of today's Czech Republic). After ordination (1615), he taught for a while at Humenné, Slovakia, and in 1619 was sent to Košice to minister to the Catholics there and in the outlying areas, who had not seen a priest for many a year.

Melchior was born in the family castle of Grodiec in Silesia, Poland, about 1584, and also entered (1603) the Society in Moravia, where Stephen was already a novice. After ordination (1616), he taught for a while in Prague, and then in 1619 he was likewise assigned to Košice. At this time, the city was a Calvinist stronghold. The two Jesuits set about their work within and outside the city. Fr. Pongrácz ministered to the Hungarians, while Fr. Grodziecki saw to the needs of those who spoke Polish and German. When the Calvinists saw that the priests' work prospered and the number of Catholics increased, so did their hatred of them.

When news arrived that the army of the Calvinist prince of Transylvania was approaching Košice (this was the time of the Thirty Years' War), both Frs. Pongrácz and Grodziecki returned to the city to be with the Catholics living there. At the same time, Fr. Mark Križevčanin (b. 1589) left Estergom to be with the Jesuits. The army easily gained control of the city on September 5, 1519, and when the military general learned that three Catholic priests were in the city, he had them placed (September 6) under house arrest. Anticipating what was before them, the priests spent the night in prayer. On the morning of September 7, the soldiers—unable to get the priests to apostatize—beat them mercilessly. Fr. Križevčanin was their first victim—they stabbed him numerous times, then rubbed flaming torches over his body and finally beheaded him. They next tortured Fr. Pongrácz in similar fashion, then suspended him from a beam and proceeded to carve his body. Fr. Grodziecki suffered the same torment as Fr. Križevčanin, and he too was beheaded. Although two of the priests died on September 7, Fr. Pongrácz was only released from his sufferings on September 8. These martyrs of Košice were canonized by Pope John Paul II in 1995.

✝ SEPTEMBER 8 ✒ Feast
Nativity of the Blessed Virgin Mary

The few historical details known about Mary's life are those found in the Gospels, but there is nothing there about Mary's birth or childhood. Mary's first appearance in the Gospels is the scene where the Archangel Gabriel announces that she is to be the Mother of God. Tradition claims that Mary was born in Jerusalem, and as early as the fifth century the Jerusalem Church commemorated Mary's birth on September 8. It seems that the commemoration arose in association with the church that was built near the Pool of Bethsaida and dedicated to the Birth of Mary. Tradition also claims that that church had been built on the site of the dwelling of SS. Joachim and Anne (see July 26), the parents of Mary. Years later, the name of the church was changed, and since the time of the crusaders it has been known as the Church of St. Anne. The final prayer in today's

Mass gives the reason why we are filled with joy at Mary's birth, for it was she who brought the dawn of hope and salvation to the world in giving birth to Christ, our Savior.

✝ SEPTEMBER 9 ✄ *Memorial*
St. Peter Claver, Priest and Religious

St. Peter Claver, the future saint of the slave trade, was born at Verdú, Catalonia, Spain, probably on June 25, 1580, and he entered the Society of Jesus in 1602. After studies in Barcelona, he went (1605) to the College of Montesión in Palma de Mallorca to study philosophy, and there he met the aged brother, Alphonsus Rodríguez (see October 31), who encouraged him to be a missionary in the New World. In 1610, Peter sailed for the missions in South America and was ordained (1616) in Cartagena, Colombia—the first Jesuit to be ordained in that city. Cartagena was a prosperous city teeming with merchants; it was also a port of entry for slaves from Western Africa. It is estimated that during Fr. Claver's years there, about 10,000 slaves passed through the port annually. The journey sometimes lasted months, and the slaves spent their days and nights chained to one another. Peter waited for the slave ships to arrive with their human cargo, and when they did, he and his interpreters, all carrying baskets of fruits, biscuits, and sweets, went aboard to greet the slaves. After comforting those on deck, Peter went down into the stench-filled holds to minister to the sick and dying. When the slaves were brought ashore, he visited them daily and gave them religious instruction, until they were sold and taken to other parts of South America. During his years working among the slaves, Peter said that he must have baptized 300,000 of them. After a lingering illness, he died in Cartagena on September 8, 1654. Pope Leo XIII canonized him in 1888, and in 1896 the same pontiff declared him special patron of missions to the black nations. In today's prayer we ask, in imitation of St. Peter Claver, for the strength to overcome all racial hatred and to love one another as brothers and sisters.

✝ *SEPTEMBER 10
Bl. Francis Gárate, Religious

Bl. Francis Gárate was born on February 3, 1857, in Spain's Basque country, in a tiny hamlet near the castle where St. Ignatius of Loyola (see July 31) was born. Francis left home when he was fourteen years of age (1871) and began working as a domestic at the Jesuit college in Orduña, and three years later he entered (1874) the Society of Jesus as a coadjutor brother. He was then appointed (1877) infirmarian at the college at La Guardia, near the Portuguese border—he had some 200 young boys under his care. He thought nothing of spending an entire night at the bedside of a sick student and then doing a full day's work the following day. After ten years, the strain on his health began to show, and in 1888 he was transferred to the University of Deusto, in Bilbao, to be doorkeeper. He filled that post for forty-one years. There is nothing remarkable in Francis's life, except that everyone took note of his limitless kindness, goodness, humility, and prayerfulness. He prayed while he worked, and he worked while he prayed. He became holy through his unfailing dedication in serving God, as today's prayer reminds us. He was practically never without a rosary in his hand. He died on September 9, 1929, and was beatified by Pope John Paul II in 1985.

✝ SEPTEMBER 12
Most Holy Name of Mary

"And the Virgin's name was Mary" (Luke 1:27). It is thus that the evangelist identifies the maiden, whom the Archangel Gabriel invites to become the Mother of God's only Son. The name "Mary" comes from "Maria," which is Greek for the Hebrew "Miriam." From reading the Old Testament, we know that Moses's sister was named Miriam (Num. 26:59) and that it was she who led the Israelite women in song and dance after their people had crossed the Red Sea (Ex. 15:20–21). Various interpretations have been given to the name, but perhaps "beloved" is the most authentic. Because the Archangel Gabriel greeted Mary with the words "Blessed are you among women" (Luke 1:28), indeed she is the most "beloved" of all creatures, for she is the one whom God chose to be the Mother of his Son.

St. Bernard, in his second sermon (*Missus est*) in praise of the Virgin Mary, says: "Let us say something about this name. . . . In dangers, anguish, and doubt, call upon Mary. Let her name be always on your lips and in your heart. The better to obtain her help, imitate the example of her life. With her as your guide, you will never go astray; by invoking her, you will not lose heart;

while she holds your hand, you will not fall; with her protecting you, you have nothing to fear; walking with you, you will not grow weary; enjoying her favor, you will reach your goal." Thanks to Bernard's sermons, devotion to the Holy Name of Mary spread through Europe, so that in 1523 the Diocese of Cuenca, Spain, was the first to be granted permission to celebrate this feast. Then Pope Innocent XI (1676–89), because of a remarkable Christian victory, extended it in 1683 to the universal Church.

For two months in 1683, Turkish troops, approximately 300,000 in number, surrounded Vienna. Because their presence was a threat to all Europe, Europe's princes came to Vienna's assistance. King John III Sobieski of Poland (reigned 1674–96) left Poland with an army of 25,000 on August 15 and marched toward Vienna. On arriving, he gathered the several small armies into one and took command—he only had 80,000 men. On the morning of September 12, a day within the octave of Mary's Nativity, he attended Mass, received Holy Communion, and when Mass was over he addressed his officers saying: "Let us march with confidence under the protection of Heaven and with the aid of the Most Holy Virgin." That day, the battle was bitter, but because the Turks were caught between crossfire, they were forced to retreat. Europe and Vienna were saved. The Christian army and world were convinced that this decisive victory was not due to military strategy but to the intercession of Mary, whose name King John had invoked before battle. The feast of the Most Holy Name of Mary was originally observed on the Sunday following Mary's Nativity, but Pius X (1903–14) changed the date to September 12, the anniversary of Vienna's liberation.

SEPTEMBER 13 ✐ *Memorial*
St. John Chrysostom, Bishop and Doctor of the Church

St. John Chrysostom was born in Antioch (now Antakya, Turkey), in about 349. His early education trained him in law and oratory. He was baptized when he was eighteen years of age, and he thought of becoming a monk. This dream, however, was not realized until 373, when he joined a group of hermits living in the mountains near Antioch. Seven years later, he returned to the city and began his studies for the priesthood. Shortly after his ordination in 386, he was assigned to preach. He became an outstanding preacher, and for twelve years he preached regularly to the people of Antioch. His homilies, which were commentaries on the Scriptures, were published, and it is because of these and his other writings that he was later declared a doctor of the Church. John was made Bishop of Constantinople (modern Istanbul) in 398, and he immediately instituted much-needed reforms in his diocese, opened hospitals, and saw that the poor were given the help they needed. His honesty and frankness in speaking out against the luxury of the imperial court and its laxity in morals earned him the hatred of the wealthy and influential, and thus he was forced into exile in June 404.

John spent three years at a frontier outpost in Armenia, but because he still had some influence in Constantinople by means of his letters, he was moved further away. On his way to his new place of exile, he was forced to walk the entire distance, over mountains, through rain, and under the burning sun. Finally, his health broke, and he died at Comana on the Black Sea on September 14, 407. From 438 on, a liturgical feast was celebrated in his honor, and ten years later his body was brought to Constantinople's Church of the Apostles. By the sixth century, the name "Chrysostom," a Greek word meaning "golden-tongued" that alludes to his eloquence, had been added to his Christian name. Then, in 1568, Pope Pius V (see May 30) declared him a doctor of the Church. The prayer in today's Mass also speaks of his eloquence and heroic sufferings.

✝ SEPTEMBER 14   ✿   *Feast*
Exaltation of the Holy Cross

The basilica built by Constantine on the site where Christ had died and had risen from the dead was dedicated on September 13, 335. By the end of the fourth century, it had become customary that on September 14, the day following the anniversary of the basilica's dedication, the relic of the wood of the true cross was exposed to the faithful for their veneration. This feast, known as the Exaltation of the Cross, quickly spread throughout the Eastern Church, and by the seventh century it was also celebrated in Rome. This feast is sometimes called The Triumph of the Cross, because by the cross Christ redeemed the world. This is the paradox: that the cross, the symbol of humiliation and of death, should become the efficacious sign of liberation and life. "Defeat" has become triumph. Our liturgy today begins with the antiphon exhorting us to glory in the cross of our Lord Jesus Christ, for he is our salvation, our life, and our resurrection.

✝ SEPTEMBER 15 ⋙ *Memorial*
Our Lady of Sorrows

The memory of the sorrows that our Lady endured standing at the foot of her Son's cross is appropriately celebrated on the day following the feast of the Exaltation of the Holy Cross. Devotion to Our Lady of Sorrows arose in the twelfth century, and in 1668 the Order of the Servants of Mary (Servites), who from their origin had a special devotion to Mary's sorrows, were granted a liturgical feast to be celebrated on the third Sunday in September. Through the preaching of the Servites, the devotion to the Seven Sorrows of Our Lady spread in the Church, and the feast was then extended to the universal Church by Pope Pius VII in 1814 to recall the sufferings that the Church and her earthly head had undergone at the hands of Napoleon Bonaparte (the pope had been held prisoner by Napoleon from 1809 to 1814), and in thanksgiving to our Lady for her ever-watchful care and through whose intercession the sufferings of the Church had come to an end. Because of Mary's sharing in her Son's sufferings on the cross, as today's opening prayer reminds us, she has also been given to us as our Mother, as today's Gospel (John 19:25–27) narrates.

✝ SEPTEMBER 16 *✐ Memorial*
SS. Cornelius, Pope and Martyr, and Cyprian, Bishop and Martyr

St. Cornelius, a Roman, was elected pope in March 251. The persecution under Decius (emperor 249–51) had just ended, but during it many Christians had denied their faith out of fear, and the debate then in progress in the Roman Church was whether these *lapsi*, as they were known, could be reconciled to the Church. Although Cornelius and many others were in favor of their readmission, there existed a rigorist party that held the opposite view. Their leader was Novatian (200–58), an important presbyter in Rome. Novatian— disappointed at Cornelius' election and at the fact that he had been passed over—set himself up as antipope (251–58). To bring peace to the Church, Cornelius called a synod (autumn 251) in Rome, at which Novatian was condemned and Cornelius's view, with Cyprian's support, was accepted as the Church's teaching. When Gallus (emperor 251–53) began his persecution of the Church in 252, he sent Cornelius into exile (June 252) to Centumcellae (today's Civitavecchia, Italy), and there the pope died in June 253. He was soon honored as a martyr.

St. Cyprian was born in Carthage (in modern Tunis), North Africa, about 210, and became a teacher of rhetoric. After his conversion (about 246), he studied the Scriptures and subsequently was ordained and then became (248) Bishop of Carthage. He survived the Decian persecution by going underground. During Pope Cornelius's dispute in Rome about readmitting those who had denied the faith during times of persecution, Cyprian agreed with the pope that these lapsed should be readmitted to the Church after doing penance, and he wrote letters to Rome giving his reasons in support of Cornelius. During the persecution (257) under Valerian (emperor 253–59), Cyprian was exiled (August 257) to Curubis, on the African coast, approximately fifty miles from Carthage. He was later brought back (August 258) to Carthage and was beheaded on September 14, 258. Cyprian's writings have always been treasured by the Church, principally because they throw light on the Church's problems in Africa. A particularly outstanding work is his *On the Unity of the Church*, a treatise on the authority of the Church and on ecclesiastical hierarchy, written (251) when the Novatianist schism had just begun. Because Cornelius and Cyprian had been friends in life and had worked together for the Church's unity, the early Christians celebrated their feasts together, as we do today.

✝ SEPTEMBER 17 ✐ *Memorial*
St. Robert Bellarmine, Bishop and Doctor of the Church

St. Robert Bellarmine was the greatest theologian of his age and an intrepid defender of the Church. He was born on October 4, 1542, in Montepulciano, in central Italy. On his mother's side, he was the nephew of Pope Marcellus II (1555). Robert entered the Society of Jesus in 1560 and did his ecclesiastical studies in Rome (1560–

63), Padua (1567–69), and Louvain (1569–70). In this last city, though he was not yet a priest, he delivered Latin sermons every Sunday to the university community. After ordination, he was appointed (1570) professor of theology at the Jesuit school in Louvain, and because this was the time when the Reformation doctrines of Luther and Calvin were fast spreading through Europe, he taught his classes with a view to answering the objections the Reformers brought against the Church. In 1577, he was transferred to Rome, where he was given the chair of "controversial theology." His lectures, which treated the theological disputes that were then dividing the Church, were eventually published under the title *Controversies*. In 1597, Pope Clement VIII made him his theological adviser; and two years later (1599), a cardinal and appointed him to serve on several congregations. In 1602, he became Archbishop of Capua, but upon the election of Pope Paul V in 1605, he was asked to remain in Rome and again be a papal adviser. He fulfilled the same office under Pope Gregory XV (1621–23). Due to failing health, he received papal permission to retire to the Jesuit novitiate in Rome, and there he died on September 17, 1621. He was canonized by Pope Pius XI in 1930. In recognition of his theological writings, Pope Pius XI also declared (1931) him a doctor of the Church. The prayer in today's Mass refers to St. Robert's God-given wisdom, which he used in defending the faith.

SEPTEMBER 19
St. Januarius, Bishop and Martyr

St. Januarius is the patron of the city of Naples. Very little is known about his life, except that he was Bishop of Benevento and that he died a martyr's death in 305, during the persecution of Diocletian (emperor 284–305). Early traditions would have it that he was born in Naples about 270, and that after a period of imprisonment—he had been arrested while visiting two of his deacons in prison—he was thrown to the wild beasts in the amphitheater of Pozzuoli, a town near Naples. Because the beasts did not touch him, he was beheaded. His body was subsequently buried in the catacombs of Naples; and later, in 1497, it was transferred to the cathedral church of Naples, where he had long been honored as the city's patron saint. The Hieronymian Martyrology (about 450) gives September 19 as the date of his martyrdom.

SEPTEMBER 20   *Memorial*
SS. Andrew Kim Taegon, Priest and Martyr, Paul Chong Hasang, Catechist and Martyr, and Their Companions, Martyrs

During Pope John Paul II's visit to South Korea in September 1984, he canonized 103 Korean Martyrs, who died between the years 1839 and 1866. The two most famous of these are SS. Andrew Kim Taegon and Paul Chong Hasang. Paul was born of Catholic parents in 1795, and went to Seoul when he was twenty years old. Because the city at that time had no priest, he took it upon himself to rebuild the Catholic Church. He did his utmost to get missionaries to come to Korea, but his many trips—a total of nine—to Peking (Beijing) were unsuccessful. He eventually wrote to Pope Pius VII (1800–23), and in 1831 the Paris Foreign Mission Society was asked to take charge of the Church in Korea. With the coming of missionaries, Paul began to study for the priesthood, but the persecution of 1839 interrupted his plans. He was arrested, tortured, and beheaded on September 22 of that year. Paul's mother and sister were included among those canonized.

Andrew Kim Taegon was born on August 21, 1821, of parents who were converts to the faith. He began (1837) his seminary studies in Macao and was ordained (1845) in Shanghai, the first native Korean to become a Catholic priest. He returned to Korea and tried to arrange for more missionaries to enter the country by eluding the border patrol. He was arrested (June 5, 1846), and after three months in prison he was beheaded on September 16, 1846, at the Han River, near Seoul. Andrew's father was included among those canonized by Pope John Paul II in the Seoul Cathedral on May 6, 1984. Of the 103 martyrs, 92 were Koreans and 11 Europeans.

✝ SEPTEMBER 21 ✍ *Feast*
St. Matthew, Apostle and Evangelist

The Apostle Matthew was a Galilean and was most probably born in Capernaum. By profession, he was a revenue officer or tax collector (Matt. 10:3), and he was working at his post when Jesus noticed him and said to him: "Follow me" (Matt. 9:3). The Evangelist Mark refers to him as Levi the son of Alphaeus (Mark 2:14), but because the description of the call of Levi is the same as the description of the call of Matthew, the individual must also be the same. Matthew is also an Evangelist, and the Gospel he composed was first written in Aramaic. Little is known about his activity after the events of Pentecost, but it is said that his early ministry was in Judea and that he then preached the gospel in Gentile territory. Early ecclesiastical writers do not agree on the lands he evangelized; some say Persia (today's Iran), others Ethiopia, and still others Parthia (in modern Iran). The same must be said about his death; some claim that he died a natural death, but others—and this is the more constant tradition in the Church—that he died a martyr's death, though the time and place remain unknown. The Hieronymian Martyrology (about 450) states that he met his martyrdom on September 21 "in Persia in the town of Tarrium," perhaps in Tarsuana.

† SEPTEMBER 23   ✎   *Memorial*
St. Pio of Pietrelcina

Francesco Forgione was born on May 25, 1887, in the small town of Pietrelcina, a short distance from Benevento in southern central Italy. His early education was no different from that of any other peasant boy of that period. At the age of sixteen years, he entered (1903) the Franciscan Capuchins; and on receiving his habit on January 22 of that year, he was given the name Pio. He then pursued the regular course of studies leading to the priesthood, which came on August 10, 1910. During his early years as a Capuchin, his health was always a source of worry to his superiors—so much so that after ordination, he spent several years convalescing at his parents' home. When he was sufficiently strong to return to community life, he was assigned (summer 1916) to teach at the minor seminary attached to the Friary of Our Lady of Grace in San Giovanni Rotondo, nestled high in the Gargano Mountains. Except for a few short interruptions, Fr. Pio spent his entire religious life at that friary. In addition to teaching, he served as spiritual director to the students and to many of the townspeople. It was during his early years there that his reputation for sanctity began to grow, for many witnessed his ecstatic trances after Mass, knew of instances of bilocation, and experienced his reading of their thoughts and hearts.

On September 20, 1918, as Fr. Pio was praying in chapel, after having celebrated Mass, he fell into an ecstasy, during which he saw a great light in the midst of which there appeared the wounded Christ. Shafts of flame then shot from the crucifix and pierced his hands and feet. He was visibly stigmatized—he bore the marks of our Lord's passion. Earlier, he had received the wound in his side on August 5. The news of his stigmatization quickly spread not only throughout central Italy, but throughout the country—with the result that not only did crowds come to the friary seeking Fr. Pio's counsel in confession, but also misunderstandings arose when some of the local clergy and unbelievers in other parts of Italy attempted to depict him as a charlatan. Fr. Pio patiently bore these trials, because he knew that it would be through these that he would achieve greater conformity with Christ crucified. His entire life was the altar, prayer chapel, and confessional, and it was in this last that he did his greatest work—there he spent his mornings and afternoons dispensing Christ's mercy and offering wise counsel. He never tired of telling his penitents to pray, for "prayer is the key that opens the heart of God." Knowing the value of prayer in one's life, he started (1947) local prayer groups, which met weekly or monthly, and prayed for the needs of the Church as well as for those of the members. These groups multiplied over the years, and today they are found throughout the world. The year 1956 saw the opening of the Home for the Relief of Suffering, a hospital that Fr. Pio had sponsored and had built with gifts and contributions from Catholics all over the world. Taking time off from his confessional duties, he frequently visited the patients, greeting each one as he passed from bed to bed.

By the mid-1960s, Fr. Pio, now in his late seventies, became more and more feeble; he suffered from arthritis, asthma, and bronchitis. These ailments, however, never kept him from the confessional. By July 1968, his physical activity was greatly curtailed. He celebrated his last Mass on September 22, and he died early the following morning. Fr. Pio carried the stigmata on his body for fifty years, and endured its pain for the same length of time, but as death approached the wounds slowly disappeared. Fr. Pio was a modern St. Francis!

Whatever effectiveness he had, it came from prayer, his daily nourishment. It is no wonder that he usually referred to himself as "a poor Franciscan, who prays." St. Pio of Pietrelcina was canonized by Pope John Paul II on June 16, 2002.

✝ SEPTEMBER 26
SS. Cosmas and Damian, Martyrs

There are numerous legends about SS. Cosmas and Damian, but what is certain is that they were martyred during the persecution of Diocletian (emperor 284–305). Tradition would have it that Cosmas and Damian were twin brothers, born in Arabia, and that they were physicians. Because they practiced their profession without charging their patients, they were called "silverless." They were arrested and martyred in Lisia in Cilicia (part of southern Turkey); their bodies were then taken to Cyrrhus in Syria, and a church was erected over them. Devotion to these martyrs had spread throughout the Church by the end of the fourth century. In Rome, Pope Felix IV (526–30) erected a basilica in their honor by converting a temple in the Roman Forum into a Christian church. September 26 is probably the date of the dedication of this Roman church, and it was probably at the time of the church's dedication that the names of Cosmas and Damian were added to the Roman Canon.

St. Vincent de Paul, Priest

St. Vincent de Paul was born at Pouy (today's Saint-Vincent-de Paul) in Gascony, France, in April 1581. He began his studies for the priesthood in 1595 and received tonsure and minor orders in 1596. He next went to Toulouse for his theology and was ordained in 1600. In July 1605, while he was aboard a ship traveling from Marseilles to Narbonne, the ship was attacked by pirates, and he and the other passengers were taken prisoners. Vincent spent the next two years as a slave in Tunisia, but eventually he escaped and made (1607) it back to France , where he took up residence in Paris and cared for a parish (1608) on the outskirts of the city. In about 1615, he decided to devote his entire life to the poor.

Two years later, Vincent founded the first Confraternity of Charity, an association of women, known as Servants of the Poor, to help the sick and the indigent. He then spent the years 1618 to 1624 preaching missions in country parishes and establishing his Confraternity of Charity in those remote areas. Seeing the good that these missions were producing, he founded (1625) the Congregation of the Mission (more commonly known as Vincentians) to evangelize France's poor rural population. He also initiated retreats for the young men soon to be ordained and later founded seminaries to provide adequate training for priests. With St. Louise de Marillac (1591–1660), he founded (1633) the Daughters of Charity, and during the Wars of Religion he organized (1639) relief services for the provinces suffering from the war. He died on September 27, 1660, and was canonized by Pope Clement XII in 1737. In 1885, Pope Leo XIII named him patron of all works of charity. Few have ever accomplished as much for the poor as did St. Vincent de Paul. The St. Vincent de Paul Societies in our parishes not only bear his name but also continue his work among the poor. The opening prayer of today's Mass speaks of St. Vincent's work for the well-being of the poor and for the formation of the clergy, both of which were close to his heart.

✝

SEPTEMBER 28
St. Lawrence Ruiz, Martyr, and His Companions, Martyrs

St. Lawrence Ruiz and fifteen others were martyred in Japan between 1633 and 1637. The group includes Asians (nine Japanese and one Filipino) and Europeans (four Spaniards, one Frenchman, and one Italian), who at various times and circumstances, spread the Christian faith in the Philippines, Formosa (now Taiwan), and Japan. After suffering a variety of tortures, fourteen were put to death by being suspended by the feet into a pit containing manure, one was burned at the stake, and another died in prison as a result of torture. All were members of the Order of Preachers (Dominicans) or were associated with it as Dominican tertiaries. Of the group, nine were priests and the remaining seven were laypersons.

St. Lawrence Ruiz was born in Binondo, Philippines, where he lived with his wife and three children. He had been educated by the Dominicans and was a member of its Confraternity of the Rosary. When the police were searching for him, for a now unspecified crime, he escaped by joining (July 1636) a missionary expedition to Japan, where he was eventually arrested for being a Christian. After lingering in a Japanese prison for a year, he was suspended over the pit and died on September 29, 1637. St. Lawrence Ruiz, the first Filipino saint, and his fifteen companions were canonized by Pope John Paul II in 1987.

✝ SEPTEMBER 28
St. Wenceslaus, Martyr

St. Wenceslaus was the son of the Christian Duke Ratislaus of Bohemia (now part of the Czech Republic), and was born at Stochov, near Prague, about 907. After his father's death in 920, Wenceslaus's mother ruled as regent. But because she was sometimes violent and unjust in her dealings with the people, Wenceslaus took over the government in about 922, when he was fifteen years of age. As duke, his main concern was peace in the country and the conversion of his subjects to Christianity. His younger brother, Boleslaus, grew more and more discontented because his brother was duke and not he, and so he started to plot against him. Boleslaus invited Wenceslaus to his estate in Stara Boleslav for a banquet on the occasion of the dedication of a church there. On the following morning, September 28, 929, as the king was on his way to attend Matins, he met his brother, who struck him; as they were struggling,

Boleslaus's henchmen rushed up and murdered the king. Wenceslaus's body was buried in the cathedral of Prague, and he was immediately venerated as a martyr and saint. St. Wenceslaus is the patron saint of the Czech Republic and is the Good King Wenceslaus of the popular Christmas carol.

✙ **SEPTEMBER 29** 🗡 *Feast*
SS. Michael, Gabriel, and Raphael, Archangels

Of the many angels who make their appearance on the pages of the Old Testament, only three are identified by name: Michael, Gabriel, and Raphael; only Michael and Gabriel appear in the New Testament. In the Book of Daniel, Michael is called "one of the chief princes" (10:13) or "the great prince, guardian of your people" (12:1), and in the New Testament epistle by Jude (9), Michael is identified as "archangel," and Revelation (12:7) depicts him as leading the good angels in battle against Satan, with the result that Satan and his minions lose their place in Heaven. Gabriel is likewise mentioned in the Book of Daniel (8:16, 9:21), but he is better known as the divine messenger who announces to Zechariah the birth of John the Baptist (Luke 1:13–20), and to Mary that she is to be the Mother of God (Luke 1:26–37). Raphael, however, appears only in the book of Tobit, where he identifies himself as "one of the seven angels who enter and serve before the Glory of the Lord" (12:15), and says that he was sent by God to cure Tobit's blindness (12:14) and to guide his son Tobiah on his journey. The three archangels are commemorated together on September 29, because on this day, according to the Hieronymian Martyrology (about 450), the basilica of St. Michael on the Salarian Way, north of Rome, was dedicated.

✝ SEPTEMBER 30 ✎ *Memorial*
St. Jerome, Priest and Doctor of the Church

St. Jerome was born in Stridon, Dalmatia (now in Croatia), in about 345. At the age of twelve years, he went to Rome to study and was baptized there when he was about nineteen. He then went to Trier (in today's Germany) to study theology, and he spent a few years (368–72) in Aquileia (northern Italy), living a quasi-monastic life with friends. He then lived for two years in the Syrian desert near Aleppo, and while there he studied Greek and Hebrew. From there, he went (374) to Antioch (now Antakya, Turkey), where he was ordained (379) a priest. He was back in Rome in 382 and became secretary to Pope Damasus I (see December 11), who asked him to revise the Old Latin version of the New Testament that was then in use; at the same time, he translated the Psalter from the Septuagint. When Pope Damasus died, Jerome left (385) Rome and went to Bethlehem, where he founded a monastery, opened a school for boys, and spent the remainder of his life writing. His *On Illustrious Men* (393–95) is a listing of 135 authors, from St. Peter to himself, who exercised an influence on Christian authors. This was the first literary history written, and it is his attempt to dignify Christians as men of letters. Jerome was one of the most learned men of his age. Between 391 and 406, he made new Latin translations of all the books found in the Hebrew Bible. His translation eventually became known as the Vulgate, and it was his greatest achievement. He likewise wrote many commentaries on various books of the Bible. He was the first biblical scholar and his scholarship was unsurpassed in the early Church. Because of his immense erudition and his distinguished writing, by the eighth century he was honored as a doctor of the Church. He died in Bethlehem on September 30, 420.

OCTOBER

OCTOBER 1   🍃   *Memorial*
St. Thérèse of the Child Jesus, Virgin and Doctor of the Church

St. Thérèse of the Child Jesus, commonly known as "the Little Flower," was born Marie Françoise Thérèse Martin in Alençon, France, on January 2, 1873. After her two older sisters, Pauline and Marie, had entered the cloistered Discalced Carmelite convent at Lisieux, where the family had moved in 1881, she also applied to enter, but because she was only fourteen years of age, her entrance had to be delayed. In the meantime, she visited Rome with her father and on that occasion she met Pope Leo XIII (1878–1903). When she told the pope of her desire to enter Carmel—hoping he would intervene in her behalf—all she received was a noncommittal "You shall enter if it be God's will." She was finally accepted in April 1888, when she was fifteen. She spent a total of nine and a half years in the convent; her life was one of humility, simplicity, and trust in God. In 1893, she was appointed mistress of novices and filled that office for four years. She contracted tuberculosis—its first signs began to appear in Holy Week 1896—

about eighteen months before her death, which occurred on September 30, 1897. Shortly before her death, she wrote her autobiography, commonly known as *Story of a Soul*, written at the request of her superior. In it, she tells others of her "Little Way" of approaching God. Her Little Way has nothing extraordinary about it; it is merely fidelity in the observance of the rule and in the performance of one's duties. Without going beyond the common order of things, Thérèse achieved sanctity. She was canonized by Pope Pius XI in 1925, and in 1997 Pope John Paul II declared her a doctor of the Church. The opening prayer of today's Mass also refers to "the way" of St. Thérèse.

OCTOBER 2   *Memorial*
Guardian Angels

It is the teaching of the Church and theologians, and in accordance with what we read in the Old and New Testaments, that the angels, who are divine messengers, exercise a particular care and protection over individuals on earth, and help them in attaining salvation. In Exodus (20:20), the Lord God told Moses, "I am sending an angel before you, to guard you on the way and bring you to the place I have prepared," and after the angel had liberated St. Peter from prison, the latter remarked, "Now I know for certain that the Lord has sent his angel to rescue me from Herod's clutches" (Acts 12:11). The common teaching of theologians is that every human being, not merely the baptized, has a special guardian angel from birth, and this they derive from Christ's words: "Do not despise one of these little ones, for I say to you that their angels in heaven always see the face of my Father, who is in Heaven" (Matt. 18:10.) Referring to the same text, St. Basil (see January 2) writes: "Every one of the faithful has an angel standing at his side as educator, and guide, directing his life" (*Against Eunomius* III, 1). Devotion to the angels began with St. Benedict (see July 11) and then steadily increased from the time of St. Gregory the Great (see September 3) to St. Bernard of Clairvaux (see August 20), who was perhaps the most eloquent exponent of devotion to the Guardian Angels. The final prayer in today's Mass speaks of the angels keeping us free from danger in this life and bringing us to the joy of eternal life. A feast in honor of the Guardian Angels was celebrated in Valencia, Spain, as early as 1411; it then spread through Spain and into France. Pope Paul V introduced it into the Roman Calendar in 1608, and Pope Clement X later (1670) set its celebration for October 2.

✠ *OCTOBER 3 ✎ *Memorial*
St. Francis Borgia, Priest

St. Francis Borgia, the oldest son of the third Duke of Gandía, was born in the family's palace in Gandía, Spain, on October 28, 1510. His great grandfather on his father's side was Pope Alexander VI (1492–1503), and his great grandfather on his mother's side was King Ferdinand the Catholic (reigned 1469–1516). Francis was educated as befitted a Spanish nobleman. While at the royal court of his cousin, Emperor Charles V (reigned 1519–58), he married (1529) Leonor de Castro of Portugal, and then in 1530 the emperor made him Marquis of Llombai and placed him in charge of the imperial household. When Empress Isabella unexpectedly died on May 1, 1539, Francis escorted the body to Granada, but when the coffin was opened for official recognition before burial, Francis no longer saw the face of a youthful queen but of one beyond recognition. He is said to have exclaimed: "Never again will I serve a master who can die on me," and from that day onward he lived an austere life.

When Francis's father died (January 8, 1543), Francis succeeded him as the fourth Duke of Gandía, and when his wife died in 1546, he decided to become a Jesuit. He was accepted into the Society of Jesus by St. Ignatius of Loyola (see July 31), but the fact was kept secret until he settled his temporal affairs and arranged marriages for his eight children. He resigned his title in favor of his eldest son, was ordained (1551) a priest, and worked as a Jesuit in Spain and in Portugal. In 1565, he was elected the third superior general of the Society of Jesus, and seven years later died in Rome on September 30, 1572. He was canonized by Pope Clement X in 1671. The opening prayer of today's Mass gives a brief summary of St. Francis Borgia's life, when it asks: Grant through his prayers that all who have died to sin and renounced the world may live for you alone.

✝ OCTOBER 4 ❧ *Memorial*
St. Francis of Assisi, Religious

St. Francis was born in Assisi, Umbria, Italy, in 1182, and was baptized John. His father was Pietro di Bernardone, a wealthy textile merchant, and after returning from a business trip to France, and to mark his esteem for that country, he began calling his son Francis. Francis's youth was spent in comfort and fine clothes. During Assisi's war with Perugia, Francis joined his city's forces. But when Assisi was defeated, Francis was unfortunately taken prisoner and remained such for a year. After his release, he volunteered to fight with the papal army in southern Italy, but while passing through Spoleto, on his way south, he had a dream in which a voice told him "to follow the master and not the man." Thus he returned to Assisi and began to change his way of life. Then in the fall of 1205, while praying in the Church of San Damiano, a short distance from Assisi, he heard a voice coming from the crucifix telling him: "Francis, go and repair my church, which as you see is in ruins." To purchase the materials needed to repair that church's fabric, he sold some of his father's cloth. Because his father did not agree with his son's action, Francis left home and spent the following two years praying, repairing churches, and visiting the poor and sick.

Sometime in 1208 or 1209, he heard a passage from Matthew's Gospel (10:5–14) read in church, in which our Lord sent his apostles out to preach and they were to take nothing with them. In imitation of this, Francis lived a life of simplicity, poverty, and humility, and constantly went about preaching God's love. His joy in following Christ was so evident and attractive that others soon joined him, and thus he wrote a rule for them, with the gospel as their way of life. He called his group Friars Minor, but they are better known as Franciscans. In 1212, he founded an order of nuns, known today as

Poor Clares, after St. Clare of Assisi (see August 11). Others also wanted to follow his manner of life—prayer and penance—and for these he established what is known as the Third Order of St. Francis.

In 1219, Francis traveled to the Middle East with the Fifth Crusade, in a vain attempt to convert Sultan Malik al-Kamil of Egypt. Then, on September 14, 1224, he received the stigmata on Mount Alvernia; he is the first individual known to have received it. Throughout his life, Francis remained a deacon—he felt himself unworthy to be ordained a priest. He died at the Portiuncula (St. Mary of the Angels), the cradle of his order, in Assisi, on October 3, 1226, and was canonized two years later (1228) by Pope Gregory IX. Francis was the most extraordinary saint of the Middle Ages and is one of the most attractive of saints. Today's opening prayer tells us that St. Francis reflected the image of Christ, through his life of poverty and humility, and asks that we too may imitate his joyful love.

✝ OCTOBER 6
St. Bruno, Priest

St. Bruno was born in Cologne in about 1030. His early studies were in his native city, and later he attended the cathedral school in Reims. Subsequently, he became a cathedral canon there and then the schoolmaster (1056). He was appointed chancellor of the Reims Diocese in 1075. When Bishop Manassès was deposed—his election was simoniacal—by Pope Gregory VII (see May 25) in 1080, the Reims see was offered to Bruno, but he declined because he was then thinking of retiring from the world. He did so about 1082 and lived a life of prayer and penance. He and two companions had a hermitage near Molesmes, where they placed themselves under the spiritual direction of St. Robert, founder of the Cistercians. Seeking still greater solitude, he and six companions went in 1084 to Grenoble in southern France, where Bruno's former pupil Hugh was bishop, and there in the valley of La Chartreuse he laid the foundation of what eventually became the Carthusian Order. In 1090, Pope Urban II, who had also been one of Bruno's students at Reims, called him to Rome to be his adviser. When the papal court moved to southern Italy, brought on by the activity of the partisans of Antipope Clement III (1080–1100), Bruno went along and later (about 1092), with the pope's permission, he retired into the wilderness of Calabria and there established another monastery. He died at his monastery in La Torre, near Catanzaro, Calabria, on October 6, 1101. In 1514, Pope Leo X granted permission to the Carthusians to celebrate a feast in honor of their founder, and in 1623 his feast was extended to the universal Church. The prayer of the Mass for today recalls the fact that St. Bruno chose to serve God in solitude.

✝ OCTOBER 6
Bl. Marie-Rose Durocher, Virgin

Bl. Marie-Rose Durocher founded the Sisters of the Holy Names of Jesus and Mary. She was born Eulalie-Mélanie Durocher on October 6, 1811, at Saint-Antoine-sur-Richelieu, a village in the Quebec Province, Canada. She made several attempts to enter religious congregations, but she was always turned down because of her poor health. Then, in 1830, when her brother was named a pastor, she became his housekeeper, and in the parish she organized (1841) the Daughters of Mary, the first such association in Canada. At this time, there were many towns in Quebec without schools, and when Bishop Ignace Bourget (1799–1885) of Montreal could not attract sisters from France to work in his diocese, he asked (1843) Eulalie to start a religious congregation for the education of children and young girls. She saw this as God's will and immediately agreed. In 1844, the Sisters of the Holy Names of Jesus and Mary came into existence, and Eulalie chose Marie-Rose as her religious name. She only had five years left to live, but during that brief period she guided her new congregation, which grew and eventually spread into the United States as well. She died at Longueuil, Quebec, on October 6, 1849, and was beatified by Pope John Paul II in 1982.

✝ *OCTOBER 6
Bl. Diego Aloysius de San Vitores, Priest and Martyr

Bl. Diego de San Vitores, who died a martyr's death on the island of Guam, was born in Burgos, Spain, on November 12, 1627. After studies at Madrid's Imperial College, he entered the Society of Jesus in 1640. He pursued his philosophical and theological studies at Alcalá de Henares and was ordained in 1651. His dream was always to go to the missions, but before this dream became a reality, he was asked to teach for the next eight years, first at Oropesa, then Madrid and Alcalá. Finally, in 1659, he was assigned to the mission in the Philippines. He left Cádiz, Spain, in May, 1660, arrived at Veracruz, Mexico, and traveled to Mexico City, where he waited eighteen months for passage to the Philippines. After leaving Acapulco in April 1662, he and his fellow missionaries arrived at their destination in July. He was stationed in Manila, where he became dean of the university, but at the same time he visited the sick in the hospitals and helped in various parishes. When a mission was opened in the Ladrones (now Marianas) Islands about 900 miles northeast of Manila, Fr. San Vitores was chosen to head it. He arrived on Guam in June 1668, and after he had evangelized there, he preached to the people on the islands of Saipan and Tinian. On April 2, 1672, he went to the village of Tumon, along with his Filipino catechist Pedro Calungsod, and while there one of his first converts, now turned apostate, struck him and his companion with a cutlass and split their heads and then threw the bodies into the sea. Diego de San Vitores was beatified by Pope John Paul II in 1985, and Pedro Calungsod was likewise beatified, but in 2000.

✝ OCTOBER 7 ✒ *Memorial*
Our Lady of the Rosary

The origin of the rosary, as we know it today, goes back to the thirteenth or fourteenth centuries. Whether it was actually initiated by St. Dominic (see August 8) is a moot question. Nevertheless, the rosary remains a favorite devotion among Catholics because it permits us to meditate on the principal mysteries of our Lord's life, passion, and resurrection. That there should be a Mass to Our Lady of the Rosary is linked with an important historical event. On October 7, 1571, the Christian fleet gained an overwhelming victory over the Turkish fleet at Lepanto (Návpaktos, Greece). The victory was attributed to the fact that, at the time of the battle, Rosary Confraternities in Rome were reciting the rosary asking our Lady's intercession with God on behalf of the Christian navy. To commemorate this victory, Pope Pius V instituted (1571) the feast of Our Lady of Victory, to be celebrated in the city of Rome, and two years later Pope Gregory XIII changed its name to that of the Most Holy Rosary. Then, in 1716, Pope Clement XI extended the feast to the universal Church in thanksgiving for another Christian victory (August 5, 1716), also over the Turks, but this time at Petrovaradin, Yugoslavia. This feast was originally celebrated on the first Sunday in October, and only in 1913 was it assigned to October 7, the anniversary of the victory at Lepanto.

✝ OCTOBER 9
SS. Denis, Bishop and Martyr,
and His Companions, Martyrs

St. Denis is today regarded as the patron of France and is said to have been the first bishop of Paris. Whatever is known of his life is had from what St. Gregory of Tours (538–93) wrote in his *History of the Franks*. About 250, Denis and six other bishops were sent by Pope Fabian (see January 20) as missionaries to evangelize Gaul (modern France). Denis established himself in the area now known as Paris. Because of his success in making converts to Christianity, Denis and his companions—Rusticus, a priest, and Eleutherius, a deacon—were arrested, imprisoned for a time, and finally beheaded. Their martyrdom took place in 258 on the outskirts of modern Paris, now known as Montmartre (Mountain of Martyrs), during the persecution of Valerian (emperor 253–59). In 475 or thereabouts, St. Genevieve built a basilica over St. Denis's tomb, and later (624) the Abbey of St. Denis was founded next to the basilica. St. Denis's relics were transferred to the abbey on October 9. Legend has it that after his martyrdom he picked up his head and walked with it for two miles, indicating where he wanted to be buried.

✝ OCTOBER 9
St. John Leonardi, Priest

St. John Leonardi was born at Diecimo, near Lucca, Italy, about 1541. He was trained as a pharmacist but decided to leave that profession and study for the priesthood. He was ordained in 1571 and immediately began teaching Christian doctrine to children, and when he needed teachers to help him, he trained them as well. Later (1579), he formed a Confraternity of Christian Doctrine. In 1573, he founded a religious congregation now known as Clerks Regular of the Mother of God. In 1603, he cofounded a seminary in Rome for foreign missions, which later became, under the auspices of Pope Urban VIII (1623–44), the College for the Propagation of the Faith. He died in Rome on October 9, 1609, after visiting the sick during an influenza epidemic, and was canonized by Pope Pius XI in 1938. Today's prayer mentions St. John Leonardi's principal apostolate, namely, that it was through his ministry that God proclaimed the good news to countless people.

✝ OCTOBER 14
St. Callistus I, Pope and Martyr

St. Callistus was born in Rome, and at one time may have been a slave. Because of his mishandling of a banking operation, his Christian master had him condemned to the salt mines of Sardinia (c. 186–89). When released, he went to live in Anzio, Italy. When Zephyrinus became pope in 199, he made Callistus his deacon and appointed him administrator of the cemetery on the Appian Way (known today as the Catacombs of St. Callistus). He succeeded Zephyrinus as pope in 217. During his pontificate, the rigorist party, under the leadership of the Antipope Hippolytus (see August 13), accused him of laxity because he favored readmitting into the Church, after suitable penance, those who had been guilty of adultery and fornication as well as those who had apostatized in times of persecution. He died on October 14, 222, seemingly in a popular uprising. He was buried in the Cemetery of Calepodius on the Aurelian Way, and he was venerated as a martyr. His tomb was discovered in 1960 in a crypt built during the pontificate of Pope Julius I (337–52).

St. John Ogilvie, Priest and Martyr

St. John Ogilvie, whose missionary career lasted only eleven months, was born in Banffshire, Scotland, in 1579. He was brought up as a Calvinist but became (perhaps in 1596) a Catholic when he was about seventeen, while studying at the Scots College in Louvain. When this school closed because of lack of funds, he transferred to the school of the Scottish Benedictines in Regensburg, Germany, but after six months he moved on to the Jesuit college at Olomouc (now in the Czech Republic). He subsequently entered the Society of Jesus in 1599, and he did his philosophical studies at Graz, Austria, and returned to Olomouc for theology. After ordination (1610), he worked in Rouen, and only in 1613 did he return to Scotland. Because those were times when Catholics were persecuted, he entered the country in disguise as a horse dealer and made his way to Edinburgh, where he carried on his priestly work. He frequently traveled to Glasgow to minister to the Catholics living there. On October 4, 1614, he was in Glasgow, where he was scheduled to receive five individuals into the Church; one of these, however, betrayed him, and he was arrested and taken to prison. He was interrogated and tortured, but never did he divulge the names of the Catholics who had befriended him or who had attended his services. After five months of imprisonment, he was tried on March 10, 1615. Because he had denied the king's supremacy in religious matters and upheld the pope's spiritual primacy, he was convicted of treason and was hanged that afternoon. Pope Paul VI canonized him in 1976.

✝ OCTOBER 15 ✎ *Memorial*
St. Teresa of Jesus, Virgin and Doctor of the Church

St. Teresa of Jesus was born Teresa de Ahumada y Cepeda in Avila, Spain, on March 28, 1515. When in her early teens, she was sent to a nearby Augustinian convent to complete her education. When she was twenty-one (1536), she entered the Carmelite convent of the Incarnation in her native city. Her first eighteen years as a nun there were not extraordinary; in fact, the convent had a somewhat relaxed lifestyle. Eventually, she became filled with the desire to strive for holiness and to realize what Carmelite convent life should be like. She looked forward to living in one that was poor and with a small number of nuns. Thus, she desired to reinstate the primitive tradition of Carmel—a more austere and penitential form of religious life. God's special graces, including mystical graces, were now more frequent, and because the convent where she lived was unsuitable for her reform movement, she sought permission to open a new one. At first, she met with opposition. But permission was finally granted, and in 1562 she moved to her new convent, named after St. Joseph. Her reform quickly spread: New convents were opened, and established convents gradually accepted her reform. She died on the night of October 4, 1582, while on a visit to her convent in Alba de Tormes. (That very night, the new Gregorian Calendar went into effect; hence, according to the new calendar, she died on October 15.) At the request of her spiritual director, she wrote an autobiography that describes the working of God in her soul, and for her sisters she wrote *The Way of Perfection* and other books on prayer and the mystical life. She was canonized by Pope Gregory XV in 1622. Because of St. Teresa's writings, Pope Paul VI declared her a doctor of the Church in 1970. Today's prayer states that the Holy Spirit raised her up to show the Church the way to perfection.

✝ OCTOBER 16
St. Hedwig, Religious

St. Hedwig, the Duchess of Silesia, was born in Andechs, Bavaria, Germany, about 1174, and was the daughter of Berthold IV, Count of Andechs. While still very young, she was married (about 1186) to Henry I, who became Duke of Silesia in 1202. Seven children were born of their union, and she admirably fulfilled the duties of wife and mother. She lived a devout interior life, cared for the poor and sick, and established hospitals. She served as peacemaking intermediary between her sons, as well as between her husband and his enemies. She brought the Franciscans and Dominicans into Silesia, and with her husband she founded and supported several new monasteries. When her husband died in 1238, she retired to the Cistercian convent at Trzebnica, in the province of Wrocław, Poland, which convent she and her husband had founded in 1202, and where their daughter Gertrude was abbess. Though living in the convent, Hedwig never became a nun; in this way, she remained free to continue disbursing her wealth to the poor and needy. There she died on October 15, 1243. She was canonized by Pope Clement IV in 1267.

✝

OCTOBER 16
St. Margaret Mary Alacoque, Virgin

St. Margaret Mary was born in Lauthecourt, France, on July 22, 1647, and entered the convent of the Visitation nuns at Paray-le-Monial in 1671. From 1673 to 1675, she was especially favored by God with mystical graces and revelations of the Sacred Heart of Jesus. Our Lord made three requests of her: (1) to spread devotion to his Sacred Heart; (2) to promote the practice of receiving Holy Communion on the first Fridays and of keeping a Holy Hour of reparation; and (3) to establish a special feast in honor of his Sacred Heart. When she tried to comply with our Lord's instructions, she at first met opposition from her superiors and sisters.

But when St. Claude La Colombière (see February 15) arrived in Paray to be the sisters' confessor, Sr. Margaret Mary informed him of our Lord's revelations, and he assured her that these were, indeed, from God and that he would assist her in realizing our Lord's requests. With the eventual appointment of a new superior of the convent, Sr. Margaret Mary was made mistress of novices. In this role, she was able to spread the devotion among the younger sisters. In 1686, the feast of the Sacred Heart was celebrated in the convent for the first time, and two years later a chapel was dedicated to the Sacred Heart. Devotion thus began to spread to other religious houses, and from there throughout

France and eventually the world. St. Margaret Mary died on October 17, 1690, and was canonized by Pope Benedict XV in 1920.

✝ OCTOBER 17 ✒ *Memorial*
St. Ignatius of Antioch, Bishop and Martyr

St. Ignatius was probably born in Syria and as Bishop of Antioch (today's Antakya, Turkey) he was the second or third successor of St. Peter in that city. During a period of persecution under Trajan (emperor 98–117), he was condemned to the wild beasts and sent under guard to Rome. On his journey to Rome, which included stages over land as well as by sea, he sent seven epistles to the Christians in various cities. These epistles, written from different stopovers on his journey, are important because they are among the first letters we have from a bishop of the early Church. In some of these, he refers to himself as Theophorus, that is, as God-Bearer. His letter to the Romans is especially famous, for while exhorting them to be faithful to Christ, he asks them not to use their influence in trying to prevent his martyrdom, because he considers himself the "wheat of God; and I must be ground by the teeth of wild beasts to become the pure bread of Christ." These words of his are reflected in today's prayer over the gifts. St. Ignatius was martyred in Rome in about 110. His feast is celebrated today because this is the day it has always been celebrated in Antioch. The Calendar of Nicomedia (about 360) gives October 17 as the date of his martyrdom.

✝ OCTOBER 18 ❧ *Feast*
St. Luke, Evangelist

St. Luke the Evangelist was born perhaps in Antioch (modern Antakya, Turkey), of a Greek-speaking pagan family. He was converted to the Christian faith and became a fellow worker of St. Paul. He was likewise a physician, because St. Paul refers to him as "our most dear physician" (Col. 4:14). Luke first met St. Paul at Troas (Acts 16:11), then accompanied him to Jerusalem (Acts 21:17), and remained with him during his imprisonment in Rome (Acts 28:14b–16; 2 Tim. 4:11). Luke handed down an account of the beginnings of the Church in his Acts of the Apostles, and from St. Paul's preaching he compiled the Third Gospel. It is uncertain where he went after St. Paul was martyred in Rome. Tradition has it that St. Luke was martyred toward the end of the first century. The prayer of the Mass today is a terse summary of his Gospel.

✝ OCTOBER 19 ❧ *Memorial*
SS. Isaac Jogues and John de Brébeuf,
Priests and Martyrs, and
Their Companions, Martyrs

Today we commemorate the martyrdom of eight French Jesuits, who had come to North America to teach the Huron and Iroquois about God. They were martyred between 1642 and 1649—three at Auriesville, New York, and five in Canada.

Martyred at Auriesville, New York

	BIRTH	DEATH
René Goupil	1608	September 29, 1642
Isaac Jogues	1607	October 18, 1646
John de La Lande	?	October 19, 1646

Martyred in Canada

	BIRTH	DEATH
Anthony Daniel	1601	July 4, 1648
John de Brébeuf	1593	March 16, 1649
Gabriel Lalemant	1610	March 17, 1649
Charles Garnier	1606	December 7, 1649
Noel Chabanel	1613	December 8, 1649

Goupil, Jogues, La Lande, and Chabanel were tomahawked to death; Daniel and Garnier were shot; Brébeuf and Lalemant were brutally and cruelly tortured to death. Six were priests, Goupil and La Lande were coadjutor brothers. They were canonized by Pope Pius XI in 1930. The opening prayer of today's Mass reminds us that these martyred missionaries consecrated the first beginnings of the faith in North America not only by their preaching of God's Word but also by the shedding of their blood.

✝ OCTOBER 20
St. Paul of the Cross, Priest

St. Paul of the Cross, founder of the Congregation of the Passion (more commonly known as Passionists), was born Paul Francis Danei in Ovada, Italy, on January 3, 1694. His years of formal education were few, but he made up for their lack by his own initiative and industry. As a young man, he led an intense spiritual life, and because he himself had felt poverty's pinch while growing up, he was naturally drawn to work among the poor. From 1717 to 1719, he served in the Venetian forces in that state's conflict with the Turks. Then, in 1720, he experienced what he called his "great vision," in which he saw himself wearing the distinctive habit of the religious congregation he would one day establish. He was ordained in 1727, and because he had such great devotion to Christ's cross, he chose thenceforth to be known as Paul of the Cross. The congregation of priests he founded in 1728 was dedicated to a life of prayer, penance, and preaching parish missions. For about thirty years (1730–60), he himself traveled throughout Italy giving missions and promoting devotion to our Lord's Passion. In 1771, he founded a contemplative order of Passionist nuns. Throughout his life, he was favored with extraordinary mystical graces. He died in Rome on October 18, 1775, and was canonized by Pius IX in 1867. His special love for the cross of Christ is mentioned in the opening prayer of today's Mass.

✝ OCTOBER 23
St. John of Capistrano, Priest

St. John was born at Capistrano, near Aquila, Italy, on June 24, 1386. He studied law at Perugia, and in 1413 he became a member of that city's civic administration. In 1415, he entered the Observant Franciscans, and after ordination (1418), he began his ministry of preaching, which took him throughout Italy. His life was one of great austerity, and he always walked barefoot to his preaching assignments.

In 1451, Pope Nicholas V sent him to Hungary and Bohemia to preach against the followers of John Hus (1369–1415). He likewise preached in Poland and Moravia (now in the Czech Republic). Because Europe was again threatened by the Turks, he preached a crusade (1455) and successfully gathered an army, which was placed under the command of the Hungarian general János Hunyadi (1407–56). When the city of Belgrade (Yugoslavia) was besieged by Turks, St. John took charge of one wing of the army, bravely withstood the Turkish onslaught, and finally gained a victory (July 22, 1456), saving the city and Europe from the Turks. He died at Ilok (in today's Croatia) on October 23, 1456. Because of his widespread preaching in Europe, he is sometimes called the "Apostle of Europe." Pope Alexander VIII canonized him in 1690. The prayer of today's Mass reminds us that it was through St. John's preaching that God's people found comfort when they were threatened by the Turks.

✝ OCTOBER 24
St. Anthony Mary Claret, Bishop

St. Anthony Claret was born in Sallent, Spain, on December 23, 1807. He was the son of a weaver, and as a youth he worked in the textile mills of Barcelona. He was ordained in 1835 and carried on his priestly ministry in Catalonia and the Canary Islands. By 1840, he had become one of his country's most popular preachers, and in 1849 he founded a congregation of preachers, the Missionary Sons of the Immaculate Heart of Mary (more commonly known as Claretians). Throughout his priestly life, he wanted to make sure that the faithful received proper instruction in the faith, and with this end in view he authored many books and pamphlets, catechisms, and devotional works. He was also instrumental in founding (1847) the Religious Library, an organization dedicated to publishing good religious literature that enjoyed remarkable success.

In 1850, he was named archbishop of Santiago, Cuba. The diocese had been without a bishop for more than a dozen years; hence, upon his arrival, he had many tasks before him. He visited each parish in his diocese, established new parishes, and reopened the seminary. He was recalled to Spain in 1857, having been appointed confessor of Queen Isabella II, and once more he traveled widely, preaching on the Eucharist and the Immaculate Heart of Mary. He was forced to leave Spain during the 1868 revolution, and he died at the Cistercian monastery at Fontfroide, near Narbonne, in southern France, on October 24, 1870. He was canonized by Pope Pius XII in 1950. The prayer of today's Mass recalls his preaching the gospel to many nations.

✝ OCTOBER 28 ✐ *Feast*
SS. Simon and Jude, Apostles

In the lists of the apostles found in the New Testament, Simon is called "the Zealot" (Matt. 10:4; Mark 3:18; Luke 6:15; Acts 1:13), and he is probably so identified as to distinguish him from Simon Peter. That he should be called the Zealot may be because he might have, at one time, belonged to the Jewish Zealot party. Jude is called "Judas, son of James" by Luke (6:16; Acts 1:13), but is called Thaddaeus by Matthew (10:3) and Mark (3:18), and he is said to have been a relative of the Lord (Matt. 13:55; Mark 6:3). It is far from certain where both of these apostles preached after Pentecost; some sources claim that Simon preached in Persia (modern Iran) and Babylonia (now Iraq), while Jude preached in Palestine and the Near East. Both Simon and Jude were martyred in the first century, and both have been commemorated in Rome on the same day since the ninth century. Jude may also be the author of one of the epistles in the New Testament.

✝ *OCTOBER 30
Bl. Dominic Collins, Religious and Martyr

Bl. Dominic was born about 1566 in the seaport town of Youghal, in County Cork, Ireland. Because Elizabeth I was then the queen of England and Ireland, Irish Catholics periodically suffered persecution. Dominic—aware that there were no career openings for young Catholic men in the Ireland of his day—went to France, and for three years (1586–89) he worked as a servant in various inns. Now that he had enough money to outfit himself as a soldier, he enlisted in the duke of Mercoeur's army, then engaged in fighting the Huguenots. Dominic's nine-year military career was a success; he advanced to the rank of captain of cavalry and was military governor of a castle. On the arrival of Spanish reinforcements to help the Catholic cause, the Spanish general gave Dominic letters of recommendation, which he presented to Philip II of Spain. Now in the service of Spain, Dominic was assigned to the garrison at La Coruña on the Bay of Biscay. During Lent 1598, the Irish Jesuit Thomas White came from the Irish College in Salamanca to hear the confessions of his countrymen in the Spanish navy. Dominic told the priest that he wanted to do something more with his life; neither the world nor the military interested him any longer. Thus, at the age of thirty-two years, he entered (December 1598) the Jesuit novitiate in Santiago de Compostela.

Two years later, Br. Dominic was assigned to accompany a certain Fr. James Archer, who was to sail as chaplain of a Spanish expedition being sent (September 1601) to help the Irish Catholics. Br. Dominic reached the Irish coast and made his way to Dunboy Castle. After the English army landed (June 6, 1602), it began its siege of the castle. After days of bombardment, the castle towers began to topple, and the defenders were forced to retreat to the cellars. Br. Collins emerged the following day, apparently to act as intermediary; he was apprehended and taken the following day to a prison in Cork. He rejected the offers placed before him; he would neither serve the queen nor give up his Catholic faith to save his life. Thus he was condemned to death. He remained in prison for three more months, and on October 31, 1602, he was taken to Youghal to be hanged. There he told the bystanders that he had come to Ireland to preach the Catholic faith and that he would willingly undergo not one but a thousand deaths for that faith. Br. Collins and sixteen other Irish martyrs were beatified by Pope John Paul II in 1992.

✝ *OCTOBER 31   *Memorial*
St. Alphonsus Rodríguez, Religious

St. Alphonsus Rodríguez was born in Segovia, Spain, on July 25, 1533. He was a wool merchant by trade, married, and had three children. It was through the death of his wife and children that God chose to lead him to an extraordinary intimate union with himself. Being a widower, he thought of the priesthood, but he was told that he was too old to begin studies. He was then about thirty-five years of age. He thus entered the Jesuits as a coadjutor brother in 1571, and later that year he was sent to the College of Montesión in Palma on the island of Mallorca, where he was made doorkeeper and remained for the next forty-six years of his life. Externally, his life had nothing extraordinary or remarkable about it. He fulfilled his monotonous job with uncommon fidelity, humility, charity, kindness, and obedience, and thus he became a saint. He encouraged the students to have devotion to our Lady and to pray the rosary, and it was he who suggested to Peter Claver (see September 9) to go to the missions in the New World. St. Alphonsus died at Palma on October 31, 1617, and only after his death was it learned how God had favored him with mystical graces, ecstasies, and visions. He was canonized by Pope Leo XIII in 1888. The prayer in the Mass today reminds us that in faithful service as lived by St. Alphonsus, God has shown us the way to joy and peace.

NOVEMBER

✝ NOVEMBER 1 ⁂ *Solemnity*
All Saints

Today we honor all those who enjoy the vision of God in Heaven, that is, the angels and those canonized and beatified by the Church, as well as all who have died in God's friendship. With God in glory today, there is a multitude of men and women, from all ages and all walks of life, who, while they lived on earth, followed Christ and are now with him for all eternity. Among these, there are also our relatives and friends. We call upon all these saints to be our intercessors with God, that by living the beatitudes as they lived them (see today's Gospel, Matt. 5:1–12), we too may learn the way of holiness and one day join them in praising God forever. Sanctity is not for the few; it is within everyone's reach. This feast goes back at least to the seventh century, for the Venerable Bede (see May 25) refers to such a feast being celebrated in England on November 1. As early as 359, the Eastern Church celebrated a feast of all martyrs on May 13. This practice was adopted by Churches in other regions, and nonmartyrs were later included in the liturgical celebration. Finally, Pope Gregory VII

(1073–85) suppressed the May 13 feast of all martyrs and decreed that the feast of All Saints would be celebrated by the universal Church on November 1.

✝ NOVEMBER 2 ✐ *Solemnity*
Commemoration of All
the Faithful Departed (All Souls)

In yesterday's feast of All Saints, we honored the Church in Heaven, and today we commemorate the Church in Purgatory—the deceased faithful who are on their way to Heaven. Their present period of purification will infallibly end with their vision of God and union with the other saints. This, then, is not a day of mourning; we rejoice because our faithful departed have been judged worthy to be with God. As early as the seventh century, certain monastic communities had specific days for commemorating the dead of their community. This practice spread, and by the ninth century it had become a commemoration of all the dead. In 998 St. Odilo, Abbot of Cluny, France, established that in his communities the commemoration of the faithful departed was to be celebrated on November 2. In the fifteenth century, the custom arose in Spain of celebrating three Masses for the deceased on November 2, and this custom prevailed throughout Spain, Portugal, and Spanish America. Then, in 1915, Pope Benedict XV—aware of the great number of deaths during World War I, which was then raging—extended to the entire Latin Church the privilege of celebrating three Masses for the deceased on this day.

NOVEMBER 3
St. Martin de Porres, Religious

St. Martin de Porres was born in Lima on December 9, 1579, the son of a Spanish father and a black mother. As a youth, he learned the basics of medical practice by helping one of the local pharmacist-physicians. He felt called to the religious life, but because he was a mulatto he thought that that way of life was not for him. Instead, he took a job—he was then fifteen years of age—doing domestic work in a Dominican monastery. During his nine years there, the monks witnessed his humility, goodness, and charity, and eventually they asked him if he would not want to become a Dominican brother. This he did in 1603. In addition to his regular tasks in the community (as barber, surgeon, and infirmarian), Br. Martin cared for the sick and the poor of the city, and when he returned home he spent his nights more in prayer than in sleep. To the people of the city and to his religious brethren, he was the living symbol of generosity and humility. He died in Lima on November 3, 1639, and was canonized by Pope John XXIII in 1962. Today's prayer mentions St. Martin's humility.

*NOVEMBER 3
Bl. Rupert Mayer, Priest

Bl. Rupert Mayer was born in Stuttgart, Germany, on January 23, 1876. After completing his secondary education in 1894, he thought of entering the Society of Jesus, but his father asked him first to be ordained, and if he were still of the same opinion then he had his permission to become a Jesuit. Rupert did his theological studies at Tübingen and Rottenburg and was finally ordained a diocesan priest in 1899. After serving as a parish priest for a year, he entered the Society of Jesus in 1900. From 1906 to 1911, he traveled throughout Germany, Switzerland, and the Netherlands giving parish missions. In 1912, he was assigned to Munich, and from then on his name became closely linked to that city. During World War I, he volunteered (1914) as an army chaplain and served until he was wounded in December 1916. After the war, he was again in Munich, working with and for the poor people who had come to the city seeking employment. He also undertook the direction of the men's sodality. Fr. Mayer witnessed the rise of Adolf Hitler (1889–1945), and while others failed to discern the falsehoods that Hitler was propagating, Fr. Mayer spoke out against him, always stressing Catholic social principles. Because he had the courage to oppose the Nazis, he was three times arrested by the Gestapo and three times imprisoned, the last in a concentration camp. He survived the war, was liberated in May 1945, and returned to his beloved Munich. Five months later he died, on November 1, 1945. He was beatified by Pope John Paul II in 1987.

✝ NOVEMBER 4 ✒ *Memorial*
St. Charles Borromeo, Bishop

St. Charles Borromeo, son of Count Gilberto Borromeo, was born at Arona, Lombardy, Italy, on October 2, 1538. He studied at the University of Pavia and earned (1559) a doctorate in civil and canon law. When his mother's brother was elected pope (Pius IV) in 1559, Charles was called to Rome, and in 1560, when he was only twenty-two years of age, he was made a cardinal, and he was named Archbishop of Milan and head of the Secretariat of State. After his ordination (1563), he lived a most austere life. When his uncle died (1565), he made Milan his residence, and from then until his death he was an exemplary bishop. He convoked synods and councils to bring the diocese into line with the prescriptions of the Council of Trent, established seminaries and colleges, and built shelters for the homeless and homes for the abandoned, as well as orphanages and hospitals. When Milan suffered from a plague (1576), he cared for the sick and buried the dead without a worry about himself. He died on November 3, 1584. In life, the people considered him the ideal pastor and shepherd; in death, they venerated him as a saint. He was canonized by Pope Paul V in 1610. The prayers today recall St. Charles's reforming activity in asking that the Church be continually renewed and in speaking of him as an example of virtue and concern for the pastoral ministry.

✝ ***NOVEMBER 5** ✍ *Feast*
All Saints and Blessed of the Society of Jesus

A few days ago, the Church celebrated the Solemnity of All Saints, and today the members of the Society of Jesus honor those of their religious family who are with God: the canonized saints, the beatified, and the countless others who, in following the prescriptions of their Institute, have attained Heaven. Holiness is everyone's goal in life, and today's feast tells us that Heaven is within everyone's reach. We do not become holy on our own; it is God who is the source of all holiness. As the Jesuits praise their brethren in Heaven for their faithfulness to God while on earth, they take encouragement, for they also labor under the same banner of Christ as their predecessors did, and because God has called them, weak though they are, to follow him, may their service be pleasing to him and may it bring them to the same goal that their brothers in Heaven now possess.

✝ NOVEMBER 9 ✐ *Feast*
Dedication of the Lateran
Basilica in Rome

The Basilica of St. John Lateran dates from about 324, when Constantine (emperor 306–37) converted a portion of the Roman palace of the Laterani into a Christian basilica and gave it to Pope Sylvester I (314–35) to become the papal residence. Because this church was the first in date and the first in dignity—it became the seat and cathedral of the Bishop of Rome—it is referred to as "the Mother and Head of all Churches, in the City and of the World," as the inscription on the church's facade indicates. The actual day of the basilica's dedication is unknown, but in the twelfth century the canons, who staffed the basilica, celebrated the anniversary of its dedication on November 9. At first, this anniversary was celebrated only in Rome, but it was later extended to the whole Church to indicate the unity among the Churches of the world and with that of the Chair of Peter. The basilica is now commonly known as that of St. John Lateran: John because it is dedicated to SS. John the Baptist and John the Evangelist, and Lateran to commemorate the family whose property it once was.

✠

NOVEMBER 10   *Memorial*
St. Leo the Great, Pope and Doctor of the Church

St. Leo was probably born in Rome about 400. He was a deacon under popes Celestine I (422–32) and Sixtus III (432–40), both of whom had entrusted him with diplomatic missions. He was elected pope in August–September 440, while on a mission to Gaul (today's France), and he was consecrated (September 29, 440) on his return to Rome. Leo is one of the three popes designated as "the Great," and he merits this title because of his teaching and his governance. His teaching is found in ninety-six sermons, which explain the major tenets of the Catholic faith. With regard to governance, he was the best administrator of the ancient Church: he consolidated Church administration and also stressed the primacy of the Roman See in his dealings with the rest of the Catholic world. He likewise urged liturgical as well as canonical and pastoral uniformity. Near Mantua, he confronted (452) Attila the Hun and persuaded him to withdraw, and on meeting the Vandal Gaiseric outside Rome, he induced (455) him to spare the city from fire and massacre. St. Leo died on November 10, 461. Pope Benedict XIV declared him a doctor of the Church in 1754. The opening prayer today echoes St. Leo's constant teaching that the Church is founded on the rock of Peter.

✠ NOVEMBER 11 ✎ *Memorial*
St. Martin of Tours, Bishop

St. Martin was born of pagan parents in Sabaria, Pannonia (today's Szombathely, Hungary), in about 316. His father was an officer in the Roman army and had moved his family to Pavia, Italy, where Martin grew up and became a catechumen. At the age of fifteen years, Martin joined the Roman army, and tradition has it that, while serving near Amiens, he shared his military cloak with a destitute beggar. Martin was later granted a vision of Christ who, clothed in the cloak he had given the beggar, encouraged him to be baptized. After Martin's discharge (356) from military service, he placed himself (about 359) under the spiritual guidance of St. Hilary of Poitiers (see January 13), and he later founded (360–61) a monastery at Ligugé, near Poitiers. This was the first monastery established in Gaul (modern France). Martin was made Bishop of Tours in 372, but he continued living a monastic life in a deserted area outside the city. He died on a pastoral visit to Candes on November 8, 397, and he was buried in Tours on November 11. His successor in the see built a chapel over his tomb, which soon became a place of pilgrimage. Martin was the first nonmartyr to be venerated as a saint and given a liturgical feast in the Church calendar. The Communion antiphon in today's Mass was chosen to recall St. Martin's charity in dividing his cloak with the beggar.

✠ NOVEMBER 12 ✒ *Memorial*
St. Josaphat, Bishop and Martyr

St. Josaphat Kuncewycz is known as the "Apostle of Union" because he gave his life to promote union between the Catholic and Orthodox Churches. He was born of Orthodox parents in Vladimir-Volynski, Ukraine, in about 1580, and while apprenticed to a merchant in Vilnius, he learned about the recent Union of Brest, which brought about (October 1596) a union of the Ruthenian Orthodox and Catholic Churches. Taken up with this idea of Church unity, he chose to become a Catholic. Then, in 1604, he entered the Holy Trinity Monastery of the Order of St. Basil in Vilnius, and on that occasion changed his name from John to Josaphat. He was ordained in 1609 and set about preaching to gain adherents—from both the Catholic and Orthodox sides—to the Union. Because he had been successful in his preaching and priestly ministry, his reputation soon spread throughout the region, and he was subsequently named superior of the Basilian monastery at Byten. Shortly afterward, he was named (1617) bishop of Vitebsk (now Vitsyebsk), Belarus, with the right to succeed to the archbishopric of Polotsk (Polatsk), Belarus. Because the archbishop died within a short time after Bishop Josaphat's appointment, the latter moved to Polotsk and immediately set about rejuvenating the archdiocese. He held synods in the principal cities, promoted reform among the clergy, and encouraged frequent administration of the sacraments and preaching, and also visiting of the sick and of prisoners.

With the appointment (1620) of a new Orthodox hierarchy in Lithuania, Bishop Josaphat met opposition to his preaching and to his work for Church union. Because of great ill-feeling against the Union in Vitebsk, he went there toward the end of October 1623, and he began a series of sermons in Vitebsk Cathedral explaining and promoting the Union. His presence there was seen as an affront to those who chose to remain Orthodox, and on November 12, 1623, an enraged mob attacked him as he stood outside the Vitebsk cathedral and he was slain. His body was then cast into the river. He was canonized by Pope Pius IX in 1867, the first Eastern Rite saint to enter the Roman Church's liturgical calendar. The Communion prayer today mentions the unity of the Church for which St. Josaphat gave his life.

✝ NOVEMBER 13   ✎   *Memorial*
St. Frances Xavier Cabrini, Virgin

St. Frances Xavier Cabrini was born at Sant' Angelo Lodigiano, Lombardy, in northern Italy, on July 15, 1850, the youngest of thirteen children. She studied (1863–68) with the Daughters of the Sacred Heart in nearby Arluno, and she completed her teacher's certification course at the age of eighteen years. She then returned home and taught for several years, first in her town's elementary school and then in Vidardo. She then transferred (1874) to Codogno, where she taught in an orphanage known as the House of Providence, operated by the Sisters of Providence. In 1877 she entered that religious congregation, but by 1880 the orphanage was closed and the sisters had to disband. Shortly thereafter, the Bishop of Lodi, Dominic Gelmini (1807–88), suggested that she found her own religious community. So, with seven girls from the orphanage, she founded (1880) the Missionary Sisters of the Sacred Heart, and within a few years, convents of her congregation were established in northern Italy and in Rome.

In the 1880s, many Italian immigrants were on their way to the United States, and fearing that they would lose their faith, if they had no Italian priests and sisters with them, Pope Leo XIII (1878–1903), together with Bishop John Baptist Scalabrini (1839–1905), asked Mother Cabrini to adopt the United States as her mission field rather than China. Together with six of her sisters, she arrived in New York on March 31, 1889, and they immediately began their work. They started schools, opened hospitals and orphanages, and taught catechism to children. Wherever there was an Italian community, the sisters went there to serve. St. Frances died in Chicago—the cause being malaria—on December 22, 1917, and was canonized by Pope Pius XII in 1946. The prayer in today's Mass speaks of her leaving Italy to work with the immigrants and how, in her charity, she cared for the sick and the frustrated.

✝ *NOVEMBER 13   🍂   *Memorial*
St. Stanislaus Kostka, Religious

St. Stanislaus Kostka was a Polish noble youth born in 1550 at the family estate of Rostków, Mazovia, Poland.

When Stanislaus was fourteen years of age, he was sent (1564) with his brother Paul to study at the recently opened Jesuit college in Vienna. There he had to endure many a trial from the hands of his brother, but this never diminished Stanislaus's resolve to live a prayerful and recollected life. When ill and longing to receive Holy Communion, Stanislaus enjoyed extraordinary favors from God. His heart was set on becoming a Jesuit, but knowing that his parents would not give their consent, he quietly left Vienna in August 1567 and walked 450 miles to Dillingen, Germany. There he met the Jesuit provincial, St. Peter Canisius (see April 27), who arranged for him to go to Rome. When Stanislaus arrived in Rome (October 1567), he was accepted by St. Francis Borgia (see October 3) and immediately began his novitiate training. In early August of the following year, he had a premonition that he would die on the 15th of that month; he became ill with a fever on the 10th, and he died on August 15, 1568, as he had foretold. He was canonized by Pope Benedict XIII in 1726. The prayer of today's Mass speaks of St. Stanislaus's generosity of heart, and hints that though his was a short life, nevertheless, it was filled with good works.

✝ *NOVEMBER 14 ✐ *Memorial*
St. Joseph Pignatelli, Priest

St. Joseph Pignatelli was born of noble parents in Saragossa, Spain, on December 27, 1737. After attending the Jesuit school in his native city, he entered the Society of Jesus in 1753, and he was ordained in 1762. For the next four years, this Spanish grandee taught his classes, visited prisons, and at times ministered to condemned convicts on their way to execution. In April 1767, King Charles III of Spain (reigned 1759–88), without ever making known his reasons, expelled the Jesuits from his kingdom and confiscated their property. The Jesuits were deported to Italy, where they settled as best they could. With the Society's suppression by Pope Clement XIV in 1773, the Jesuits now took on a variety of tasks in various dioceses—teaching in seminaries, doing parish work, and filling chaplaincies. Throughout these years, Fr. Pignatelli maintained contact with most of them, looking forward to the time when they could all be reunited. When he learned that the Society was never suppressed in the territory of Catherine the Great of Russia (reigned 1762–96), he immediately wrote and associated himself with them, but he continued to work in Italy. He lived in exile for forty years, regrouping the former Jesuits and awaiting the day when the Society could be restored throughout the world. He was not to see that day, for he died on November 15, 1811, three years before the Society's restoration by Pope Pius VII on August 7, 1814. Fr. Pignatelli was canonized by Pope Pius XII in 1954. The opening prayer in the Mass today refers to his courage and strength in uniting his scattered brethren.

✝ NOVEMBER 15
St. Albert the Great, Bishop and Doctor of the Church

St. Albert the Great was an eminent scientist, philosopher, and theologian and is called "the Great" because of his immense erudition. He was born in Lauingen, near Ulm, Germany, in about 1200. He entered the Order of Preachers (Dominicans) in 1223, and after theological studies in Germany, he was ordained to the priesthood. For the next seven or so years, he taught theology in various Dominican houses of study. Then, in about 1241, he went to the University of Paris, where he earned his master's degree and later lectured (1245–48). He then moved to Cologne and there opened his order's first *studium generale* in Germany. Among his Cologne students was St. Thomas Aquinas (see January 28). Albert subsequently became provincial (1253–57) of the German Dominicans, and in 1260 he was named bishop of Regensburg. He resigned two years later to return to teaching and writing. During his lifetime, he was regarded as a man superior in every branch of learning and was called the wonder and miracle of his age. In addition to his philosophical and theological writings, he wrote treatises on physics, meteors, minerals, sleep, breathing, and botany. In recognition of his theological expertise, he was invited to attend the second Council of Lyon (1274). He died in Cologne on November 15, 1280. Pope Pius XI canonized him in 1931 and declared him a doctor of the Church. Today's opening prayer mentions that in St. Albert human wisdom and divine faith were combined, and asks that the advance in human knowledge deepen our love of God.

NOVEMBER 16
St. Margaret of Scotland

St. Margaret, the daughter of the Anglo-Saxon Prince Edward Atheling and Princess Agatha of Hungary, was born at Reska, Hungary, in 1046. Her early education was at home, but when her father was recalled (1057) to England, by her great-uncle Edward the Confessor (reigned 1042–66), she lived at the royal English court. Because her father had died shortly after his arrival in England, and due to the Norman victory at the Battle of Hastings (1066), she tried (1067) to return to Hungary, but was shipwrecked off the coast of Scotland. There she married (1070) Malcolm III, the king of Scotland, and bore him eight children. Together with her husband, she initiated a series of reforms that changed the religious life of Scotland. She founded (about 1074) Holy Trinity Abbey at Dunfermline, and she restored the abbey at Iona as well as other churches. Queen Margaret, however, was especially known for her goodness and love toward the poor and the sick. She died in Edinburgh on November 16, 1093, was buried in the abbey church at Dunfermline, and was canonized by Pope Innocent IV in 1250. St. Margaret was named patron of Scotland in 1673. The opening prayer of today's Mass speaks of her special love for the poor and describes her as a living sign of God's goodness.

NOVEMBER 16
St. Gertrude, Virgin

St. Gertrude, known as "the Great," was born in Eisleben, Thuringia, Germany, on January 6, 1256, and was entrusted to the care of the Cistercian nuns at nearby Helfta Abbey, when she was but five years of age. There she was educated and eventually entered the monastery. When she was twenty-five, she underwent a mystical experience (January 27, 1281), which she called her "conversion," and from that time onward she lived a life of contemplation, rich in extraordinary mystical experiences. These experiences she recorded, over an eight-year period, in her *Revelations*. The monastic liturgy also served as the source for her spiritual life. She was also one of the first to promote devotion to the Sacred Heart of Jesus. She died at Helfta on November 17, 1301 or 1302. Her cult was first authorized in 1606 and then extended to the entire Church by Pope Clement XII in 1738.

*NOVEMBER 16   ✿   Memorial
SS. Roch González, John del Castillo, and Alphonsus Rodríguez, Priests and Martyrs

St. Roch González was born in Asunción, Paraguay, in 1576, was ordained a diocesan priest, and subsequently entered (1609) the Society of Jesus. He was first assigned to evangelize the Indians, and he was later placed in charge of various "reductions" (i.e., Indian settlements directed by Jesuits) along the River Plate, where he supervised the construction of houses for the Indians and founded schools and built churches. While teaching the Indians the essentials of farming, he also taught them the fundamentals of the Catholic faith. In time, the reductions in Paraguay became ideal Christian communities. Because of his success in peacefully bringing the Indians together and Christianizing them, a local witch doctor, seeing that his influence was waning, decided that the missionaries had to die. On November 15, 1628, Fr. González was in Caaró (in today's Brazil), and as he left the chapel after celebrating Mass, the witch doctor and his henchmen attacked him and another Jesuit, Fr. Alphonsus Rodríguez (b. 1598), a Spaniard, and martyred them. A day later, the murderers went to the reduction at Iyuí, and there they killed another Spanish Jesuit, Fr. John del Castillo (b. 1596). The three martyrs were canonized by Pope John Paul II in 1988. When today's prayer speaks of a hundredfold in a harvest of justice and peace, it summarizes what St. Roch González and his companions were trying to accomplish in the Jesuit reductions of South America.

✠ NOVEMBER 17   ✑   *Memorial*
St. Elizabeth of Hungary, Religious

St. Elizabeth, the daughter of King Andrew II of Hungary (reigned 1205–35), was born in today's Bratislava (now in Slovakia) in 1207. When she was about four years of age, she was betrothed (1211) to Ludwig, son of Herman I, Landgrave of Thuringia (Germany), and was sent there to be raised with her future husband at the Thuringian court. On the death of his father, Ludwig became Landgrave in 1221, and during that year his marriage to Elizabeth (now fourteen years of age) was solemnized. Three children were born of this marriage. Besides being wife and mother, Elizabeth gave of herself and of her wealth to serve God by relieving the needs of the poor. Near their Wartburg castle, she founded a hospital, which she regularly visited to feed and wash the patients. After her husband's death during the crusade of 1227—he died in Otranto after contracting the plague—she provided for her children, gave up her possessions, and took (March 1228) the habit of the Third Order of St. Francis. She then built a hospital in Marburg, where she herself nursed the sick and cared for the poor. She died in Marburg during the night of November 16–17, 1231, at age twenty-four. Four years after her death, she was canonized (1235) by Pope Gregory IX. The prayer in the Mass today recalls St. Elizabeth's honoring Christ in the poor of this world.

✝ NOVEMBER 18
Dedication of the Basilicas of
SS. Peter and Paul, Apostles

Over the tombs of the Apostles Peter and Paul in Rome, Constantine (emperor 306–37) built two basilicas. The one over St. Peter's tomb on Vatican Hill was built about 324 and was dedicated about 326. The one over St. Paul's tomb on the Ostian Way was built about the same time as that of St. Peter, but because it proved too small to hold all the pilgrims that visited it, it was rebuilt and dedicated again in 390. By the eleventh century, the dedication of St. Peter's was celebrated annually on November 18, and in the following century this commemoration also included that of St. Paul's. This celebration, however, remained a local feast for Rome until 1568, when Pope Pius V placed it in the universal Roman Calendar. When St. Peter's had to be rebuilt in the sixteenth and seventeenth centuries, Pope Urban VIII dedicated the new basilica on November 18, 1626. St. Paul's was likewise rebuilt, due to a fire in 1823, and it was dedicated by Pius IX on December 10, 1854. By commemorating the dedication of these basilicas of SS. Peter and Paul in Rome, we honor the princes of the apostles, and in today's prayer we ask that the Church always enjoy the protection of the apostles, because it first received the faith of Christ through them.

✝ NOVEMBER 18
St. Rose Philippine Duchesne, Virgin

St. Rose Philippine Duchesne was a courageous pioneer and persevering missionary. She was born in Grenoble, France, on August 29, 1769, and despite her father's opposition, she entered (1788) the Visitation Convent of Sainte-Marie-d'en-Haut. Later, because of the French Revolution, the community was dispersed (1792) and, thus, she returned home and spent her time teaching neglected children and caring for the sick. When peace returned, she purchased (1801) the convent building from the government and tried to bring the Visitation Sisters together again, but this proved impossible. Having heard of a new congregation, the Sisters of the Sacred Heart, she offered (1804) herself and the building to the founder, St. Madeleine Sophie

Barat (1779–1865). Then, in 1818, her dream of missionary work in the New World came true. Bishop Louis Du Bourg (1766–1833) of the Louisiana Territory requested sisters to teach Indian and French children in his diocese. Mother Rose Philippine asked to go; she and four companions landed in New Orleans in May 1818. They made their way to St. Louis, and that September she opened, at St. Charles, near St. Louis, the first free school for girls west of the Mississippi. Life on the frontier was far from easy; the sisters lived and taught in unheated log cabins. In succeeding years, more schools were opened; parish schools, schools for Indian girls, and schools for boarding students. In 1840, when Mother Rose Philippine was in her seventies, she was sent to help start a school among the Potawatomi Indians in Sugar Creek, Kansas. She did not teach—she was never able to learn their language—but she cared for their sick. The Indians called her "Woman-Who-Prays-Always." In 1842, she was recalled to St. Charles, and she died there on November 18, 1852. She was canonized by Pope John Paul II in 1988.

✝ NOVEMBER 21 ✍ *Memorial*
Presentation of the Blessed Virgin Mary

The Eastern Church celebrated a feast commemorating Mary's entrance into the Temple in conjunction with the anniversary of the dedication (November 21, 543) of a new basilica in honor of Mary built near the Temple in Jerusalem. In time, the feast became known as the Presentation of Mary in the Temple, recalling an incident not found in the four canonical Gospels but described in another early writing known as the Protoevangelium of James. According to this tradition, the parents of Mary, Anne and Joachim, presented their three-year-old daughter to God in the Temple, where she was then reared and educated with other girls under the tutelage of holy women. The French knight, Philippe de Mézières (1327–1405), became acquainted with this feast on a visit to the Holy Land, and when he returned to France he promoted its celebration. When Pope Gregory XI, then residing in Avignon, heard of it, he introduced it at Avignon in 1373, and Sixtus V later (1585) extended its celebration to the universal Church.

✠ NOVEMBER 22   🖎   *Memorial*
St. Cecilia, Virgin and Martyr

St. Cecilia was one of the most venerated martyrs of the early Church in Rome, and by the end of the fourth or beginning of the fifth century, a church in the Trastevere quarter of the city was named in her honor. As early as 545, her feast was celebrated there on November 22. That a maid named Cecilia was martyred and buried in the cemetery of Callistus is certain. Nothing else, however, is known about Cecilia, except what is found in a life written some two centuries after her death and, hence, not quite reliable. Legend has it that Cecilia was a young Roman who had been condemned for her Christian beliefs and ordered to be suffocated in an exceedingly hot steam bath in her home. Because she remained unharmed, she was to be beheaded. She endured three strokes of the sword and died three days later. In 821, Pope Paschal I had her body transferred from the cemetery to her church, which is still one of the favorite churches in Rome. The fact that her name is found in the Roman Canon indicates the popularity of her cult.

☩ NOVEMBER 23
St. Clement I, Pope and Martyr

St. Clement was the third pope (about 91–101) after St. Peter. St. Irenaeus (see June 28) stated that Clement, who had been born in Rome, knew SS. Peter and Paul (see June 29) and had witnessed their preaching. Besides the fact that Clement was pope, the only other thing known about him with any certainty is that he wrote (about 96) an epistle to the Church in Corinth, where dissension had broken out. This epistle is the most important first-century Christian document outside the New Testament. It records the Church of Rome's concern for a community founded by St. Paul and indicates the unity that existed between those Churches. We also find in the letter the earliest testimony to the martyrdoms of SS. Peter and Paul. So revered was this letter that in some places it was read in church and treated as a part of the New Testament itself. Tradition has it that Clement was exiled by Trajan (emperor 98–107) to the Crimea, where he was forced to work in the quarries with other Christians. He was later thrown into the sea and drowned, having had an anchor placed around his neck. St. Clement has always been revered as a martyr.

✝ NOVEMBER 23
St. Columban, Abbot

St. Columban was born at Leinster, Ireland, about 543. He studied under St. Sinell at Cleenish in Lough Erne, and then he entered the monastery at Bangor. He subsequently taught for about thirty years in that monastery's school, and in about 591, St. Comgall of Bangor (516–602) sent him and twelve companions as missionaries to the Continent. They went to Gaul (today's France), and there they preached to pagans. Columban eventually settled in Burgundy, having been invited by the Merovingian King Childebert II (reigned 575–96), and there he established three monasteries, one of which was Luxeuil, of which he was abbot. It was for these houses that he composed his rule. He spoke out against the laxity of the local clergy and the immorality at the court of King Theuderic II (reigned 596–613), and he introduced the strict Celtic manner of Penance. He himself compiled two Penitentials (manuals for confessors stipulating penances for specified sins). When expelled from Burgundy in 610, Columban went and preached in the vicinity of Zurich. But he was likewise driven out (612) from there, because he opposed the people's pagan practices. He then went to Bobbio, Italy, and in a valley of the Apennines he founded a monastery that became, in time, a famous center of learning. St. Columban died at Bobbio on November 23, 615, and is regarded as the greatest of the Irish missionary monks.

✝ *Bl. Michael Augustine Pro,*
Priest and Martyr

Bl. Michael Augustine Pro was a Mexican, born in Guadalupe de Zacatecas on January 13, 1891. He entered the Society of Jesus in 1911, but because of the political upheavals and growing anti-Catholicism in his country, he and other young Jesuit students had to leave (1914) their homeland. He continued his studies with the Jesuits in California before going to Spain and Belgium for further studies leading to the priesthood (1925). The Catholic Church in Mexico was suffering a most severe persecution under the atheistic government of its president, Plutarco Elías Calles, a rabid anti-Catholic, when Fr. Pro returned to Mexico City in July 1926. Because Catholic priests were hunted as criminals, Fr. Pro carried on his priestly ministry in secret. And because churches were closed, he set up Communion stations in various parts of the city, where the people gathered once a week and to whom he regularly brought Holy Communion. Thus for little more than a year he ministered to his fellow Mexicans, all the while praying that he might be accepted by God as a sacrifice for the faith in his country. His prayer was finally answered, for he was arrested on November 18, 1927, and on the morning of November 23, he was taken into the prison yard—in his right hand he grasped his crucifix and in his left his rosary. He looked around and saw rifles pointing at him. Having refused the blindfold, he stretched out his arms in the form of a cross, and when the order to fire was given, his last prayer before martyrdom was "Viva Cristo Rey!" "Long live Christ the King!" He was beatified by Pope John Paul II in 1988.

✝ NOVEMBER 24 ✎ *Memorial*
St. Andrew Dung-Lac, Priest and Martyr, and His Companions, Martyrs

Today we commemorate 117 saints who were martyred in the territory we now know as Vietnam. Christianity was first established in that land during the early years of the seventeenth century, but the succeeding years were far from peaceful for Catholics. Between 1625 and 1886, about 260 years, 53 different decrees of persecution were promulgated and about 130,000 Catholics were martyred for their faith.

Of the 117 canonized in 1988 by Pope John Paul II, 6 died between the years 1745 and 1799, and the other 111 between 1835 and 1862. The manner of their deaths varied; 74 were beheaded, others were crucified, strangled, burned alive, quartered, or died in prison as a result of torture. Of the 117, 96 were Vietnamese, 11 were Spaniards, and 10 French. In the group there were 8 bishops, 50 priests, 1 seminarian, 16 catechists, and 42 lay people, one of whom was a woman.

St. Andrew Dung-Lac, who heads the list of these martyrs, was born in 1795 in Bac Ninh, in the north of Vietnam (then known as Tonkin). His parents were so poor that they sold him to a catechist, who took the child to the Catholic mission. There the child was baptized, given the name Andrew, and reared. In time he became a catechist, then studied theology, and eventually was ordained (1823). His priestly years coincided with the years of brutal persecution under the Tonkinese ruler Minh Mang (1820–41). While serving as a pastor in a small village, Andrew was arrested, but his parishioners secured his release after paying a ransom to city officials.

Andrew then changed his name from Dung to Lac and went to another part of Tonkin to continue ministering to Catholics. There he was again arrested (November 10, 1839). His release was once more secured by paying a ransom. His freedom was short-lived, however, for soon afterward, as he was getting off a river boat, a man offered his hand to help him get ashore. The man, a government official, recognized the priest and called out: "Look! We have caught a master of religion!" Andrew was immediately arrested (November 16, 1839) and taken to a prison in Hanoi. Because he refused to deny his faith by stepping on a crucifix, he was beheaded on December 21, 1839. The memorial of these 117 Vietnamese martyrs is celebrated on November 24, because a number of them were martyred together on that day.

✝ NOVEMBER 25
St. Catherine of Alexandria, Virgin and Martyr

Most of what we read about St. Catherine is legend. All we can be certain of is that she lived in Alexandria, was a virgin, and died a martyr. Even the century of her death is uncertain. When historical facts are so few, it is no wonder that legend takes over, and the more popular the saint, the more involved the story becomes. Catherine is said to have been born of a patrician family. She became acquainted with Christianity through her extensive reading and was eventually baptized. When Emperor Maximinus ordered Christians to pay homage to pagan gods, Catherine, then only eighteen years of age, presented herself before him, publicly reproached him for his tyrannical decree, and spoke to him about the true God and showed that his gods were none at all. Unable to respond to her logical argument, the emperor summoned his philosophers—fifty in number—to answer the maiden's claims. Overcome by Catherine's wisdom and syllogistic reasoning, the philosophers were converted to Christ. As a result, the emperor had them burned alive, and ordered Catherine beaten and put in prison.

While Catherine was in prison, the emperor's wife, yielding to curiosity, went to visit her, and she too was soon won over to Christianity by Catherine's discourse. Hearing of his wife's apostasy, the emperor ordered Catherine to be placed between two rotating wheels, each with sharp protruding spikes. As soon as Catherine was placed between them, the wheels broke into countless pieces, injuring bystanders. Finally, she was beheaded. Tradition maintains that she was martyred on November 24 or 25, 305, and shortly thereafter angels took her body to Mount Sinai, where a monastery dedicated to her was subsequently built.

Catherine's cult was very strong in the East from the tenth century onward, and it was introduced in the West with the return of the crusaders and remained popular until the eighteenth century. St. Catherine is listed among the Fourteen Holy Helpers, and she is invoked by philosophers, scholars, lawyers, students, and wheelers.

✝ *NOVEMBER 26 🌿 *Memorial*
St. John Berchmans, Religious

St. John Berchmans was born at Diest, Belgium, on March 13, 1599, and after attending the Jesuit college in Mechlin, he decided to enter (1616) the Society of Jesus. With his novitiate training over, he was sent (1618) to Rome to the famous Roman College. He enjoyed his three years of philosophy and did so well that when he completed his program in 1621, he was asked to defend the entire course of philosophy in a public disputation. Having applied himself so thoroughly for his final examination and then for the disputation, he so weakened his health that he fell ill in early August, 1621. Unable to shake his fever, he grew weaker by the day. Then, on the morning of August 13, he died. Extraordinary accomplishments are not required for holiness, and there was nothing extraordinary in John's short life. It was his ordinary deeds done extraordinarily well that brought him to sanctity. The Jesuits in Rome were convinced that John was a saint, and immediately after his death they began collecting data for his canonization. Pope Leo XIII canonized him in 1888. Because St. John Berchmans saw God's will in every little facet of daily living, the prayer today refers to him as a cheerful giver who was always eager to seek God and to do his will.

✝ NOVEMBER 30 ⌀ *Feast*
St. Andrew, Apostle

St. Andrew was a Galilean, born in Bethsaida (John 1:44) and a fisherman by trade (Mark 1:16). He was a disciple of John the Baptist, and it was John who first pointed out the Lord to him (John 1:35–36). After Andrew had met the Lord and talked to him, he introduced his brother, Simon Peter, to the Lord as well (John 1:40–42). Andrew and Peter became disciples when the Lord saw them casting their nets into the sea of Galilee, and said to them "Come after me," as today's Gospel (Matt. 4:18–22) narrates. It is said that after Pentecost Andrew preached the gospel in northern Greece, at Epirus (now part of modern Greece), and Scythia (today's Kazakhstan), and tradition has it that he was crucified at Patras (Greece). After hanging on the cross for two days, he died on November 30, in about 70. Devotion to St. Andrew spread in the East, and his feast was celebrated in Rome during the pontificate of Pope Simplicius (468–83), who converted a building on Rome's Esquiline Hill into a church honoring him. St. Andrew is the patron of Scotland and of Russia.

✝ LAST SUNDAY IN
ORDINARY TIME ⌀ *Solemnity*
Our Lord Jesus Christ the King

Pope Pius XI, on December 11, 1925, published his Encyclical Letter *Quas Primas*, in which he instituted the feast of Christ the King. At that time the pope likewise decreed that it was to be celebrated on the last Sunday of October. In the 1969 revision of the liturgical calendar after Vatican Council II, the feast was transferred to the last Sunday in Ordinary Time. From Christ's birth until his death on the cross, he was acknowledged as a king. When the Magi arrived in Jerusalem, they asked of Herod: "Where is he who has been born King of the Jews?" (Matt. 2:2). And on his cross, Pilate affixed the notice for all to read, "Jesus of Nazareth, King of the Jews." The Archangel Gabriel, at the time of the Annunciation, told Mary that her son would be given "the throne of his father David, and he will reign over the house of Jacob for ever; and of his kingdom there will be no end" (Luke 1:31–33). Throughout our Lord's public life, he preached the Kingdom of God—this, in fact, was the core of his teaching, and when Pilate asked him "Are you a king?" his answer was: "For this was I born and for this I have come into the world to bear witness to the truth" (John 18:37). Today we acknowledge our Lord's royal sovereignty over us and over the world; we also express our gratitude to him, for it is by his life and death that we have been redeemed and are promised a place in his eternal Kingdom.

DECEMBER

☩ ***DECEMBER 1**   *❧*   *Memorial*
SS. Edmund Campion, Robert Southwell, Priests and Martyrs, and Their Companions, Martyrs

Today we commemorate the ten canonized and eighteen beatified Jesuit martyrs of England and Wales. All were martyred on their native soil between 1581 and 1679, at a time when the Catholic Church was the object of fierce persecution.

St. Edmund Campion was born in London on June 25, 1540, and for a time taught at Oxford University. After becoming reconciled (1572) to the Catholic Church, he entered (1573) the Society of Jesus in Rome, and was one of the first Jesuits to be assigned (1580) to the English Mission. England, at the time of his arrival there, was a land where the Mass was prohibited and priests were hunted as traitors. He secretly ministered to English Catholics for a year, and he was then captured on July 16, 1581, and imprisoned in the Tower of London. Because he refused to apostatize and accept the religion established by Queen Elizabeth I (reigned 1558–1603), he was hanged, drawn, and quartered at Tyburn, London, on December 1, 1581.

St. Robert Southwell, one of England's better poets, was born at Horsham St. Faith, near Norwich, in 1561. He became a Jesuit in Rome in 1578, and he returned to England as a missionary in 1586. He secretly labored among the English Catholics for six years, until he was captured on June 25, 1592. He suffered imprisonment for two and a half years, during which time he was brutally tortured. He was condemned to death because he was a priest, and he was hanged, drawn and quartered at Tyburn, London, on February 21, 1595.

The ten saints commemorated today were canonized by Pope Paul VI in 1970; of the eighteen blessed, three were beatified in 1886, thirteen in 1929, and two in 1987.

Saints	BIRTH	DEATH
Edmund Campion	1540	December 1, 1581
Alexander Briant	1553	December 1, 1581
Robert Southwell	1561	February 21, 1595
Henry Walpole	1558	April 7, 1595
Nicholas Owen	?	March 2, 1606
Thomas Garnet	1575	June 23, 1608
Edmund Arrowsmith	1585	August 28, 1628
Henry Morse	1595	February 1, 1645
Philip Evans	1645	July 22, 1679
David Lewis	1616	August 27, 1679

Blessed	BIRTH	DEATH
Thomas Woodhouse	1535	June 19, 1573
John Nelson	1535	February 3, 1578
Thomas Cottam	1549	May 30, 1582
John Cornelius	1557	July 4, 1594
Roger Filcock	c. 1570	February 27, 1601
Robert Middleton	1570	April 3, 1601

Blessed, continued	BIRTH	DEATH
Francis Page	?	April 20, 1602
Ralph Ashley	?	April 7, 1606
Edward Oldcorne	1561	April 7, 1606
Thomas Holland	1600	December 12, 1642
Ralph Corby	1598	September 7, 1644
Peter Wright	1603	May 19, 1651
William Ireland	1636	January 24, 1679
John Fenwick	1628	June 20, 1679
John Gavan	1640	June 20, 1679
William Harcourt	1609	June 20, 1679
Anthony Turner	1628	June 20, 1679
Thomas Whitbread	1618	June 20, 1679

✝ DECEMBER 3   ✦   **Feast*
St. Francis Xavier, Priest

St. Francis Xavier is the best known missionary since the time of the apostles. He was born in Navarre, Spain, on April 7, 1506, and studied at the University of Paris, where he met (1529) St. Ignatius of Loyola (see July 31) and joined his group. He sailed from Lisbon for India in April 1541. Once he arrived (May 1542), he set out to preach to the pearl fishers on India's Fishery Coast. In 1544, he began his extensive missionary journeys, preaching, and baptizing. After opening a mission station, he left it for other missionaries to continue, while he himself went on to new areas or lands. From India, he went on to Malaya (1545) and to the Moluccas (1546), and on August 15, 1549, he landed in Japan, the first Catholic missionary to enter that country. Later, when he heard about China, he also desired to go there. In

September 1552, he was on the small island of Sancian, off the coast of China, unsuccessfully trying to arrange passage to the mainland. There he fell ill on November 21 and died on December 3. He was canonized by Pope Gregory XV in 1622, and in 1927 Pope Pius XI made him patron of missions. Francis Xavier was not the first missionary to go to the East, but he was the first to meet with success in establishing permanent Christian communities in the several lands he visited. Today's prayer hints at his success when it says that God opened a door to Asia when he sent St. Francis Xavier to preach the gospel.

✝

DECEMBER 4
St. John of Damascus, Priest and Doctor of the Church

St. John was born in Damascus of Christian parents in about 675. After his schooling was completed, he gained a position in the caliph's court, but when the caliph became hostile toward Christians, John resigned (about 710) and went to the Holy Land. There he became a monk in the monastery of St. Saba, near Jerusalem, and was ordained. He taught in the monastery, preached in Jerusalem, and spent much of his time writing theological treatises. When the Iconoclast controversy erupted (725) in the East, he vigorously opposed it, defended the veneration of images, and in his writings offered sound theological arguments for his position. He died on December 4, about 749. Shortly after his death, he was condemned (754) by an iconoclastic synod, but the Second Council of Nicaea (787) officially approved his teaching on images. Of his many writings, the most important is his *Exposition of the Orthodox Faith*, which is a synthesis of the teaching of earlier Church Fathers on the principal themes of the Christian faith. By the end of the eighth century, he was honored as a saint. Pope Leo XIII declared him a doctor of the Church in 1890. When today's prayer mentions the true faith he taught so well, it is referring to his writings.

✝ DECEMBER 6
St. Nicholas, Bishop

St. Nicholas has always been one of the more popular saints of the Church. Nonetheless, the only certain fact we know of his life is that he was Bishop of Myra in ancient Lycia (now modern Dembre in Turkey), during the first half of the fourth century. Tradition has it that he was born in Patara in Lycia, in about 270, and that he died on December 6, between 345 and 352. Justinian I (emperor 526–65) built a church in his honor during the early sixth century. In 1087, Italian soldiers stole the saint's body from Myra and transported it by sea to Bari, and the saint's cult then spread quickly throughout Italy and the rest of Europe. Numerous legends arose about his liberality, the most famous being his secretly providing dowries for three poor girls. Thus he is often depicted with three bags of gold. Because of this legend, St. Nicholas became, in Europe, the secret bringer of presents to children on the eve of his feast. In

English-speaking countries, his name has become corrupted into Santa Claus, the bringer of gifts to children on Christmas Eve. St. Nicholas is the patron of Russia.

✝ DECEMBER 7   🖋 *Memorial*
St. Ambrose, Bishop and Doctor of the Church

St. Ambrose was born of an aristocratic Roman family in Trier, Germany, in about 339. His father was praetorian prefect of Gaul (modern France), and after the father's death, the family moved to Rome, where Ambrose studied (361–65) law. He entered (about 365) the civil service as a lawyer, and later (about 370) was named governor of Aemilia-Liguria in nothern Italy, with his headquarters in Milan. As governor, he proved himself an honest and upright official, and his personal life was blameless. When the bishop of Milan died, and when a suitable successor could not be found, the people unanimously chose Ambrose, though he was still a catechumen. He was baptized, ordained, and then consecrated bishop on December 7, 374. He immediately began his study of theology, and his lifestyle was a model of austerity. As bishop, he championed orthodoxy against the Arians, staunchly advocated the rights of the Church against the civil power, and was an exemplary shepherd of souls. It was by hearing Ambrose's sermons that Augustine (see August 28) was converted (386) and baptized in Milan in 387. Ambrose wrote many important dogmatic, exegetical, moral, and ascetical works, and in recognition of these he is honored as one of the four great doctors of the Latin Church. He likewise wrote several Latin hymns, which are still used in the Liturgy of the Hours. He died on Holy Saturday, April 4, 397. His memorial is celebrated on the anniversary of his episcopal consecration.

✝ DECEMBER 8 ✐ *Solemnity*
Immaculate Conception of the Blessed Virgin Mary

Bl. Pope Pius IX, on December 8, 1854, issued the bull *Ineffabilis Deus*, in which he solemnly proclaimed and defined Mary's Immaculate Conception: "The doctrine which holds that the most Blessed Virgin Mary from the first moment of her conception was, by the singular grace and privilege of Almighty God, in view of the merits of Christ Jesus the Savior of the human race, preserved free from all stain of original sin, is revealed by God and is therefore firmly and constantly to be believed by all the faithful." Mary, by a unique grace, was preserved from the stain which all children of Adam contract at the very moment of their conception in their mother's womb. Inasmuch as Mary was chosen to be the mother of Jesus, the Sinless One, this special grace was granted her in view of her Son's future merits. Though reference to Mary's immaculate conception is not found in the Gospels, nevertheless, it is implicitly contained in the exceptional holiness (Luke 1: 28, 42) required of her to be the mother of Christ (see Luke 1:30–31). The early Fathers of the Church unanimously speak of Mary's holiness, and St. Ephrem (306–73), in one of his hymns, is the first to give explicit testimony: "No blemish in you, my Lord, and no stain in your Mother." By the seventh century, the Eastern Church celebrated the feast of Mary's Conception. By the eighth century, it was generally held among the faithful of the East that her conception was immaculate. The feast was subsequently introduced in Spain and Italy and then throughout the rest of Europe. In 1568, when Pope Pius V's Missal appeared, he extended the feast of the Immaculate Conception to the universal Church. In 1846, the U.S. bishops, gathered at the Sixth Provincial Council of Baltimore, chose the Immaculate Conception as the patronal feast of the United States.

✠ DECEMBER 9
St. Juan Diego, Hermit

Juan Diego, known in his native tongue as Cuauhtlatóhuac ("he who speaks as an eagle"), was born in Tolpetlac, a small village north of Guadalupe, Mexico, in about 1474. He was married, a landowner, and an artisan who made and sold mattresses. He had been baptized, with his wife, by early Franciscan missionaries. At the time of our Lady's apparitions to him, his wife had already died and he had been living a fervent Christian life. On December 9, 1531, our Lady appeared (see December 12) to him on Tepeyac Hill, not far from Mexico City, and instructed him to tell the bishop to erect a church on the site. When Bishop Juan de Zumárraga asked for proof that the message had indeed come from the Virgin, Juan Diego opened his cloak and let the flowers, which our Lady had told him to gather on the hill, fall at the bishop's feet. At the same time, an image of our Lady was seen imprinted on the cloak. These apparitions of the Virgin had a tremendous effect on Juan Diego's later life. He despoiled himself of his property and belongings and dedicated his days to helping other Mexicans and to living a life of prayer and penance near the shrine. He died in 1548. Since his death, the Mexican faithful, without interruption, have acknowledged Juan Diego's holiness and considered him their intercessor in Heaven. On the occasion of a papal visit to Mexico, Pope John Paul II, on July 30, 2002, canonized Juan Diego and officially numbered him among the saints.

✝ DECEMBER 11
St. Damasus I, Pope

St. Damasus was a Roman, born about 305; he was a deacon under Pope Liberius (352–66), and accompanied the pope when he went into exile (355). When Liberius died (September 24, 366), Damasus was elected his successor and was consecrated on October 1, 366. As pope, Damasus combated heresies (Arianism, Apollinarianism) and carried out liturgical reforms. During his pontificate, Latin became the principal liturgical language in Rome. He was the first pope to call the See of Rome the Apostolic See, and he emphasized that the Bishop of Rome's preeminence over other bishops derives from his being Peter's successor. He provided housing for the papal archives and commissioned St. Jerome (see September 30), his secretary, to revise the then-existing Latin translation of the New Testament. He also promoted the cult of the martyrs, restored their tombs in the catacombs, and enhanced them by writing elegant Latin inscriptions for them. He died in Rome on December 11, 384. Today's prayer reminds us that St. Damasus loved and honored the martyrs.

✠ DECEMBER 12 ◢ *Feast*
Our Lady of Guadalupe

The shrine of Our Lady of Guadalupe, on the outskirts of Mexico City, is the most famous shrine of our Lady in the Western Hemisphere, and today we commemorate her appearances to a native Mexican convert, St. Juan Diego (see December 9), on Tepeyac Hill. On December 9, 1531, our Lady appeared to him and asked that a church be built on the site, and on December 12 she again appeared and urged him to take her message to the bishop. To offer proof that he was our Lady's messenger, she told him to gather the flowers he found blooming there in mid-December. When Juan Diego stood before Bishop Juan de Zumárraga, he opened his cloak, and as the flowers cascaded to the floor, those present saw on the rough cloth an image of our Lady— the image still preserved at the shrine. The first sanctuary was built in about 1533; the second was begun in 1556; and the third was built in 1695. The present basilica dates from 1976. In 1746, Our Lady of Guadalupe became the patroness of Mexico, and in 1754 Pope Benedict XIV established December 12 as the feast. In 1945, when Pope Pius XII was speaking of Our Lady of Guadalupe, he called her "Queen of Mexico and Empress of the Americas." The pope went on to say that the image on the cloak was done "by brushes that were not of this world." The prayer in the Mass today affirms that by the Virgin Mary's appearance at Tepeyac, God has brought blessings to the Americas.

✝ DECEMBER 13 ✍ *Memorial*
St. Lucy, Virgin and Martyr

St. Lucy is said to have been martyred in Syracuse, Sicily, about 304, during the persecution under Diocletian (emperor 284–305). Devotion to her in Sicily was popular by the fifth century, and from there, during the following centuries, it spread to Rome and northern Italy. Her name is found in the Roman Canon, and it was probably placed there by Pope Gregory the Great (see September 3). Whatever else is said about St. Lucy's martyrdom is derived from an account of her death written about two centuries later and is hence of questionable reliability. The Hieronymian Martyrology (about 450) gives the date of her death as December 13. The name Lucy means "light," and this is most probably why she had been invoked, especially during the Middle Ages, against blindness and in cases of eye disease. She is often portrayed with two eyes on a dish. The prayer of the Mass today makes a play on her name when it asks God to fill us with joy and light so that we may one day contemplate his glory with our eyes.

✝ DECEMBER 14 ✿ *Memorial*
St. John of the Cross, Priest and Doctor of the Church

St. John's family name was Yepes, and he was born of poor parents in Fontiveros, Spain, on June 24, 1542. He entered the Carmelite Order in 1563 and then studied at Salamanca and was ordained in 1567. Soon after ordination, he met St. Teresa of Jesus (see October 15), who told him that she and her religious sisters were restoring the primitive Carmelite Rule. Because John was then searching for a more austere form of religious life, he adopted St. Teresa's reform and began (1568) a monastery of his own. It was at this time that he changed his name to John of the Cross. Because he and his followers wore sandals, they became known as Discalced Carmelites. John's reformed group soon grew in numbers, but because some of the other Carmelites wanted to put a stop to its expansion, they seized him (December 2, 1577) and imprisoned him in Toledo. After nine months of imprisonment, he escaped (August 1578) and made his way to his discalced monastery. For the remainder of his life, he guided his monasteries and wrote spiritual treatises. He is especially renowned for his mystical poetry and his ascetical writings. He died in Ubeda, Spain, on December 14, 1591, and was canonized by Pope Benedict XIII in 1726. Recognizing the influence that St. John of the Cross's mystical writings have had in the Church, Pope Pius XI declared him a doctor of the Church in 1926. John's two most famous works, *The Ascent of Mount Carmel* and *The Dark Night*, are hinted at in today's opening prayer when it says that

God had led him to the mountain that is Christ, through the dark night of renunciation and burning love for the cross.

✝ DECEMBER 21
St. Peter Canisius, Priest and
Doctor of the Church

See April 27.

✝ DECEMBER 23
St. John of Kanty, Priest

St. John, whose family name was Wacienga, was born in Kanty, in the Diocese of Cracow, on June 23, 1390. He studied at the Cracow Academy, earned a master's degree, and was ordained (1416) a priest. For a time, he was rector (1421–29) of the Templars' school at Miechów, but then he returned to the Cracow Academy to teach philosophy. In 1443, he received his doctorate in theology and lectured on that subject at the academy. He was a devoted and conscientious professor, but he had a greater reputation for sanctity than for brilliance in lecturing. Throughout his life, he was always generous and compassionate to the poor. He died in Cracow on Christmas Eve, December 24, 1473, and was buried in the church near the academy where he had taught. He was canonized by Pope Clement XIII in 1767. When today's opening prayer speaks of understanding and kindness to others, it reflects St. John's charity and interest in the poor.

✟ DECEMBER 25 ✄ Solemnity
Nativity of the Lord (Christmas)

On this day, we celebrate the birth of our Lord, Jesus Christ, born of the Virgin Mary. Both Matthew (2:1) and Luke (2:4, 6–7) speak of his birth as taking place in Bethlehem, thus indicating his Davidic ancestry. The actual date of Christ's birth is unknown, nor can the year be determined exactly. However, Matthew (2:1) and Luke (1:5) place Christ's infancy during the reign of King Herod the Great, and because Herod died in 4 B.C., Jesus must have been born in about 7 or 6 B.C. By the end of the fourth century, the Church liturgically celebrated the Lord's nativity. In the East, this was commemorated on January 6 (together with the feast of the Epiphany), whereas in the West it was celebrated on December 25. This latter date was chosen in the West because that was the date when the Roman festival of the winter solstice (Natalis Solis Invicti) was held. Because Christ is the Sun of Justice, Christians replaced the pagan feast with their own religious festival. By the fifth century, the Eastern Church was observing the Western Church's custom, and within centuries all Europe followed. The custom of multiple Masses on Christmas is equally of ancient custom. In her account of her visit to the Holy Land (in about 400), the pilgrim Aetheria relates that the Midnight Mass of Christ's Nativity was celebrated (January 6) in Bethlehem and that following this the congregation went to Jerusalem to celebrate a second Mass in the church on Calvary. By the time of Pope St. Gregory the Great (see September 3), the custom in Rome was to celebrate three Christmas Masses (midnight, dawn, and day), at three different stational churches. The custom of three Masses on Christmas still remains today.

✝ DECEMBER 26 ✎ *Feast*
St. Stephen, First Martyr

According to the New Testament accounts, St. Stephen was the first to give his life in witness for his faith in Christ. The Church, from her earliest days, judged that the commemoration of her first martyr should be on the day after the celebration of Christ's birth. When the apostles decided that there was a need for deacons in the Church, Stephen was the first of seven chosen; he was said to have been "filled with faith and the Holy Spirit" (Acts 6:5–6). As a result of his preaching, he was falsely accused and arrested (Acts 6:12–14); he was then dragged out of the city and stoned to death (Acts 7:54–59), as the first reading for today's Mass relates. Stephen's cult quickly took hold in the East, and the early *Martyrology of Nicomedia* (361) gives his feast as December 26. When today's opening prayer says that St. Stephen prayed for those who killed him, this is a reference to his final words, "Lord, do not hold this sin against them" (Acts 7:60).

✝ DECEMBER 27 ✎ *Feast*
St. John, Apostle and Evangelist

St. John was a Galilean, a son of Zebedee and the brother of James (Matt. 4:21); his mother was probably Salome (Mark 15:40 and Matt. 27:56), who may have been the sister of our Lady (John 19:25). John was a fisherman by trade, and he and his brother James were with Simon (Luke 5:10) when they were called from their boats and nets to follow Christ (Matt. 4:21–22). During John's years with the Lord, he was privileged to witness the raising of Jairus's daughter (Mark 5:37), our Lord's Transfiguration (Mark 9:2), and his agony in the Garden of Gethsemane (Mark 14:33). It was John who stood at Jesus's cross, and it was to him that our Lord entrusted his mother (John 19:26–27). John likewise went with Peter to the tomb on the first Easter morning and found it empty, as today's Gospel reading (John 20:2–8) narrates. Besides being one of the Twelve Apostles, John was also an evangelist. After Pentecost, he settled in Ephesus (in today's Turkey), but at the time of Domitian (emperor 81–96) he was exiled to the island of Patmos (Greece), where he wrote the Book of Revelation (Rev 1:9). He subsequently returned to Ephesus under Nerva (emperor 96–98), and there, in his old age, wrote his Gospel and three epistles. John died at Ephesus in about 100. The prayers in the Mass today recall that through his Gospel St. John has passed on to us the mysteries of the Word that God had revealed to him. Of the four evangelists, John is the only one who refers to Jesus as "Word" (John 1:1–14).

✝ DECEMBER 28 ✍ *Feast*
Holy Innocents, Martyrs

The Jewish historian Flavius Josephus (37–100) considered King Herod (73–4 B.C.) to have been a "man of great barbarity." Even if Herod had not slain other individuals—which he did and in great numbers—the slaughter of the Innocents in Bethlehem would admirably prove Josephus's statement. Today's Gospel reading (Matt. 2:13–18) relates how Herod "ordered the massacre of all the boys two years old and under in Bethlehem and its environs." The actual number of children killed on that occasion is unknown. In centuries past, the number was given in the thousands, even up to 14,000, obviously to emphasize Herod's cruelty. At the time of Christ, however, Bethlehem was but a small town, and judging from the number of people who probably lived there, together with the number of births a year, demographers think that the number of male children massacred might have been between twenty and thirty. Though the number is less, it does not lessen Herod's barbarity. These children were venerated as martyrs as early as the fourth century—martyrs, not because they died for Christ, but because they died in place of Christ. Theirs was, as the prayer after Communion indicates, a wordless profession of faith in Christ, and thus they were crowned with life at his birth.

✝ DECEMBER 29
St. Thomas Becket, Bishop and Martyr

St. Thomas Becket was born of Norman parents in London in 1117 or 1118. After his schooling was finished, he became a member of Archbishop Theobald's staff at Canterbury. In 1154, King Henry II of England (reigned 1154–89) made Thomas his chancellor, and both king and chancellor worked together in great harmony.

When Archbishop Theobald died, King Henry, looking for someone who would do whatever he wanted, chose (1162) his friend Thomas to to be the new Archbishop of Canterbury. Opposition, however, soon arose between king and archbishop; Henry wanted to have complete control of the Church, and Thomas, knowing that his duty was now primarily to God, fought for the Church's freedom and rights. When Henry moved to have Thomas arrested, Thomas went (1164) into exile in France. When their differences were reconciled, he returned to England during the summer of 1170. But the king immediately returned to his old tricks, and Thomas excommunicated him. Henry responded by sending four knights to Canterbury; they found Thomas in his cathedral, and there they murdered him on December 29, 1170. Thomas was immediately venerated as a martyr, and countless miracles were reported at his tomb. He was canonized by Pope Alexander III in 1173. St. Thomas Becket's tomb in Canterbury Cathedral was a center for pilgrimages until 1538, when King Henry VIII had the saint's tomb dismantled.

✝ SUNDAY AFTER CHRISTMAS,
OR DECEMBER 30 ✎ *Feast*
Holy Family of Jesus, Mary, and Joseph

When God the Father ordained that his only Son should be born an infant in Bethlehem, he likewise chose that his Son should be brought up within a human family. In celebrating the Feast of the Holy Family, we celebrate the "hidden years" of the life of Mary, Joseph, and Jesus. These years are hidden not only because they were lived in out-of-the-way Nazareth, but also because the Gospels are, but for a single incident, silent about them. After the Holy Family's return from Egypt and going to Nazareth (Matt. 2:19–23), the only incident we know of during this long period is when Mary and Joseph found Jesus among the teachers in the Temple (Luke 2:48–52). In the eyes of the people who lived in Nazareth, theirs was an ordinary family— Mary and Joseph did the normal things that parents do. Joseph worked as carpenter and provided for the family; Mary ran the household, doing the necessary everyday chores of a mother. And Jesus was obedient to them; he helped about the house, and after Joseph's death, he took over the carpentry business and provided for his mother. Their life was no less humdrum than our own. The Holy Family is the model for all Christian families—a model because Mary, Joseph, and Jesus were faithful in their devotion to and love for each other and because they lived their lives in peace and harmony.

✝

DECEMBER 31
St. Sylvester I, Pope

When St. Sylvester, a Roman by birth, became pope on January 31, 314, Constantine was emperor (306–37). In the previous year (313), Constantine, by the Edict of Milan, had officially recognized the Catholic Church and brought all persecution against the Church to an end. The emperor was favorable to Christianity, but he himself postponed his baptism until he was on his deathbed. It was during Sylvester's peaceful pontificate that the Church had her first rapid growth and that the basilicas over the tombs of SS. Peter and Paul were built by Constantine. It was also Sylvester who received from the emperor the property (the Lateran) that became the official residence of the popes until the Middle Ages. Though Sylvester did not attend the Council of Nicaea (325), called by Constantine, he sent representatives to it. Because his pontificate coincided with the years when Constantine was emperor, countless legends arose regarding pope and emperor, such as the pope's curing the emperor of leprosy. These, however, are no more than stories. Sylvester died on December 31, 335, and was buried in the Cemetery of Priscilla on Rome's Salarian Way.

Glossary

Albigenses: a heretical sect in southern France during the twelfth and thirteenth centuries, centered around the city of Albi. They were also called Cathari (from the Greek *katharoi,* meaning "pure"), and they taught Neo-Manichaean dualism. According to this teaching, there are two principles, one good and the other evil. The Christian God is the creator of spirit-being only, and the devil, who is a rival god, created matter. The human soul, created by God, is imprisoned in matter by the devil, and because all matter is evil, salvation is liberation from matter. Marriage is therefore to be avoided because it involves the body.

Antioch: the city dates back to 300 B.C., the year of its founding. It is located in southeastern Turkey and is known today as Antakya. It was the administrative center of the Seleucid Kingdom until 64 B.C., when the Romans made it the capital of their Syrian province. St. Peter was the founder of the Church there and was her first bishop. The city became a center of Christianity; for a time St. Paul made it his headquarters, and it was there that the disciples were first called Christians (Acts 11:26). The first renowned figure of the early Church, other than the apostles, to be associated with the city was St. Ignatius of Antioch (see October 17).

antipope: the term given to an individual who illegitimately sets himself up as a rival to the legitimately elected pope and claims to exercise the office of the Roman Pontiff. In the history of the Church, there have been approximately thirty-seven antipopes. The earliest is said to have been St. Hippolytus (see August 13).

apostasy: the name given to that act whereby a baptized Catholic both inwardly and outwardly abandons the beliefs once professed. The individual is then known as an apostate.

Apostolic Fathers: the earliest Christian ecclesiastical writers, who were either contemporary with the apostles or lived during the period immediately afterward, that is, late first and early second centuries; for example, Clement I of Rome (see November 23), Ignatius of Antioch (see October 17), and Polycarp of Smyrna (see February 23).

Arianism: a fourth-century heresy, named after the Alexandrian priest, Arius (d. 336), who promoted the heresy in the East. Arianism is a basic denial of the divinity of Christ. With other Christians, Arius taught that the Son was begotten by the (unbegotten) Father. But he then argued that because the Son was begotten, then he had a beginning, and hence there was a time when he was not. If the Son had a beginning, it follows that he is not eternal and, therefore, the Son cannot be God. The Father alone is true God. Arius's teaching was opposed by St. Athanasius (see May 2), who taught that the Son, being begotten of the Father, is consubstantial (of the same substance as) with the Father, and that therefore the Son is God. St. Athanasius's teaching was upheld at the First Council of Nicaea (325), and both Arius and his teaching were condemned. Arianism, however, continued in the East until it was again proscribed by the Council of Constantinople (381).

Assumption: the doctrine that Mary, the mother of Jesus, when her life on earth had come to an end, was taken (assumed) body and soul into heaven. The theological foundations of this doctrine are implicit in the New Testament and explicit in the writings of the Fathers of the Church. In the Roman Catholic Church, the feast of the Assumption is celebrated on August 15; in the Eastern Churches, the feast is called the Dormition of Our Lady. This doctrine was defined by Pope Pius XII on November 1, 1950.

beatification: the official papal declaration that a deceased individual, now called "blessed," may be honored with public cult in a particular region, country, or religious institute. This declaration, however, follows a detailed canonical investigation into whether a Servant of God had, during life, practiced heroic virtue or had suffered a true martyrdom, and whether after death authentic miracles have occurred through the Servant's intercession with God on behalf of a given person. Beatification is a prerequisite for canonization.

Beatitudes: a series of blessings found in the New Testament and spoken by Jesus during his Sermon on the Mount as recorded in Matt. 5:3–12, and in his Sermon on the Plain as recorded in Luke 6:20–23. They are called the Beatitudes because each begins with the words "blessed are." Luke has four blessings, whereas Matthew has nine. In general, the Beatitudes describe the blessed state of those possessing certain qualities necessary for life in the Kingdom of God.

bull: a papal letter or document to which was attached a *bulla,* that is, a leaden seal. The seal indicated that the document was authentic; in time, the document itself became known as a bull. Starting in the fifteenth century, the term bull was reserved for more important documents, such as dogmatic pronouncements, etc. In 1878, the leaden seal for bulls was set aside, except for the more important and solemn documents, and a red ink stamp with the name of the current pope encircling the heads of SS. Peter and Paul came into use. Bulls are usually cited by the first words of their Latin text (e.g., Pope Benedict VIII's *Unam sanctam* of 1302).

canonization: the official papal declaration that a blessed (one who has been beatified) is included in the list (canon) of the saints and may be honored with a public cult throughout the universal Church. Before the tenth century, it was the custom for bishops, in their respective dioceses, to declare a deceased holy person a saint. The first papal canonization in Rome was that of St. Ulrich, Bishop of Augsburg, in 973, and it was not until the middle of the twelfth century that canonizations were reserved to the Holy See. For a blessed to be canonized, another miracle has to be authenticated through the blessed's intercession with God.

Cappadocian Fathers: a title reserved for the three great theologians who were natives of ancient Cappadocia—a district in east central Anatolia (central modern Turkey) that became a part of the Roman Empire in 190 B.C., after the Roman victory at Magnesia (in modern Greece)—namely, St. Basil the Great (see January 2), his friend St. Gregory Nazianzen (see January 2), and his brother St. Gregory of Nyssa (c. 335–94). All three are famous for their contributions to Trinitarian theology.

catacombs: subterranean cemeteries outside ancient Rome, consisting of connected tunnels with *loculi* carved into the walls to receive the tombs. Because Roman law forbade burials within the city, the dead were interred beyond the city limits. The earliest catacombs date from the third century. Not far from Rome's center, there are approximately forty early Christian catacombs.

Chalcedon, Council of: the Fourth Ecumenical Council, held October 8–31, 451. The council was convoked by Marcian (emperor 450–57) to deal with the heretical teaching that the Constantinopolitan monk Eutyches (c. 375–454) had been propagating. Eutyches maintained that there were not two natures in Christ but only one. At the time of the Son's incarnation, his human nature was totally absorbed by his divinity, and therefore Christ was not of the same substance as other humans beings. In response, the Fathers at the Council of Chalcedon taught that Christ was perfect God and perfect man, that he was consubstantial with the Father in his divinity and consubstantial with man in his humanity. Furthermore, Christ must be acknowledged in two natures without any commingling or change or division or separation, and the distinction between the natures is in no way removed by their union but rather the specific character of each nature is preserved and they are united in one person and one hypostasis. With this council, the Christological controversies of the fourth and fifth centuries came to an end.

communion of saints: an article of faith found in the Apostles' Creed, which refers to the mutual sharing in help, satisfaction, prayer, and other good works as well as the communication among all the faithful whether members of the Church on earth (Church Militant), in purgatory (Church Suffering), or in heaven (Church Triumphant). This communion is made possible because all the baptized in the Church are united with Christ, the head.

Constantinople: ancient Byzantium, founded c. 660 B.C., modern Istanbul, Turkey. On his becoming sole emperor, Constantine (emperor 306–37) transferred (328) his capital from Italy to Byzantium, for greater facility in governing his vast empire. He named (330) the city after himself, and soon afterward the city became known as "New Rome." Some of the greatest names of the Eastern Church were patriarchs of Constantinople; for example, SS. Gregory Nazianzen (see January 2) and John Chrysostom (see September 13). Four Ecumenical Councils were held in the city (381, 553, 680–81, and 869–70). The Turks captured the city in 1453, and the capital of the Ottoman Empire was transferred there in 1457. The name Istanbul was officially adopted in 1930.

cult: the honor or reverence shown toward another who is acknowledged as being more excellent and superior. In the religious sphere, it is externally expressed by rites or ceremonies through which an individual worships God or venerates the saints.

Doctor of the Church: a special title given to certain authors in the Church, whose writings have had great influence in the Church. To be given such a title, there are three requirements: great sanctity, eminent learning, and the individual must be proclaimed such by a pope or an Ecumenical Council. Only canonized saints are numbered among the doctors of the Church, for example, SS. Augustine (see August 28), Bernard (see August 20), and Teresa of Jesus (see October 15).

Ephesus, Council of: the Third Ecumenical Council of the Church. The council was convoked by Theodosius II (emperor 408–50) on November 19, 430, and opened on June 7 of the following year. The purpose of the council was to deal with the teaching of Nestorius (381–451), patriarch of Constantinople, who denied that the Virgin Mary was the Mother of God (Theotokos) and maintained that she was merely the mother of the human Christ. In this matter, the Church's principal advocate was St. Cyril of Alexandria (see June 27).

Eucharist, the: the sacrament in which the body and blood, soul and divinity of Jesus Christ are really and truly present under the signs of bread and wine. The conversion of the substance of the bread and wine into the substance of Christ's body and blood, while the appearances of the bread and wine remain, is called transubstantiation and it takes place during the consecration of the Mass. Because the Eucharist is confected during the Mass, the Mass is called the Eucharistic Celebration.

Fathers of the Church: the name given to certain ecclesiastical writers of Christian antiquity, that is, from the end of the first century to that of the eighth. The earliest are the Apostolic Fathers (see above), then the Apologists (e.g., St. Justin; see June 1), those who wrote before the Council of Nicaea (e.g.: St. Cyprian, see September 16; Origen, c. 185–c. 254; and Tertullian, c. 160–after 220) and those after Nicaea (SS. Jerome, see September 30; Basil, see January 2; and Athanasius, see May 2).

Fatima: a small village in central Portugal, southeast of Leiria. It was here that on six occasions the Blessed

Virgin Mary appeared to three shepherd children in 1917. Since then, it has become one of the more famous Marian shrines in the world (see May 13).

Heaven: where God dwells with the angels and saints (the elect), that is, those who, because of their faithful following of the teaching of Jesus Christ, have achieved eternal communion of life and love with the Most Blessed Trinity and all the blessed. Heaven is the state of supreme, definitive happiness, the ultimate end and fulfillment of humankind's deepest longings.

Hell: the state of definitive self-exclusion from communion with God and the blessed. It is where the fallen angels dwell and those who have died unrepentant of their grievous sins. Hell is eternal, and its chief punishment is eternal separation from God.

Immaculate Conception: the belief that the Virgin Mary, from the first moment of her conception in her mother's womb, was preserved free from original sin. Thus, by singular privilege, she inherited human nature in an untainted condition, and this privilege was granted her so that she could be the fitting mother of Jesus Christ. Furthermore, it was granted in view of her Son's future merits. Though this belief was commonly held in the Church from time immemorial, it was only in 1854 that Pope Pius IX defined it as a dogma of the Roman Catholic Church (see December 8).

Jansenism: a religious movement with unorthodox tendencies and prevalent in France and the Low Countries during the seventeenth and eighteenth centuries. The name is derived from that of Cornelius Jansen (1586–1638), professor of theology at the University of Louvain and later bishop of Ypres, whose book *Augustinus* was published posthumously. The book dealt with the theology of grace of St. Augustine (see August 28). The author, however, espoused an extreme interpretation of St. Augustine's positions on grace and predestination, with the result that he offered the reader a pessimistic view of the human condition and a rigorous interpretation of the Christian life. In 1653, Pope Innocent X, by his constitution, *Cum occasione*, condemned five propositions taken from the book.

lay investiture: In the eleventh century, when bishops were appointed to their respective sees, they were given possession of ecclesiastical property by their feudal overlords. This was done by investing them with the crozier and ring. These symbols, however, became equivocal, for the overlords began to interpret this investiture as their granting the bishops not only ecclesiastical property but also ecclesiastical jurisdiction. Thus, the overlords acted as if the bishops and the Church in their territory were under their control, and hence they deposed and appointed bishops on their own. Thus, lay investiture infringed upon the rights of the Church, which alone had power to appoint bishops and grant ecclesiastical jurisdiction.

Lourdes: a town on the Gave de Pau River in southwestern France, lying at the foot of the Pyrenees, eleven miles southwest of Tarbes. It was here that the Blessed Virgin Mary appeared to Bernadette Soubirous. The eighteen appearances took place between February and July 1858. Lourdes is now the most famous of the world's Marian shrines (see February 11).

Manichaeism: a religious movement founded by Mani (216–274), which espouses a dualistic understanding of the world. Good and evil are uncreated principles; matter, which was created by the evil principle, is therefore evil; but spirit, having been created by the good principle, is good. Thus good and evil, matter and spirit, and light and darkness are in eternal conflict. The movement perdured well into the Middle Ages and found adherents in the Albigenses.

Marcionism: a religious sect founded by Marcion (+ c. 160) that proposed the existence of two Gods, namely, the Creator-Judge of the Old Testament, and the one revealed by Jesus. The God of the Old Testament was the cause of the world and of evil, whereas the Father of Jesus was a forgiving and a saving God. Because there is no common ground between these two Gods, it follows that the New Testament has to be disassociated from Judaism. Furthermore, the Old Testament is devoid of any revelation of the Christian God. Marcion believed himself to be recovering authentic Christianity. He was excommunicated in 139 or 140.

Maronite Church: an Eastern Rite community within the Roman Catholic Church, mainly located in Lebanon. The Church is named after St. Maron of Cyr (+ 423), a Syrian monk. Its liturgy belongs to the Syro-Antiochene family, which is the Syriac version of the Liturgy of St. James. The Maronite Church is the only Oriental Church that does not have a non-Catholic counterpart, and it is well represented in the United States.

martyr: a person who willingly suffers death for the faith. The word martyr derives from the Greek *martys,* meaning "witness." Thus, in dying the martyr witnesses to the true faith. It is not the death nor the manner of death that makes a martyr, but the reason why the martyr willingly undergoes that death. St. Augustine wrote: "It is the reason why, not the suffering that constitutes the martyr" (*Epist.* 89.2).

Monophysitism: the name given to the heresy taught by the monk Eutyches (c. 375–454). He taught that there was but one nature (*mono physis*) in Christ, for at the time of his incarnation, his humanity was totally absorbed by his divinity (see Council of Chalcedon, above).

Montanism: a second-century heresy begun by the prophet Montanus, who taught that the Holy Spirit, whom Jesus promised to his Church prior to his return to Heaven, was now manifested in the person of Montanus and his prophets and prophetesses. The Montanists maintained that when they spoke, it was the Spirit who was actually speaking. Their prophetic utterances were to be taken as additions to the teaching of Christ and, thereby, the Church, with the coming of Montanus, now possessed a fuller revelation. In preparation for Christ's Second Coming, the Montanists discouraged marriage and encouraged fasting. This heresy continued in the East until the time of Justinian I (emperor 527–65). At one time, it had a great following in Carthage.

Nicaea, Council of: the First Ecumenical Council of the Church, held at Nicaea (today's Iznik, northwestern Turkey) from May 20 or June 19 to about August 25, 325. It was convoked by Constantine (emperor 306–37) to respond to the heretical teaching of the Alexandrian priest Arius (see Arianism, above). Nicaea was also the site of the Seventh Ecumenical Council, which was held from August to October 787 and dealt principally with the problem of iconoclasm.

Orthodox Churches: the term refers to those Eastern Churches that accept the teachings of the Council of Chalcedon, but which, beginning in the eleventh century (i.e., from 1054), have become separated from Rome and do not recognize the juridical primacy of the pope, e.g., the Russian Orthodox and Greek Orthodox Churches.

Purgatory: the intermediate state between the death of the just believer and the final judgment; a state where there is expiation for sins already forgiven, but also looking forward to ultimate fellowship with God in Heaven. All who die in God's grace are assured of eternal salvation, but if they are still imperfectly purified, then to attain the holiness necessary to enter into the joy of Heaven, they must undergo a period of purgation after death. Hence, Purgatory is the state of final purification of the elect, which is totally different from the punishment of the damned in Hell.

Reformation: a religious movement in the Western Church of the sixteenth century, intending to reform and correct abuses then existing in the Catholic Church. The movement—the basis for the formation of Protestantism—had more than religious effects, for it extended itself into the political, economic, and social spheres as well. Its most important leaders were Martin Luther (1483–1546) in Germany, and John Calvin (1509–1564) and Huldrych Zwingli (1484–1531) in Switzerland.

sacrament: an outward sign, instituted by Christ to give grace. There are seven sacraments (Baptism, Confirmation, Eucharist, Penance, Orders, Last Anointing, and Marriage), and each has its perceptible signs (words and actions), which with the action of Christ and the power of the Holy Spirit make present the grace they signify. Because the Eucharist contains the body and blood, soul and divinity of Jesus Christ, it is referred to as the Blessed Sacrament.

stigmata: the Greek word for "marks." According to Church usage, these are marks that appear on an individual's body and are similar to the marks that Christ himself suffered during his passion, namely, in his hands, feet, and side. The earliest known case of the stigmata is that of St. Francis of Assisi (see October 4); in more recent times, St. Pio of Pietrelcina (see September 23) received the stigmata.

Trent, Council of: the Nineteenth Ecumenical Council, opened at Trent, Italy, on December 23, 1545, and closed there on December 4, 1563. The council was convoked by Pope Paul III to clarify Catholic doctrine, as well as to legislate a thorough reform of the Church in light of the criticisms made by the Reformers, especially by Martin Luther (1483–1546). The principal issues treated at the council were Scripture and tradition; original sin and justification; the sacraments in general and Baptism; the Eucharist and the Sacrifice of the Mass; Communion under both species; marriage; the jurisdiction of a bishop; indulgences; and the establishment of seminaries.

Vatican: today, an independent papal state within the commune of Rome that covers an area of 108.7 acres, and was created by the Lateran Treaty of February 11, 1929. Here Constantine (emperor 306–37) built the first basilica over the tomb of St. Peter (see November 18), and here the Roman pontiff resides. It is also the administrative headquarters of the Roman Catholic Church and the home of the Vatican Library and Archives.

Vulgate: the Latin translation of the Bible made by St. Jerome (see September 30). The name "Vulgate" comes from the Latin expression *versio vulgata*, that is, the popular or widespread edition.

Western Schism: the period from 1378 to 1417 when Western Christendom was divided between two and then (from 1409) three papal obediences. Upon the death of Pope Gregory XI in 1378, Urban VI was elected his successor. Because certain cardinals found Urban's manner of government not to their liking, they gathered at nearby Anagni, and on September 20, 1378, they elected Cardinal Robert of Geneva as antipope with the name Clement VII, who chose to reside at Avignon. Thus two obediences came into existence, that of Rome and Avignon. After about thirty years of confusion as to which pope was legitimate, it was suggested that both popes, then reigning, resign and open the way to a new election. Neither of the popes, however, would resign. As a result, some cardinals from both obediences met in Pisa, and on June 26, 1409, they elected Alexander V, thus creating a third obedience. Finally, Sigismund, king of the Romans (1410–37), in his desire to bring peace to the Church and Europe, urged John XXIII (successor to Alexander V of the Pisan line) to convoke a council to meet at Constance. There, Gregory XII (of the Roman line) resigned, and Benedict XIII (of the Avignon line) and John XXIII were deposed. The cardinals, now free to advance toward an election, on November 11, 1417, chose Cardinal Oddo Colonna, who became Martin V. Thus the Western Schism came to an end.

Bibliography

*Biographies of individual saints
or blessed are not included.*

Bibliotheca Sanctorum; 12 vols. Rome: Istituto Giovanni XXIII nella Pontificia Universitá Lateranense, 1960–1970.

Butler's Lives of the Saints: New Full Edition, rev. by Paul Burns; 12 vols. Collegeville, Minn.: Liturgical Press, 1995–2000.

Catholicisme, Hier, Aujourd'hui, Demain, ed. G. Jaquemet et al. Paris: Letouzey et Ané, 1948– .

Diccionario Histórico de la Compañía de Jesús. Biográfico-Temático, ed. Charles E. O'Neill and Joaquín M. Domínguez; 4 vols. Rome and Madrid: Institutum Historicum Societatis Iesu/Universidad Pontificia Comillas, 2001.

Dictionnaire de Spiritualité, Ascètique et Mystique, Doctrine et Histoire, ed. M. Viller et al.; 17 vols. Paris: Beauchesne, 1937–94.

Dictionnaire d'Histoire et de Géographique Ecclésiastiques, ed. A. Baudrillart et al. Paris: Letouzey et Ané, 1912– .

Dizionario degli Istituti di Perfezione, ed. G. Pelliccia and G. Rocca. Rome: Edizione Paoline, 1974– .

Enciclopedia Cattolica; 12 vols. Florence: G. C. Sansoni, 1948–54.

Enciclopedia dei Papi; 3 vols. Rome: Istituto della Enciclopedia Italiana, 2000.

Farmer, D. H. *The Oxford Dictionary of Saints,* 3d ed. New York: Oxford University Press, 1993.

Kelly, J. N. D. *The Oxford Dictionary of Popes.* New York: Oxford University Press, 1986.

Musurillo, Herbert, ed. *Acts of the Christian Martyrs.* Oxford: Clarendon Press, 1972.

————. *Fathers of the Primitive Church.* New York: New American Library, 1966.

New Catholic Encyclopedia; 14 vols. New York: McGraw-Hill, 1967.

Quasten, Johannes. *Patrology;* 3 vols. Utrecht: Spectrum, 1951–60.

Tylenda, Joseph N. *Jesuit Saints and Martyrs: Short Biographies of the Saints, Blessed, Venerables, and Servants of God of the Society of Jesus.* Chicago: Loyola University Press, 1998.

————, ed. *Portraits in American Sanctity.* Chicago: Franciscan Herald, 1982.

INDEX

DATE DUE
